My
iPad®

SIXTH EDITION

Gary Rosenzweig

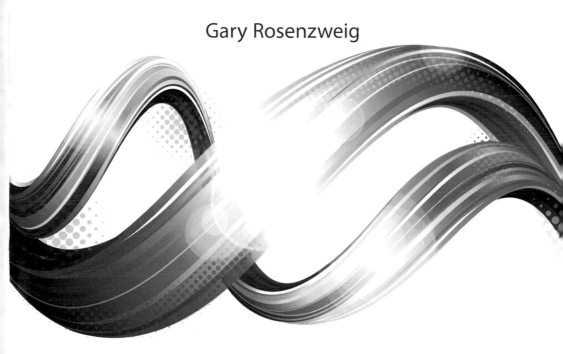

800 East 96th Street,
Indianapolis, Indiana 46240 USA

My iPad®

Copyright © 2014 by Pearson Education, Inc.

ISBN-13: 978-0-7897-5102-7
ISBN-10: 0-7897-5102-X

Library of Congress Control Number: 2013948635

Printed in the United States of America

First Printing: November 2013

Trademarks

All terms mentioned in this book that are known to be trademarks or service marks have been appropriately capitalized. Que Publishing cannot attest to the accuracy of this information. Use of a term in this book should not be regarded as affecting the validity of any trademark or service mark.

Warning and Disclaimer

Every effort has been made to make this book as complete and as accurate as possible, but no warranty or fitness is implied. The information provided is on an "as is" basis. The author(s) and the publisher shall have neither liability nor responsibility to any person or entity with respect to any loss or damages arising from the information contained in this book.

Special Sales

For information about buying this title in bulk quantities, or for special sales opportunities (which may include electronic versions; custom cover designs; and content particular to your business, training goals, marketing focus, or branding interests), please contact our corporate sales department at corpsales@pearsoned.com or (800) 382-3419.

For government sales inquiries, please contact governmentsales@pearsoned.com.

For questions about sales outside the U.S., please contact international@pearsoned.com.

Editor-in-chief
Greg Wiegand

Senior Acquisitions Editor and Development Editor
Laura Norman

Managing Editor
Kristy Hart

Project Editor
Lori Lyons

Proofreader
Kathy Ruiz

Indexer
Erika Millen

Editorial Assistant
Cindy Teeters

Cover Designer
Mark Shirar

Compositor
Bronkella Publishing

Technical Editor
James Floyd Kelly

Graphics Technician
Tammy Graham

Contents at a Glance

Table of Contents

About the Author

Gary Rosenzweig is an Internet entrepreneur, software developer, and technology writer. He runs CleverMedia, Inc., which produces websites, computer games, apps, and podcasts.

CleverMedia's largest site, MacMost.com, features video tutorials for Apple enthusiasts. It includes many videos on using Macs, iPhones, and iPads.

Gary has written numerous computer books, including *ActionScript 3.0 Game Programming University*, *MacMost.com Guide to Switching to the Mac*, *Special Edition Using Director MX*, and *My Pages (for Mac)*.

Gary lives in Denver, Colorado, with his wife, Debby, and daughter, Luna. He has a computer science degree from Drexel University and a master's degree in journalism from the University of North Carolina at Chapel Hill.

Website: http://garyrosenzweig.com

Twitter: http://twitter.com/rosenz

More iPad Tutorials and Book Updates: http://macmost.com/ipadguide/

Acknowledgments

Thanks, as always, to my wife, Debby, and my daughter, Luna. Also thanks to the rest of my family: Jacqueline Rosenzweig, Jerry Rosenzweig, Larry Rosenzweig, Tara Rosenzweig, Rebecca Jacob, Barbara Shifrin, Richard Shifrin, Barbara H. Shifrin, Tage Thomsen, Anne Thomsen, Andrea Thomsen, and Sami Balestri.

Thanks to all the people who watch the show and participate at the MacMost website.

Thanks to everyone at Pearson Education who worked on this book: Laura Norman, Lori Lyons, Tricia Bronkella, Kathy Ruiz, Kristy Hart, Cindy Teeters, Mark Shirar, and Greg Wiegand.

We Want to Hear from You!

As the reader of this book, *you* are our most important critic and commentator. We value your opinion and want to know what we're doing right, what we could do better, what areas you'd like to see us publish in, and any other words of wisdom you're willing to pass our way.

We welcome your comments. You can email or write to let us know what you did or didn't like about this book—as well as what we can do to make our books better.

Please note that we cannot help you with technical problems related to the topic of this book.

When you write, please be sure to include this book's title and author as well as your name, email address, and phone number. We will carefully review your comments and share them with the author and editors who worked on the book.

Email: feedback@quepublishing.com

Mail: Que Publishing
ATTN: Reader Feedback
800 East 96th Street
Indianapolis, IN 46240 USA

Reader Services

Visit our website and register this book at quepublishing.com/register for convenient access to any updates, downloads, or errata that might be available for this book.

Learn to tap, swipe, flick, and pinch your way through the iPad's interface.

Learn to use the iPad's physical switches.

In this chapter, you learn how to perform specific tasks on your iPad to become familiar with the interface.

Getting Started

Before you learn how to perform specific tasks on your iPad, you should become familiar with the interface. If you have used an iPhone or iPod touch, you already know the basics. But if the iPad is your first touch-screen device, you need to take time to become accustomed to interacting with it.

Generations of iPads

The first thing you may want to do is identify which iPad you have and what features are available to you. There have been many versions of the iPad: the iPad, the iPad 2, the 3rd and 4th generation iPads, the iPad Air (5th generation iPad) and two generations of the iPad mini.

Identifying Your iPad

The following table shows the major differences between these iPads:

iPad Comparison Chart

Model	Released	Display Size	Screen Resolution
iPad	April 2010	9.7-inch	768x1024
iPad 2	March 2011	9.7-inch	768x1024
3rd Generation	March 2012	9.7-inch	1536x2048 Retina
4th Generation	November 2012	9.7-inch	1536x2048 Retina
iPad mini 1st Generation	November 2012	7.9-inch	768x1024
iPad Air	November 2013	9.7-inch	1536x2048 Retina
iPad mini 2nd Generation	November 2013	7.9-inch	1536x2048 Retina

Model	Front Camera	Rear Camera	Processor	Connector
iPad	None	None	A4	30-pin
iPad 2	0.3MP/VGA	0.7MP/720p HD	A5	30-pin
3rd Generation	0.3MP/VGA	5MP/1080p HD	A5X	30-pin
4th Generation	1.2MP/720p HD	5MP/1080p HD	A6X	Lightning
iPad mini 1st Generation	1.2MP/720p HD	5MP/1080p HD	A5	Lightning
iPad Air	1.2MP/720p HD	5MP/1080p HD	A7	Lightning
iPad mini 2nd Generation	1.2MP/720p HD	5MP/1080p HD	A7	Lightning

iPad Capabilities Chart

Model	iOS 7-Compatible	Siri-Compatible	AirDrop
iPad	No	No	No
iPad 2	Yes	No	No
3rd Generation	Yes	Yes	No
4th Generation	Yes	Yes	Yes
iPad mini 1st Generation	Yes	Yes	Yes
iPad Air	Yes	Yes	Yes
iPad mini 2nd Generation	Yes	Yes	Yes

The 3rd and 4th generation iPads, the iPad Air, and the 2nd generation iPad mini use a very different display than the previous versions. They are the same size, but a higher resolution. Instead of 768 pixels across and 1024 vertically, they contain 1536 and 2048, giving you four times as many pixels. This means photographs and text are crisper and clearer. In fact, you can't even distinguish the individual pixels with your eye unless you hold the iPad very close.

Another difference between iPads is the cameras. The original iPad had no camera at all. The 2nd and 3rd generations had cameras, but the more recent iPads have a rear-facing camera that is capable of much higher resolution for both still photos and video.

Each iPad has also become a little more powerful with a faster processor at its heart. The latest iPad has the 64-bit A7 processor, which gives it the capability to handle voice dictation and render beautiful graphics for games.

iOS 7

The primary piece of software on the iPad is the operating system, known as iOS. This is what you see when you flip through the screens of icons on your iPad and access the various default apps such as Mail, Safari, Photos, and iTunes.

This book covers iOS 7, the version released in September 2013. There have been seven generations of the software that runs iPhones and iPads. The original iPhone OS was developed for the first iPhone. The third version, iOS 3, worked on iPhones and the iPad. This latest version, iOS 7, works on the iPad 2 and newer. If you have an original iPad, you can only use up to iOS 5. Many of the features and tasks in this book work the same in iOS 5 and iOS 6, but you will not be able to use the latest features such as the new Maps app or Siri. To find out which version you are using and to learn how to update, see "Keeping Your iPad Up-To-Date" in Chapter 3.

The iPad Buttons and Switches

The iPad features a Home button, a Wake/Sleep button, a volume control, and side switch.

Wake/Sleep button

Side switch

Volume control

Home button

The Home Button

The Home button is probably the most important physical control on the iPad and the one that you will use the most often. Pressing the Home button returns you to the Home screen of the iPad when you are inside an application, such as Safari or Mail, and you want to get back to your Home screen to launch another app. You can also double press the Home button to jump to the app switching screen that we'll look at in Chapter 15.

Where's the Quit Button?

Few, if any, apps on the iPad have a way to quit. Instead, think of the Home button as the Quit button. It hides the current app and returns you to your Home screen. The app is actually still running, but hidden, in the background. To completely quit an app, see "Quitting Apps," in Chapter 15.

The Wake/Sleep Button

The primary function of the Wake/Sleep button (sometimes called the On/Off button) at the top of your iPad is to quickly put it to sleep. Sleeping is different than shutting down. When your iPad is in sleep mode, you can instantly wake it to use it. You can wake up from sleep by pressing the Wake/Sleep button again or pressing the Home button.

Peek a Boo!

If you are using the Apple iPad Smart Cover (see Chapter 18), your iPad will go to sleep when you close it and wake up when you open it, as long as you use the default settings.

The Wake/Sleep button can also be used to shut down your iPad, which you might want to do if you leave your iPad for a long time and want to preserve the battery life. Press and hold the Wake/Sleep button for a few seconds, and the iPad begins to shut down and turn off. Confirm your decision to shut down your iPad using the Slide to Power Off button on the screen.

To start up your iPad, press and hold the Wake/Sleep button for a few seconds until you see the Apple logo appear on the screen.

When Should I Turn Off My iPad?

It is normal to never turn off your iPad. In sleep mode, with the screen off, it uses little power. If you plug it in to power at night or during longer periods when you aren't carrying it with you, you don't need to ever shut it down.

The Volume Control

The volume control on the side of your iPad is actually two buttons: one to turn the volume up, and the other to turn it down.

Your iPad keeps two separate volume settings in memory: one for headphones and one for the internal speakers. If you turn down the volume when using headphones and then unplug the headphones, the volume changes to reflect the last settings used when the headphones were not plugged in and vice versa. A bell icon and a series of rectangles display on the screen to indicate the level of volume.

The Side Switch

The switch on the side of your iPad can do one of two things: It can be set as a mute switch or an orientation lock. You can decide which function this button performs in your iPad's settings. See "Setting Side Switch Functionality" in Chapter 2.

If you choose to use this switch as a mute switch, it will mute all sound if switched to the off position. You will see a speaker icon appear briefly in the middle of the screen when you do this. A line through the icon means you just muted the sound; otherwise, you just unmuted your iPad. By default, the iPad comes with the switch configured to mute.

If you choose to use this switch as an orientation lock, it will do something else entirely. Your iPad has two primary screen modes: vertical and horizontal. You can use almost every default app in either orientation. For example, if you find that a web page is too wide to fit on the screen in vertical orientation, you can turn the iPad sideways and the view changes to a horizontal orientation.

When you don't want your iPad to react to its orientation, slide the iPad side switch so that you can see the orange dot, which prevents the orientation from changing. When you need to unlock it, just slide the lock off.

This comes in handy in many situations. For instance, if you are reading an ebook in bed or on a sofa while lying on your side, then you may want vertical orientation even though the iPad is lying sideways.

Orientation and Movement

I know I said there were only four physical switches on your iPad, but there is another one: the entire iPad.

Your iPad knows which way it is oriented, and it knows if it is being moved. The simplest indication of this is that it knows whether you hold it vertically with the Home button at the bottom or horizontally with the Home button to one of the sides. Some apps, especially games, use the screen orientation of the iPad to guide screen elements and views.

Shake It Up!

One interesting physical gesture you might perform is the "shake." Because your iPad can sense movement, it can sense when you shake it. Many apps take advantage of this feature and use it to set off an action, such as shuffling songs in the Music app, erasing a drawing canvas or as an "undo" function.

Screen Gestures

Who knew just a few years ago that we'd be controlling computing devices with taps, pinches, and flicks rather than drags, key presses, and clicks? Multitouch devices such as the iPhone, iPod Touch, and the iPad have added a new vocabulary to human-computer interaction.

Tapping and Touching

Since there is no mouse, a touch screen has no cursor. When your finger is not on the screen, there is no arrow pointing to anything.

A single, quick touch on the screen is usually called a "tap" or a "touch." You usually tap an object on the screen to perform an action.

Occasionally you need to double-tap—two quick taps in the same location. For instance, double-tapping an image on a web page zooms in to the image. Another double-tap zooms back out.

Pinching

The screen on the iPad is a multitouch screen, which means it can detect more than one touch at the same time. This capability is used with the pinch gesture.

A pinch (or a pinch in) is when you touch the screen with both your thumb and index finger and move them toward each other in a pinching motion. You can also pinch in reverse, which is sometimes called an "unpinch" or "pinch out."

An example of when you would use a pinch would be to zoom in and out on a web page or photograph.

Dragging and Flicking

If you touch the screen and hold your finger down, you can drag it in any direction along the screen. This action often has the effect of moving the content on the screen.

For instance, if you are viewing a long web page and drag up or down, the page will scroll. Sometimes an app will let you drag content left and right as well.

What if you have a long web page or a list of items inside an app? Instead of dragging the length of the screen, lifting your finger up, and moving it to the bottom to drag again, you can "flick." Flicking is like dragging, but you move quickly and lift your finger off the screen at the last moment so that the content continues to scroll after you have lifted your finger. You can wait for it to stop scrolling or touch the screen to make it stop.

Pull Down and Release to Update

A common gesture is to tap in a list of items, drag down, and release. For instance, you would do this in Mail to get new messages. You would also do this in Twitter to get new tweets. Many Apple and third-party apps use this gesture to let you signal that you want to update the list of items. So if you don't see an obvious "update now" button, try this gesture.

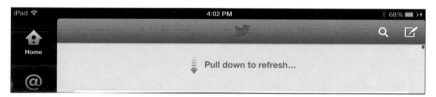

Four-Finger Gestures

You can perform one of three special functions by using four or five fingers at a time on the screen. If you put four or five fingers on the screen and pinch them all together, you will be taken out of your current app and back to the Home screen, similar to just pressing the Home button.

You can swipe left or right using four or more fingers to quickly page between running apps without going to the Home screen first. Swiping up with four fingers will bring you to the multitask switcher. See "Viewing Currently Running Apps" in Chapter 15.

iPad Screens

When using a desktop computer, you can usually see multiple windows on the screen that represent different applications, documents, and controls. The iPad doesn't use a window metaphor like this, but instead usually displays a full screen dedicated to a single purpose.

The Lock Screen

The default state of your iPad when you are not using it is the lock screen. This is just your background wallpaper with the time at the top and the words Slide to Unlock at the bottom. You can see the date under the time. The battery status is at the top right, and you can also see it under the time, alternating with the date, if the iPad is currently charging. There is also a small button at the bottom right for quick access to the camera app. The top and bottom of the screen show short bars to allow you to access the Notifications Center at the top and the Control Center at the bottom.

We look at customizing what appears on the lock screen in Chapter 2, as well as the Control Center and the Notifications Center later in this chapter.

By default, you see the lock screen when you wake up your iPad. Sliding your finger from left to right near the words Slide to Unlock takes you to the Home screen or to whichever app you were using when you put the iPad to sleep.

The Home Screen

Think of the Home screen as a single screen but with multiple pages that each features different app icons. At the bottom of the Home screen are app icons that do not change from page to page. The area resembles the Mac OS X Dock.

The number of pages on your Home screen depends on how many apps you have. The number of pages you have is indicated by the white dots near the bottom of the screen, just above the bottom icons. The brightest dot represents the page you are currently viewing. You can move between pages on your Home screen by dragging or flicking left or right.

We'll look at adding more apps to your iPad in Chapter 15.

An App Screen

When you tap on an app icon on the Home screen, you run that app just like you would run an application on your computer. The app takes over the entire screen.

At this point, your screen can look like anything. If you run Safari, for instance, a web page displays. If you run Mail, you see a list of your new email or a single incoming email message.

Home Screen Searching

If you are on your Home screen looking at page one of your app icons, you can drag from the center of the screen downward to bring up a Search iPad field at the top and a keyboard at the bottom. This allows you to search your iPad for apps, contacts, events, and other information.

You can type in anything to search for a contact, app, email message, photo, and so on. You don't have to define what type of thing you want to search for.

1. From the Home screen, tap in the center of the screen and drag down. Don't start at the very top of the screen, as that will bring up Notifications Center instead.

2. Type a search term using the on-screen keyboard.

3. You see a list of items on your iPad that match the search term. Tap the Search button on the keyboard to dismiss the keyboard and complete the search.

4. Tap the X in the search field to clear the search and start again.

5. Tap any of the items to go to the appropriate app and view the content.

The Settings Screen

One of the apps that you have on your iPad by default is the Settings app. With the Settings app, you can control several basic preferences for your iPad. (See Chapter 2 for more on customizing settings.)

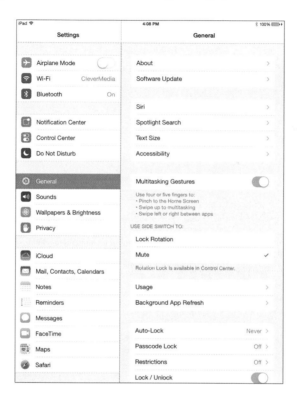

This is really just another app screen, but it is worth singling out as you'll need it to customize most aspects of your iPad.

Interacting with Your iPad

Now let's examine the different types of on-screen interface elements, the on-screen keyboard and how to use it, and specialized interactions such as text editing and copy and paste.

Common Interface Elements

Several interface elements are more complex than a simple button. In typical Apple style, these elements are often self-explanatory, but if you have never used an iPhone or iPod touch before, you might find some that give you pause.

Switches

A switch is like a simple button, but you need to tap only the switch to activate it. A switch gives you feedback about which state it is in.

For example, two switches indicate whether the Sound Check and Group By Album Artist features of the Music app are on or off. Tapping on either switch changes the position of the switch.

Toolbars

Some apps have a set of buttons in a toolbar at the top of the screen that are general controls. Each button is nothing more than a word or two that you can tap on to trigger an action. The toolbar might disappear or the buttons might vary depending on the mode of the app. An example of a toolbar is in the Videos app, which lets you switch between Movies, TV Shows, and Music Videos at the top. There is also a button to return to the main Store screen. But this toolbar can change. For instance, if you add some of your own video clips to your iPad, a new Home Movies item will be added to this toolbar.

Menus

Often tapping a single button in a toolbar brings up more buttons or a list of choices, which are like menus on your Mac or PC. The choices in the list are usually related. For example, a button in Safari gives you many different ways to share a web page.

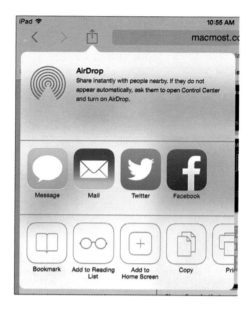

Tab Bars

Sometimes you see a row of buttons at the bottom of the screen that function similarly to toolbars, but each button represents a different mode for the
app. For instance, at the bottom of the App Store app, you see a Tab bar that
you use to switch between various lists of apps: Featured, Top Charts, Near
Me, Purchased, and Updates.

Using the On-Screen Keyboard

The interface element you might interact with the most is the on-screen keyboard. It pops up from the bottom of the screen automatically whenever you
need to enter some text.

The default keyboard has only letters and the most basic punctuation available. There are two shift keys that enable you to enter uppercase letters. You also have a Backspace key and a Return key.

Is There a Quicker Way to Capitalize?

So to capitalize a word, you tap the Shift key and then type the letter, right? You can. But a faster way is to tap the Shift key; then, without letting your finger off the screen, drag it to the letter and release in a single tap, slide, release action.

You can do the same with numbers and punctuation by tapping the .?123 key and sliding and releasing over the key you want.

To enter numbers and some other punctuation, tap the .?123 key to switch your keyboard into a second mode for numbers and punctuation.

To return to the letters, just tap the ABC key, or tap the #+= key to go to a third keyboard that includes less frequently used punctuation and symbols.

There are other keyboard variations. For instance, if you type in a location that needs a web address, a keyboard that doesn't have a spacebar appears that instead has commonly used symbols such as colons, slashes, underscores, and even a .com button. Instead of a Return key, you might see an action word like "Search" written on that key—tapping it will perform an action like searching the web. All keyboards include a button at the bottom right that enables you to hide the keyboard if you want to dismiss it.

You can also split the keyboard and/or move it up away from the bottom of the screen. Just tap and hold the keyboard button at the bottom-right corner of the keyboard. It has a little keyboard icon on it. Then select Undock or

Split. The first will simply move the keyboard to the middle of the screen. The second will do that as well, but will also split the keyboard into two halves. You can then drag the keyboard up and down by tapping, holding, and dragging on that same keyboard button. Drag it all the way back down to the bottom to dock it to the bottom again. You can also split the keyboard by placing two fingers on the keyboard and dragging them apart, and then rejoin it by dragging the fingers together.

Dictating Text

If you have a 3rd generation iPad or newer, or an iPad mini, you can also dictate text using your voice rather than typing on the keyboard. Almost any time you see a keyboard you should also see a small microphone button to the left of the spacebar. Tap that and you will be prompted to speak to your iPad. You will need to be connected to the Internet through a Wi-Fi or cellular connection for this to work.

1. Any time you see the default keyboard, you will see the microphone button to the left of the spacebar. Tap it to begin dictating.

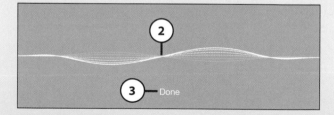

2. The keyboard is replaced with a waveform line that vibrates as you speak. Speak a few words or a sentence or two.

3. Tap Done when you are finished speaking. After a few seconds your spoken words will be translated into text and inserted as if you had typed them.

Speak somewhat slowly and clearly, and in segments about the length of a sentence for best results. Of course this feature isn't perfect. Pay careful attention to what is transcribed and correct any mistakes using the keyboard. Over time you will get better at speaking in a way that minimizes mistakes.

DICTATION TIPS

The dictation button will appear any time a standard keyboard is present in any app. You can use it in Notes, Pages, or any writing app. You can use it in search fields and text entry fields on the web. But you cannot use it when there are specialty keyboards like the ones used to enter in email addresses, web URLs, telephone numbers, and so on. So, for instance, you can use it in the Contacts app to speak a name or address, but not to enter an email address.

You need to be connected to the Internet for dictation to work. Your iPad sends the audio to Apple's servers, which handle the transcription and send the text back to your iPad. If you are not connected, it won't work.

Dictation works according to your language set in Settings, General, International. Not all languages are supported, but Apple is adding more all the time.

You can indicate the end of a sentence by saying "period" or "question mark." You can also speak other punctuation like "comma" or "quote."

You can also speak commands like "new line" or "cap" to capitalize the next word. There is no official list of what the dictation feature supports, and since the transcription takes place on Apple's servers they can change how it handles commands at any time.

Editing Text

Editing text has its challenges on a touch-screen device. Even though you can just touch any portion of your text on screen, your finger tip is too large for the level of precision you usually get with a computer mouse and cursor. To compensate, Apple developed an editing technique using a magnifying glass area of the screen that you get when you touch and hold over a piece of text.

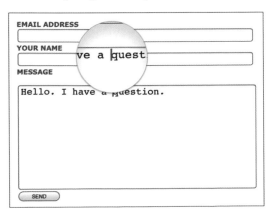

EMAIL ADDRESS

YOUR NAME

ve a quest

MESSAGE

Hello. I have a question.

SEND

For example, if you want to enter some text into a field in Safari, touch and hold on the field. A circle of magnification appears with a cursor placed at the exact location you selected.

When you find the exact location that you want to indicate, release your finger from the screen. Then a variety of options display, depending on what kind of text you selected, such as Select, Select All, and Paste. You can ignore the options presented and start typing again to insert text at this location.

Copy and Paste

You can copy and paste text inside an app, and between apps, on your iPad. Here's how you might copy a piece of text from one document to another in the Notes app.

Notes

1. Launch Notes. If you don't have any notes yet, create one by typing some sample text.

2. Touch and hold over a word in your note. The Select/Select All pop-up menu appears.

3. Choose Select.

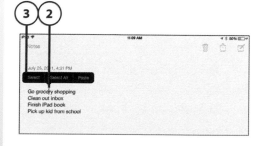

4. Some text appears highlighted surrounded by dots connected to lines. Tap and drag the dots so the highlighted area is exactly what you want.

5. Tap Copy.

6. Tap the new note button to create a new note.

7. Tap the empty document area once to bring up a pop-up menu with the Paste command.

8. Tap Paste to insert the copied text.

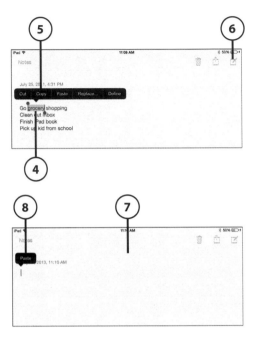

Using Siri

Siri is a voice-activated assistant that was first introduced in 2011 on the iPhone 4S. You can use your voice and speak commands to your iPhone and Siri will respond. It will either give you information or take action using one of the apps on the iPhone.

To use Siri on your iPad, you need to make sure you have Siri turned on in the Settings app under General settings. Then, you use the Home button to activate Siri.

1. In your Settings app, tap the General settings.

2. Make sure Siri is turned on.

3. Press the Home button to exit Settings.

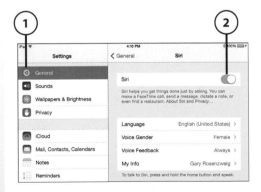

4. Press and hold the Home button for about a second. The Siri interface will pop up, showing a waveform line at the bottom of the screen that reacts to the sound of your voice.

5. The help button brings up a list of examples of things you can ask Siri.

6. Speak clearly at a normal pace and say "How's the weather outside?" After a short delay, the words you spoke will appear and Siri will attempt to perform an action based on those words.

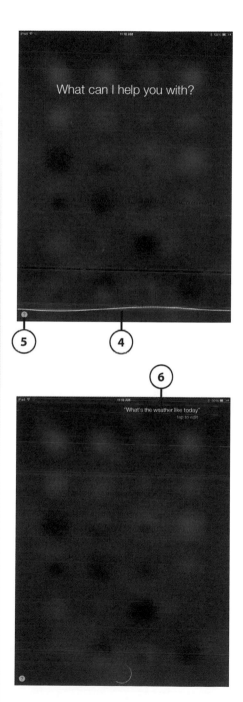

7. In this case, a short weather forecast will appear.

8. Siri also responds with a statement and will speak it audibly. The text of the response will typically appear above the response.

9. You can ask Siri another question by tapping the microphone button at the bottom of the screen.

SIRI TIPS

To use Siri, you must have a connection to the Internet. It can be a Wi-Fi connection or a mobile connection. When you speak text, the audio is transmitted to Apple's servers to convert it to text and interpret the command. The results are sent back to your iPad.

It is best to speak clearly and to limit background noise. Using Siri in a quiet room works better than in a crowded outdoor space or in a car with the radio on, for instance.

Because Apple's servers control Siri, they can update Siri's capabilities at any time. For example, originally Siri did not understand a request for local sports scores, but after an update this functionality was added.

You can use Siri to perform many tasks on your iPad without typing. For example, you can search the Web, set reminders, send messages, and play music. Throughout the rest of this book, look for the Siri icon for tips on how to use Siri to perform a task related to that section of the book.

Using Notifications Center

To move between pages on your Home screen, you swipe left and right. But you can also pull down and pull up two special screens from any Home screen, or just about any screen at all, even if you are in an app.

Swiping from the very top of your screen downward pulls down the Notifications Center.

1. Swipe down from the top of the screen to pull down the Notifications Center. If you are having trouble, try placing your finger above the screen, outside of the actual screen area, and moving your finger down onto the screen, continuing all the way down.

2. In large type at the top of the screen, you will see today's date.

3. Under that, you may see a summary of today's weather, depending on your settings for the Notifications Center.

4. More information about today are summarized under the weather.

5. A preview of your calendar events for the day are shown. You can tap on an event to open the Calendar app and go right to it.

6. If you have any items set for today in the Reminders app, you will see them here. You can tap them to open the Reminders app.

7. If you have more information than can fit on the screen, you can swipe up to see it. This screen shows information about tomorrow as well as today.

8. Tap All to see other notifications, such as incoming email, Messages, and App Store updates.

9. Tap Missed to see events and other information from earlier in the day.

10. Tap the flat arrow at the bottom of the screen and drag up to the top of the screen to close the Notifications Center. You can also just press the Home button at the bottom of your iPad.

You can customize the Notifications Center in the Settings app, deciding exactly what appears in it. We look at that in Chapter 2.

Using Control Center

The Notifications Center comes down from the top of your iPad's screen, but the Control Center comes up from the bottom.

1. To bring up the Control Center, swipe up from the very bottom of the screen. If you are having trouble, try starting below the screen and swiping up onto the screen area all the way to the top.

2. The upper-left corner of the Control Center is a complete set of music playback controls. You see the name of the song playing and can pause or resume the song, and move the white line to jump around inside the song. You can also skip to the next or go back to the previous song.

3. Below the playback controls is a volume slider.

4. The first in a set of buttons in the middle of the Control Center is a switch that lets you quickly turn on Airplane mode. This shuts off all Wi-Fi, Bluetooth, and cellular data connections.

5. The next button lets you toggle on and off the Wi-Fi connection.

6. Likewise, you can toggle on and off the Bluetooth connection that you may be using with wireless headphones, a keyboard, or to connect to a wireless audio speaker.

7. You can quickly switch to Do Not Disturb mode, which silences all notifications such as incoming messages.

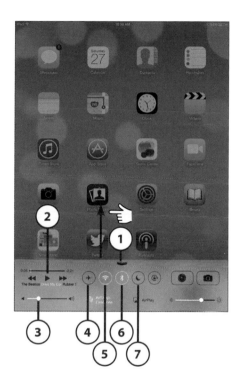

8. This switch locks the iPad's orientation to the current state—horizontal or vertical. In Chapter 2, you learn how to use the iPad's side switch for this, which then changes this Control Center button to a mute switch instead.

9. This button is a shortcut to take you to the Clock app.

10. This is a shortcut to take you to the Camera app.

11. If you have an iPad that supports AirDrop, this button lets you turn AirDrop on or off. We'll look at AirDrop in Chapter 3.

12. The AirPlay button lets you choose a device to stream audio or video to, assuming you have such a device connected to your network. We'll look at AirPlay in Chapter 16.

13. The bottom-right corner of Control Center lets you adjust the brightness of the iPad's screen.

14. To dismiss Control Center, you can tap the flat arrow at the top and drag down. You can also tap the screen above Control Center or simply press the Home button.

There's not much that Control Center does that cannot be done in the Settings app or the Home screen. Control Center simply provides quick access to a variety of functions.

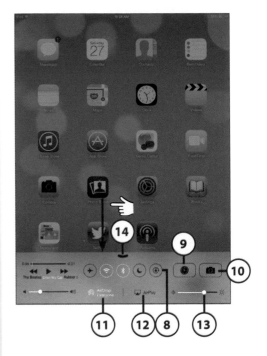

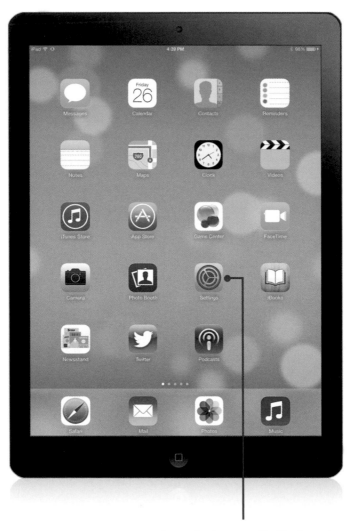

Customize how your iPad looks and
works through the Settings app.

In this chapter, you learn how to change some of the settings on your iPad such as your background images, sounds, passcode, and how some apps behave.

→ Changing Your Wallpaper
→ Getting Details About Your iPad
→ Setting Alert Sounds
→ Password Protecting Your iPad
→ Setting Parental Restrictions
→ Setting Side Switch Functionality
→ Setting Your Date and Time
→ Modifying Keyboard Settings
→ Do Not Disturb Settings
→ Privacy Settings
→ Notification Center Settings

2

Customizing Your iPad

Like with any relationship, you fall in love with your iPad for what it is. And then, almost immediately, you try to change it.

It's easier, though, to customize your iPad than it is your significant other because you can modify various settings and controls in the Settings app. You can also move icons around on the Home screen and even change how the Home button works.

Changing Your Wallpaper

The wallpaper is the image behind the icons on the Home screen and on the lock screen, so make sure it's something you like.

1. Tap the Settings icon on your Home screen.

2. Choose Wallpapers & Brightness from the Settings on the left side of the screen.

3. Tap the Large Wallpaper button that shows previews of your lock and home screens.

Settings

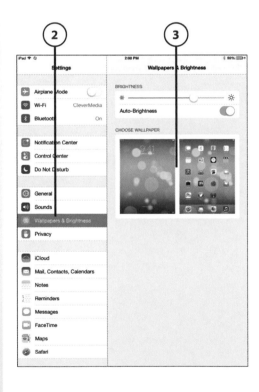

4. If you want to use one of Apple's dynamic wallpapers, tap here. Dynamic wallpapers are patterns that slowly animate.

5. If you want to select an image from your photo library—either of a photo you took with your iPad or one you synced from your computer—tap one of the groups of photos listed.

6. If you want to use one of Apple's default wallpaper images, tap here.

7. Choose an image from the category you selected in step 4, 5, or 6.

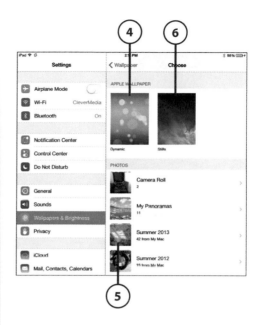

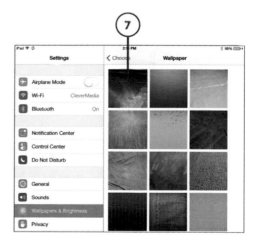

8. You'll see the full image in a pre-view covering the entire screen.

9. Choose Set Lock Screen to set this image as the background of your lock screen.

10. Choose Set Home Screen to set this image as the background for your Home screen.

11. Choose Set Both to make the image the background for both screens.

12. Tap Cancel at the bottom-left corner of the screen to go back to the wallpaper icons.

Adjusting the Wallpaper Image

You can touch and drag in a photo to move to other areas of the image so you can choose the part of the image you want as your wallpaper. You can also pinch to zoom in and out on your photographs.

Getting Details About Your iPad

One of the many things in the Settings app on the iPad is an About section, from which you can learn details about your iPad.

1. Tap the Settings icon on your Home screen.

Settings

2. Tap General from the list of settings on the left.

3. Tap About, the first item at the top of the list of General settings.

4. Tap Name to change the name of your iPad as it is seen in iTunes and iPhoto when you sync with your computer and various other instances.

5. See how many songs, videos, photos, and apps you have.

6. See the total capacity of your iPad and the amount of space available.

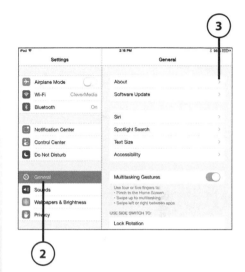

Why Am I Missing Space?

Notice in the example here that the capacity of the iPad is shown as 13.3GB. However, that particular model is advertised as a "16GB" model. The discrepancy between the two is because of space used by the operating system and other system files.

7. The version number tells you which version of the iPad operating system you are running. Check this to make sure you are running the latest version of iOS.

8. The model number tells you exactly which iPad you own if you happen to get it serviced or perhaps to report a bug to a third-party app developer.

9. The serial number, Wi-Fi address, and Bluetooth address are unique to your iPad. Apple may ask for your serial number if you are sending your iPad in for repairs. The Wi-Fi number is what you need if you are asked for a "MAC address" or "Ethernet address" for your iPad.

Another Model Number?

If you tap the Legal button and then the Regulatory button on the About screen, you are taken to another screen that lists another model number for your iPad. For the 4th generation iPad, Wi-Fi only model, this is A1458. The models A1459 and A1460 represent the AT&T and Verizon 3G models. When you are buying third-party accessories for your iPad, the specifications for those accessories may say "compatible with model X." In that case, X may represent either model number.

Setting Alert Sounds

Your iPad can be a noisy device with various events that trigger alert sounds. Just typing on the on-screen keyboard can produce a series of clicks.

Here's how to adjust your iPad's alert sounds.

1. Tap the Settings icon on the Home screen.

2. Tap Sounds from the list of settings on the left.

3. Adjust the volume of system sounds, like FaceTime ringtones and notification alerts. This does not affect the volume of music or video.

Settings

4. When this is turned on, the volume in step 3 can change by using the buttons on the side of the iPad. If you turn this off, you can still use the buttons to adjust the volume of music and video when those are playing, but otherwise the side volume controls won't affect the system sound volume.

5. Tap any of these settings to set the sound that plays when an event occurs. You can choose ringtones, alert tones, or custom tones for any of the events. Ringtone refers to FaceTime calls and Text Tone refers to the Messages app.

6. Switch the Lock Sounds on or off. When this setting is on, a sound plays when you unlock the Lock screen.

7. Switch Keyboard Clicks on or off.

How About Custom Sounds?

Any sound event can play a ringtone rather than a plain alert sound. You will see a list of "Alert Tones" that are built into iOS, as well as a list of ringtones, which include the built-in ringtones and any custom ringtones. You can add your own custom ringtones in iTunes on your Mac or PC and then sync them with your iPad. After the sync, you will see them listed when selecting an alert sound. See "Syncing Music," in Chapter 3. By obtaining or creating your own custom ringtones, you can set your alert sounds to anything you want.

Password Protecting Your iPad

Password protecting your iPad is a great way to make sure that someone else can't access your information or use your iPad.

1. Tap the Settings icon on the Home screen.

2. Tap General from the list of settings on the left.

3. Tap Passcode Lock.

Settings

Even More Security

To lock your iPad automatically when you aren't using it, choose Auto-Lock from the General Settings and set your iPad to automatically lock at 2, 5, 10, or 15 minutes. You can also choose to never have it auto-lock. Of course, you can manually lock your iPad at any time by pressing the Wake/Sleep button at the top.

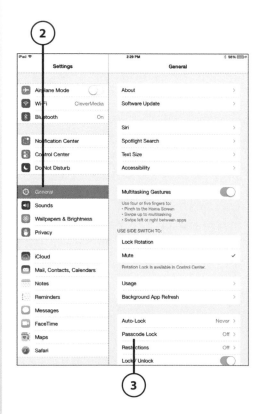

4. Tap Turn Passcode On to activate this feature. You then are prompted to enter a passcode.

5. Type in a four-digit passcode that you can easily remember. Write it down and store it in a safe place—you can run into a lot of trouble if you forget it, most likely needing to erase your iPad and restore it from your last backup.

6. You will be asked to re-enter your passcode.

7. Tap the Require Passcode button and choose the delay before a passcode is required. If you choose anything other than Immediately, someone else using your iPad can work on it for that period of time before needing to enter the code.

8. Tap Simple Passcode to switch from using a 4-digit number to a longer password that can include both letters and numbers, if you want additional security; otherwise, your password will consist of 4 digits. Tap Turn Passcode On.

9. Turn off Siri to disable the ability to use Siri from the Lock screen.

10. Turn on Erase Data if you want to erase the iPad data after 10 failed passcode attempts.

11. Press the Wake/Sleep button to confirm your new settings work. Then press the Home button and Slide to Unlock. The Enter Passcode screen displays.

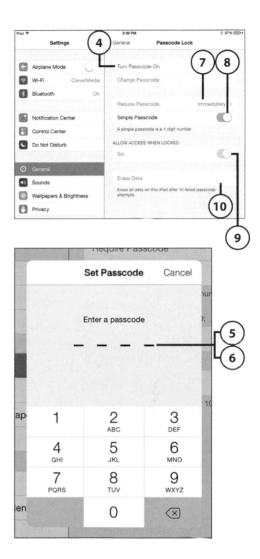

You Forgot Your Passcode?

Well, it wouldn't be secure if there were a way to get around the passcode, so you're out of luck until you can connect your iPad to your Mac or PC and use iTunes to restore it. Hopefully, this never happens to you.

Setting Parental Restrictions

If you plan to let your kids play with your iPad, you might want to set some restrictions on what they can do.

1. Tap the Settings icon on the Home screen.

2. Tap General.

3. Tap Restrictions.

Settings

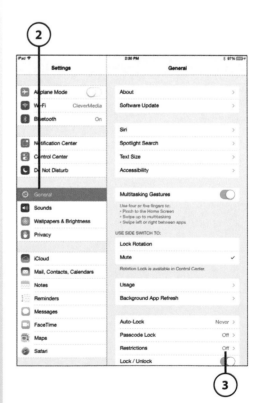

4. Tap Enable Restrictions to turn restrictions on.

5. Type in a four-digit code and then re-enter the code when prompted. Remember this code, or you can't turn off or change restrictions later.

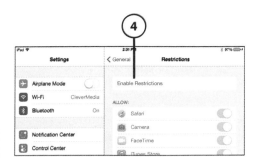

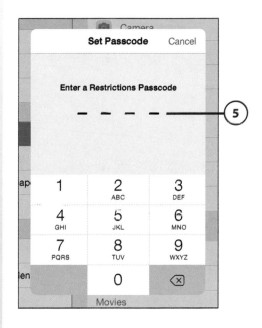

6. To remove the Safari, Camera, FaceTime, iTunes, and iBookstore apps from your Home screen, turn the switches to off. The user of the iPad will not be able to access these apps.

7. The Installing Apps switch prevents new apps from being installed.

8. Turn Deleting Apps on to prevent the user from removing apps.

9. Another way to access information on the Internet is to ask Siri. Turn this switch off to prevent that.

10. Turn AirDrop off to prevent the use of AirDrop for transferring photos and other data to or from this iPad.

11. The Allowed Content settings enable you to restrict access to various content based on ratings systems and filters. Each works slightly differently depending on the type of content and the way that content is rated. But you can also turn off each of these completely.

12. You can choose to turn off the In-App Purchases switch completely, or require a password for each purchase, or require the password once every 15 minutes. These settings help parents by preventing kids from making purchases from within an app, such as a game, using their iTunes account.

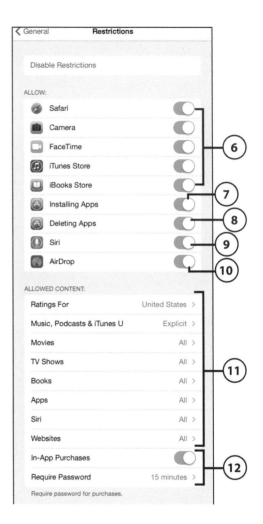

13. Tap Location Services to enable or disable location-based functions of all apps, including Find My Phone.

14. All of the Privacy settings control the use and editing of stored information. For instance, you can set it so Contacts can be accessed fully, allowing changes, or accessed without allowing changes. Each subcategory gives you a list of apps that use the information, and you can turn each app's access to that information on or off. For instance, you can allow Pages and Keynote to access your photos, but not the Facebook app.

15. Tap Accounts to disallow adding or changing Internet accounts, such as email, contacts, and calendar events.

16. Turn Background App Refresh off to stop apps from updating in the background.

17. The Volume Limit settings allow for a maximum volume limit to be set and adjusted.

18. Select options in the Game Center functions you want to allow. This will only affect games that use Game Center to communicate with other players. Some apps use their own system of communication or other systems, like Facebook.

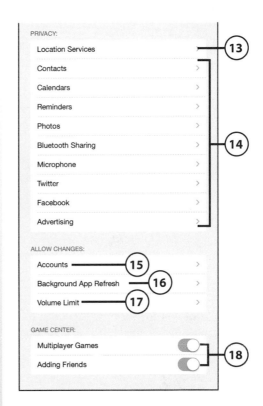

Privacy Settings

The permission settings in step 14 are also available outside of parental controls. You can select Privacy on the left side of the Settings app and then view all the apps that have requested access to contacts, events, reminders, photos, and your location. You can review and deny access to these apps. See "Privacy Settings" later in this chapter.

>>>Go Further

SETTINGS NOT REMEMBERED

It would be nice if you could just switch Restrictions on and off, so you could hand off your iPad to Junior after quickly turning them on, but the settings are reset each time. So you need to set the switches each time after turning Restrictions back on.

Setting Side Switch Functionality

The switch on the side of your iPad can be used for one of two things: muting the sound or locking the screen orientation. Whichever one you choose for the switch, the other will then appear in the Control Center as a button. See "Using Control Center" in Chapter 1. So either way, you have fairly quick access to both functions.

1. Tap the Settings icon on the Home screen.

Settings

2. Tap General.

3. Tap Lock Rotation if you want your side switch to be an orientation lock switch.

4. Tap Mute if you want the side switch to mute the volume on the speakers and earphones.

Setting Your Date and Time

You can set the date, time and time zone for your iPad and even choose whether to display the time in 12- or 24-hour mode.

1. Tap the Settings icon on the Home screen.

Settings

2. Tap General.

3. Scroll down to the bottom of the General Settings list and tap Date & Time.

4. Turn the 24-Hour Time switch on to show the time in 24-hour format (military time). Turn it off to revert to 12-hour format.

5. Turning Set Automatically on syncs the date and time with the Wi-Fi network or cellular network that the iPad is connected to.

6. Tap the Time Zone button and then enter the name of your city, or a nearby city, to set the zone.

7. To manually set the time, tap the date and time shown to bring up a set of controls underneath.

8. The controls are four "wheels" that you can spin by dragging up and down. You can set the day, hour, minute, and AM or PM.

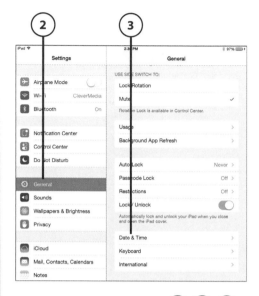

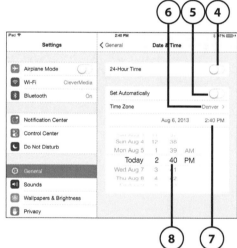

Modifying Keyboard Settings

If you use your iPad for email or word processing, you will use the on-screen keyboard a lot. The keyboard does several things to make it easier for you to type, but some of these might get in the way of your typing style. Use the following steps to modify the keyboard settings to your preferences.

1. Tap the Settings icon on the Home screen.

2. Tap General.

3. Scroll down to the bottom of the General Settings list and tap Keyboard.

4. Turn Auto-Capitalization on to automatically make the first character of a name or a sentence a capital letter.

5. Turn Auto-Correction on to have mistyped words automatically corrected.

6. Turn Check Spelling on or off to control whether possible misspellings are indicated.

7. Turn Enable Caps Lock on or off. By default, this is off. When Caps Lock is enabled, you can double-tap the shift key to lock it.

8. Turn on the "." Shortcut if you want a double-tap of the spacebar to insert a period followed by a space.

9. Use the Keyboards button to choose a different keyboard layout. In addition to keyboards commonly used in other countries, you can switch to a Dvorak keyboard or one of several other alternatives to the traditional QWERTY keyboard.

10. If you want to lock the keyboard so it can never be split and moved up vertically, then switch this to off. See, "Using the On-Screen Keyboard," in Chapter 1.

11. You can add your own shortcuts. For instance, you can set it so when you type "omw," it will instantly expand to "On my way!" Add your own shortcuts for things you commonly type.

Settings

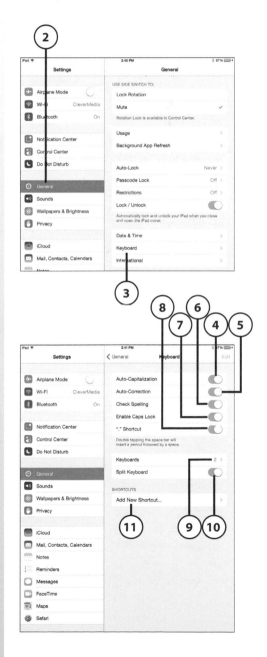

12. After you add a second keyboard in step 9, you now see a special key that lets you switch between keyboards. So, you can have both an American English keyboard and a Dvorak keyboard selected in Settings, and tap here to switch between them.

SMILE!

>>>Go Further

When you look at the list of special keyboards, you'll mostly see ones for various languages. But there is one special keyboard called Emoji that is something different. If you add that one, you can switch to a keyboard that features smiling faces and other little graphics you commonly see in text messages. You can actually use these little pieces of clipart in many apps, although some, like Pages, do not support them.

Do Not Disturb Settings

Your iPad is trying to get your attention. It beeps and rings with notifications, FaceTime calls, messages, and event alarms. In fact, it might be hard to have it nearby when trying to sleep or enjoying some time "offline."

Do Not Disturb is a mode where your iPad quiets down. Most audible alerts are silenced. You can set your iPad to enter this mode manually with the Do Not Disturb settings, or set a predefined block of time each day.

1. Tap the Settings icon on the Home screen.

Settings

2. Tap Do Not Disturb on the left.

3. You can turn on Do Not Disturb mode manually with this switch.

4. Tap Scheduled for Do Not Disturb mode to automatically start and end at a specific time. For instance, you can set it to start at 10 p.m. and end at 7 a.m. so you aren't disturbed while sleeping.

5. Tap here to use time and date controls to set the start and end times.

6. Tap Allow Calls From to allow FaceTime calls and messages from specific people by selecting a group in your contacts list.

7. Turn on Repeated Calls so that someone can reach you in an emergency by calling twice within three minutes.

8. Do Not Disturb can work at all times, or only when you have your iPad locked. Tap the desired setting so that a blue checkmark appears next to it.

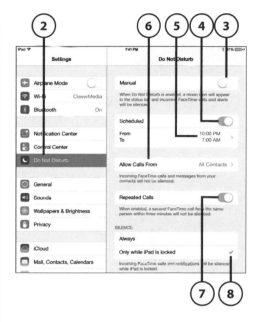

Privacy Settings

Information on your iPad can flow between apps. For instance, your Mail app will use email addresses from your Contacts app to allow you to easily address messages.

You may not want all apps to have access to all your information. Sure, sharing email addresses between Contacts and Mail makes sense, but does that game you just downloaded really need access to your contacts, or photos, or calendar events? Privacy settings allow you to see which apps have access to what and to turn off those connections, if you like.

1. Tap the Settings icon on the Home screen.

2. Tap Privacy on the left.

3. The list includes different sources of information, such as your contacts, location, reminders, and even your Twitter and Facebook accounts. Select any one to see which apps have access to that information.

4. After you select an app, you see the list of apps that have permission to use the data.

5. Tap the switch to turn access on or off for each app.

Settings

Notification Center Settings

Apps communicate with you through the Notifications Center. See "Using Notifications Center" in Chapter 1. There you receive alerts telling you all sorts of things: incoming email, new messages, game events, news items, and so on.

The Notification Center settings is where you decide how important each type of notification is, and how it should be displayed, if at all.

1. Tap the Notifications Center category in Settings.

2. Use these switches to configure whether notifications and the summary of today's events should be shown in Notifications Center while you are on the lock screen. This information would be available to anyone holding your iPad, even if they have not entered your passcode to get past the lock screen.

3. Use these switches to configure what information should be available in the Today View portion of the Notifications Center screen.

4. You can have all the items in the Notifications Center sorted by time, or sorted manually in an order you specify, by tapping one of these options.

5. If you choose the manual option in step 4, tap Edit at the top right of the screen to be able to arrange the apps listed on this screen. Set them in the order you want them to appear in Notifications Center.

6. Tap an app to edit its settings.

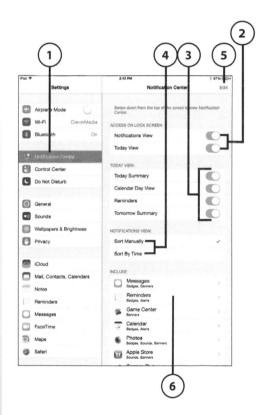

7. Choosing the None alert style means that neither a banner nor alert will appear.

8. Choosing Banners means that a drop-down banner will appear when the app has a message, and it will go away on its own after a few seconds. These do not interrupt your work when they appear.

9. Choosing Alerts means that a box pops up in the middle of the screen when the app has a message, and you must dismiss it to continue.

10. Turning on Badge App Icon means that the icon will show a number over it when there is a message.

11. Many apps let you set the specific sound used. Tap Alert Sound to specify the sound the app uses.

12. Turn off Show in Notifications Center to exclude these alerts from the Notifications Center screen completely. You will still see the alert when it happens, but it will no longer be in the list when you access Notifications Center.

13. Tap Include to choose how many alerts appear in the list in Notifications Center.

14. Show on Lock Screen means that alerts from this app appear, even when the iPad is locked.

15. Turn off Show Preview so that the small preview of the message does not appear with the alert.

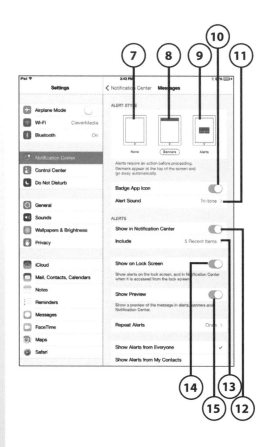

16. Tap Repeat Alerts to configure whether the alert will repeat after a few minutes, and how many times. It is useful to have an alert repeat in case you missed it the first time.

17. Tap Show Alerts from My Contacts to remove the blue check-mark beside Show Alerts from Everyone. For the Messages app, this turns off alerts for those not in your contacts list.

Each app has its own set of settings, so take a few minutes to go through them all and see what options are offered. As you add new apps to your iPad, any that use the Notifications Center will be added to this list, so it is a good idea to review your settings occasionally. When a new app wants to send you notifications, it first must ask you for permission. This is where you can go to revoke that permission later on.

It's Not All Good

Lock It Down

Notifications Center and Control Center put a lot of power on the Lock Screen. You can see a lot of information and control portions of your iPad without ever needing to enter your passcode.

If you prefer to have all of that power hidden behind the passcode, then turn off both options under Access On Lock Screen in the Notifications Center settings. Also turn off Access on Lock Screen in the Control Center settings.

Adding More and More Apps

The Settings app adds new items as you add new apps to your iPad. Some third-party apps do not add a component in the Settings app, so don't be alarmed if you don't see an app you added in the Settings list.

Sync your music and
information with your
Mac or PC computer.

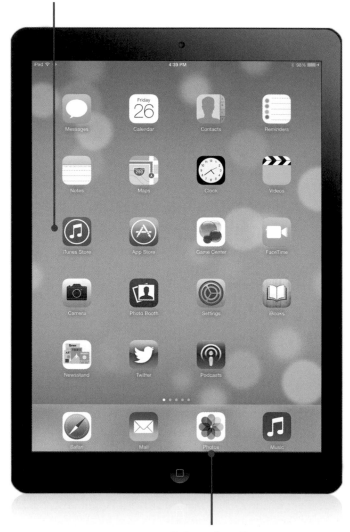

Put your favorite
photos on your iPad.

In this chapter, you find out how to connect your iPad to your local Wi-Fi network. You also see how to sync your iPad with your Mac or Windows computer and with Apple's iCloud service.

→ Setting Up Your Wi-Fi Network Connection

→ Setting Up Your 3G/4G Connection

→ Syncing Using iCloud

→ Syncing with iTunes

→ Syncing Photos with iTunes

→ Keeping Your iPad Up-To-Date

→ Sharing with AirDrop

Networking and Syncing

Your iPad connects you to the world. You can surf the web, view all sorts of information, communicate with friends, and share photos. But first, you must connect your iPad to the Internet. You can do that using a Wi-Fi connection. Some iPads also have the capability to connect to a mobile network.

Setting Up Your Wi-Fi Network Connection

One of the first things you need to do with your iPad is to establish an Internet connection.

Chances are that you did this when you started your iPad for the first time. It should have prompted you to choose from a list of nearby Wi-Fi networks. But you need to do this again if you first used your iPad away from home or need to switch to use another Wi-Fi network.

To connect your iPad to a wireless network, follow these steps.

Settings

1. Tap the Settings icon on the Home screen.

2. Choose Wi-Fi from the list of settings on the left.

3. Make sure that Wi-Fi is turned on.

4. Tap the item that represents your network. (If you tap on the blue-circled i button next to each network, you can further customize your network settings.)

I Don't Have a Wireless Network

If you don't have a Wi-Fi network but do have high-speed Internet through a telephone or cable provider, you have several options. The first is to call your provider and ask for a new network modem that enables wireless connections. Some providers might upgrade your box for free or a small cost.

Another option is to keep your current box and add a wireless base station of your own, such as the Apple Airport Extreme base station.

5. If the network is protected by a password, you will be asked to enter the password. Once you enter the password, your iPad will remember it. So if you switch between two locations, like work and home, you will be asked to enter the password for each the first time you use that connection. From that point on, your iPad will automatically log on to each connection as you move around.

>>>Go Further

SECURITY? YES!

Your wireless network at home should have security turned on. This means that you should see a padlock next to it in the list of Wi-Fi networks on your iPad. When you select it for the first time, you should be asked to supply a password.

If you don't require a password, seriously consider changing your Wi-Fi network box's settings to add security. The issue isn't simply about requiring a password to use your Internet connection. It is about the fact that a secure network will send encrypted data through the air. Otherwise, anyone can simply "sniff" your wireless connection and see what you are doing online—such as using credit cards and logging on to websites and services. See your network equipment's documentation to set up security.

Setting Up Your 3G/4G Connection

If you have an iPad with 3G/4G capabilities, you can set it up to use AT&T, Verizon, or any other compatible network. You can purchase a monthly data plan or purchase service in shorter increments.

1. Tap the Settings icon on the Home screen.

2. Tap Cellular Data on the left.

3. Turn on Cellular Data. In addition, if you have a 3rd generation iPad, turn on Enable LTE for the faster 4G connection.

4. Tap View Account.

Settings

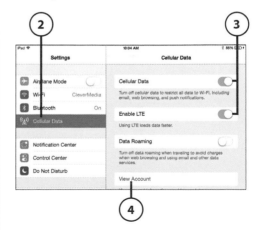

5. You have three options to set up an account with AT&T. Other carriers may offer different options. The first one is to set up a completely new account. If you choose this, skip to step 8.

6. Another option is to add your iPad's data plan as an additional service to your existing AT&T plan. Use this if you are already an AT&T customer. You will be prompted for your mobile phone number, zip code, passcode, and social security number to complete the setup.

7. This option is for those who already have an iPad data plan but want to transfer it from an old iPad to a new one.

8. To set up a new account, you are prompted for some basic information. You need to enter all your basic information and specify an email address for your account and a password.

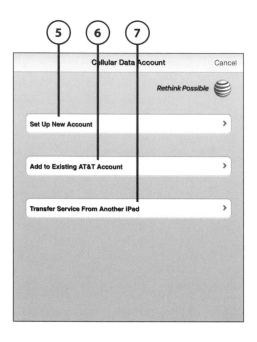

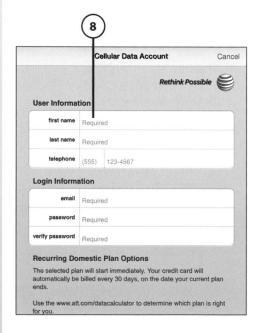

9. Choose a data plan that best fits your needs

10. Enter your credit card information. When you are done, you have to approve the service agreement and confirm your purchase. Still, it beats going to the mall and dealing with a salesperson at a mobile phone store, right?

It may take a few more minutes for your 4G service to activate. After establishing 4G service, you can return to this section of the Settings app to view your usage and modify your plan. Then you can see your pay details and status.

Working with Wi-Fi and 3G/4G

After you establish a 3G/4G plan, your iPad should still connect to your Wi-Fi networks when it is in range and use 3G/4G when it cannot find a Wi-Fi network. You can also return to Settings and turn on or off Cellular Data to specifically prevent your iPad from using the 3G/4G network. This is handy when you are completely out of mobile data range but have local Wi-Fi; for instance, you might be on an airplane flight. Of course, for take-off and landing, you will most likely be asked to use the Airplane Mode available in the Settings as well. That mode comes in handy when you want to quickly take your iPad "off the grid" and have it connected to absolutely nothing.

Looking at the top-left corner of your iPad's screen, you can tell which sort of connection you are currently using. You will see the Wi-Fi symbol, a fan of four curves, when you are connected to Wi-Fi. If you have a 3G/4G plan you will see the name of your network next to it, such as "AT&T," plus a series of bars that show your connection strength. But you are only using that connection if the characters "3G," "4G," or sometimes "LTE" are shown.

It's Not All Good

Watch for Data Roaming

In the Cellular Data settings, you can turn Data Roaming on or off. This is what enables your iPad to connect to wireless data networks that are outside of your data plan, such as networks in other countries. If you leave Data Roaming on and your iPad connects to such a network, you may find a surprise bill in the mail. You can avoid extra charges by leaving Data Roaming off or by purchasing a plan from AT&T for International data roaming.

Syncing with iCloud

When you think of your contacts, calendar events, and email messages, you may be tempted to think of that information as being "on your iPad" or "on your computer." But today this information is usually in both places, and more. This is referred to as "the cloud"—when the actual location of the information isn't important as long as it is where you need it, when you need it.

As an iPad user, you have access to several different cloud services, most notably Apple's system called iCloud. It is a free service that offers email, contacts, calendar, and other types of data stored on Apple's servers and automatically synced to your iPad and the other Apple devices you may own.

Or, you could choose to use other cloud services, such as Gmail or Yahoo!, for mail and calendar events. There's no reason to pick just one—you can use both iCloud and Gmail on your iPad, for instance.

When you use cloud services, you get automatic syncing as long as you have a connection to the Internet. For example, add a contact to your iPad and your iPhone will automatically update to show that new contact. Let's look at how to set up an iCloud account, or link to one you've already created.

1. Go to the Settings app.

Settings

2. Select iCloud settings.

3. If you have never set up an account with Apple before, then tap Get a Free Apple ID to set one up. Any account you have with Apple, such as an iTunes account, would be an Apple ID, and you should use that instead of starting a new account.

4. If you already have an Apple ID, even if you have never used iCloud before, then enter your ID and password. Apple IDs can be any email address, not just an @icloud.com email address.

5. Tap Sign In to access your account. If your account has only been used for things like iTunes in the past, then you will be prompted to set up the new iCloud part of your account.

6. If you think you have used an email address to log on to iTunes or some other Apple service before, but you can't remember the password, then tap Forgot Apple ID or Password to reset your password.

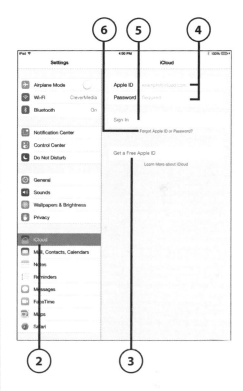

It's Not All Good

Don't Confuse ID with Email

An Apple ID is a unique identifier that allows you to log in to your iCloud account. It can be an Apple email address, like myipadbook@icloud.com, but it can also be a non-Apple email address, like myipadbook@gmail.com. In the former case, the ID is the same as your iCloud email address. But in the latter case, the ID is just an ID. Your email account would be a Gmail account and have nothing to do with your iCloud account.

7. You can use your iCloud email on your iPad. This would typically be an @icloud.com (or old @me.com or @mac.com) email address. These addresses are part of the free iCloud service. If you happen to be using a non-Apple email address as an Apple ID, note that this setting has nothing to do with that email account.

8. If Contacts is on, iCloud stores all your contacts so they automatically sync with the iCloud servers and then to your other Apple devices.

9. Likewise, iCloud can store your calendar events when the Calendars switch is on.

10. Turn on Reminders to have the Reminders app use iCloud to store reminders and automatically sync them with your other devices.

11. Safari can sync over iCloud as well. Things like your bookmarks, tabs, and reading list would sync across devices when the Safari switch is on.

12. Turn the Notes switch on so that Notes can also sync over iCloud.

13. iOS 7 allows you to store some passwords while using Safari so you don't need to enter them each time. Syncing these over iCloud means that you can also access these passwords on other Apple devices. Tap Keychain to configure this setting. We'll look at Keychain further in Chapter 7.

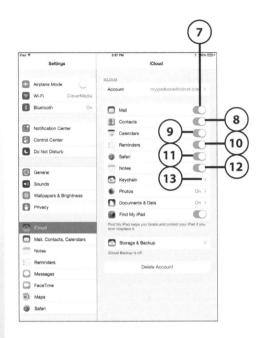

14. The Photos option enables you to configure Photo Stream for storage and sharing. We'll look at Photo Stream further in Chapter 9.

15. Some other Apps, like Pages, Numbers, and Keynote, can store documents using iCloud. This way you can access the same document using the same app on your other devices. The files are transferred to iCloud and then to each device without you needing to take any action. Tap Documents & Data to make sure switches for these apps are turned on, if you use them.

16. Find My iPad is an option that lets you locate your iPad on a map using another Apple device or the iCloud.com website. Be aware that if your Location Services are not on, this feature will not work.

17. If you don't have a desktop computer to use to back up your iPad, you can enable iCloud backups by tapping Storage & Backup. Most of your critical information, such as contacts and events, are stored in iCloud anyway if you have them enabled. However, a full backup makes it easier for you to recover from a lost or broken iPad.

It's Not All Good

iCloud.com

In addition to syncing between devices, much of your iCloud information is available if you go to iCloud.com and log in using your Apple ID. You can do this on any computer. So even if you are using your iPad as your only computing device, there still is another way to get to your data should you need it.

Syncing with iTunes

With iOS 7 and iCloud, the iPad can be a truly stand-alone device, no desktop computer needed. If you use a computer, however, you may still want to sync your iPad with it. There are several advantages to doing so:

- Each day you sync your iPad, iTunes stores a backup of its content. You can restore all your data from these backups if you lose your iPad.

- Syncing with a computer is a good way to get a large number of photos from your collection on your iPad.

- Syncing is how you get your music stored in iTunes onto your iPad. If you have a large collection of music, you can opt to copy only a selection of it to your iPad at any one time. You can also do this with iCloud if you use an optional pay service from Apple called iTunes Match.

- It can be easier to arrange your app icons on the Home screen pages using iTunes, rather than doing it on your iPad.

You might get a message on your computer the first time you connect your iPad and open iTunes, asking if it is okay to sync your iPad to this computer. The message won't reappear.

After connecting the first time, iTunes should automatically open when you connect your iPad. While connected, you can always resync to apply changes by clicking the Sync button in iTunes.

You can also check Sync over Wi-Fi connection in your iPad's options in iTunes. This allows you to sync when your iPad isn't connected by the cable. It only needs to be on the same network as your Mac or PC that is running iTunes.

Syncing Options

After your device is in sync, you can change some general options for your iPad from the Summary screen in iTunes. Most of the options are self-explanatory, such as Open iTunes When this iPad Is Connected.

1. Using iTunes 11, look for the devices button at the top right. If you have only the iPad connected, it should show the name of the iPad there, and you can click it and skip step 2. If you have enabled the left sidebar in the View menu of iTunes, then your iPad will appear in that sidebar instead.

2. A list of devices appears. Click on your iPad.

3. You can configure your backups. iCloud backups are convenient for those without regular access to a computer, but it uses Internet bandwidth and can be a problem if you have a slow connection. Backing up to your computer is the best option if you regularly sync to your computer anyway.

4. You can set your iPad to connect via Wi-Fi. From then on, you only need to be on the same network as your computer to sync with iTunes.

5. A handy graph of your iPad's storage is shown.

6. Any changes you make on this screen or any other iTunes sync screen will require that you click Apply to re-sync with the new settings.

One option that dramatically changes how your iPad syncs is Manually Manage Music and Videos, which turns off automatic syncing of music and videos and enables you to simply drag and drop songs and movies from your iTunes library onto the iPad icon on the left. (You might need to scroll down the Summary page to locate this checkbox if your screen size is too small to show the entire page at once.)

As we look at some of the syncing options for the iPad, the Mac version of iTunes is used as an example. The Windows version of iTunes is similar but not exactly the same.

>>>Go Further

BACK IT UP!

Perhaps the most important part of syncing with your computer is backing up your data. Everything you create with apps, every preference you carefully set, and every photo you take could be gone in a second if you drop your iPad or someone swipes it. Even a hardware failure is possible—the iPad isn't perfect.

Choosing This Computer is your best option. This saves all your data on your computer in a backup file. Try to do it once per day. With a good backup you can replace a lost iPad and restore all your data from the backup. It works incredibly well.

You can always plug your iPad into your Mac or PC, launch iTunes, and Control+click (right-click on Windows) your iPad in the left sidebar and select Backup. But it also happens automatically once per day if you set up the sync.

Your other option is iCloud. This will back up your data wirelessly to iCloud. It is your only option if you are not going to sync your iPad with a computer. But it does use up your data storage allotment in your iCloud account, so you may need to upgrade your iCloud account to allow for more data.

Even so, backing up to iCloud is a great alternative, especially if you travel often and use your iPad for critical tasks.

Syncing Music

The easy way to sync music is to select Entire Music Library In iTunes on your computer. If you have more music than can fit on your iPad, though, you must make some choices. Syncing Movies, TV Shows, Podcasts, Tones (ringtones for messaging and FaceTime), iTunes U, and Books all work in a similar way to syncing music, so you can apply what you learn in these steps to those items as well.

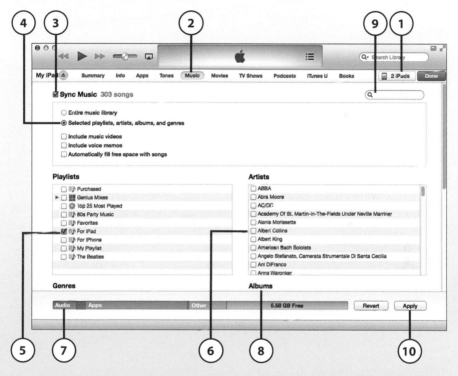

1. Select your iPad at the top of the iTunes window. If you have more than one iOS device, you may have to select your iPad from a short list.

2. Click the Music button of your iPad's settings in iTunes.

3. Select Sync Music, if it isn't already turned on.

4. Click the Selected Playlists, Artists, and Genres button.

5. Check off any playlists in the Playlists section that you want to include.

6. Check off any artists for which you want to include every song by that artist.

7. Check off any genres to include in their entirety.

8. Check off any albums you want to include.

9. Use the search box to quickly find specific artists.

10. Click the Apply button if you want to apply the changes now.

One Copy Only

Note that songs are never duplicated on your iPad. For instance, if the same song appears in two playlists and is also by an artist that you have selected to sync, the song only has one copy on your iPad. But it appears in both playlists and under that artist, album, and alphabetical list of all songs.

The Kitchen Sync

In addition to Music, you can also sync your Tones, Movies, TV Shows, Podcasts, iTunes U, and Books in a similar way. Each type of media has its own way of syncing, but they are all similar to music. For instance, Tones lets you sync all tones or selected tones, and then you select them individually. There are no playlists for Tones. Movies, TV Shows, and Podcasts can be included in playlists, so syncing options there let you sync by playlist if you like. Explore each page of your syncing settings to see which options you have.

>>>Go Further

MORE WAYS TO SYNC

iTunes Match is a service from Apple. For an annual fee, you can sync your music collection with Apple's servers. Then you can access all your music on your iPad by turning on iTunes Match in the Music settings in the Settings app. When you do this, you no longer need to sync your music. Instead, you see all your music on your iPad, and it will download from Apple's servers when you want to listen to a particular song.

Visit www.apple.com/itunes/itunes-match/ to find out more about Apple's iTunes Match service.

You can also sync your music and videos manually. This sounds like a lot of work, but it can be an easier way to sync your music for many people. If you check off Manually Manage Music and Videos on the iTunes Summary screen for your iPad, you can then drag and drop music from your iTunes music library on to your iPad. It requires a bit of knowledge about how the iTunes interface works, however. You'll need to choose View, Show Sidebar so you can see your iPad in the left sidebar. Then you can look at the Music item listed to see which songs are there. Switch to your iTunes Music library to see what songs you have on your computer and simply drag and drop songs, albums, or artists from the iTunes Music library to your iPad in the left sidebar.

Syncing Photos

The process for syncing photos from your computer to your iPad is very similar to how you move music, videos, and other data to your iPad. So let's use photos as an example. The steps here are very similar if you want to sync something else, like movies, to your iPad. You would just choose the Movies tab in iTunes instead of the Photos tab.

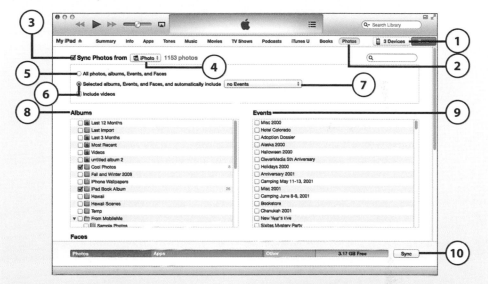

1. Select your iPad.

2. Choose the Photos tab at the top.

3. Click the checkbox to indicate that you want to sync photos.

4. You can choose from any applications that are compatible with iTunes and store photos. For instance, on Mac you can choose iPhoto and also Aperture if you use it. You can also simply select a folder to use as the location for your photos. The rest of the steps here assume you are using iPhoto.

5. Click All photos, albums, Events, and Faces to sync all your photos. Only do this if you have a fairly small collection.

6. Choose Selected albums, Events, and Faces, and automatically include button to select which albums and events to sync.

7. You can also have a number of recent events, or photos taken over a recent period of time, automatically sync. For instance, you can have it sync all events from the past 6 months.

8. Choose which albums you want to sync. Albums are collections of photos, like music playlists, that allow you to compile your favorite or related photos into a group.

9. You can also select individual iPhoto events.

10. When you are satisfied with your selections, click Sync to begin the transfer.

No Duplicates

Like with music, you get only one copy of each photo, no matter how many times the photo appears in albums, events, and faces. The photos appear in all the right places but take up only one spot in memory on your iPad.

It's Not All Good

One Way Only

As with the iPhone and iPod touch, syncing photos works only one way. For the photos you sync from your computer to your iPad, you cannot pull photos from your iPad back to your computer. The original is on your computer, and there is merely a copy on your iPad. So, it is important that you maintain your real photo library on your computer and remember to back it up.

Syncing music, movies, and other items works basically the same way. For instance, with music you can choose albums, artists, playlists or simply your entire music collection. With movies you can choose individual videos or everything.

Syncing Apps

iTunes keeps your apps on your computer and your iPad in sync and helps you organize them.

Note that you cannot run apps on your computer, just store them. You can store all of the apps you have downloaded and purchased on your computer and only have a subset of those set to sync on to your iPad.

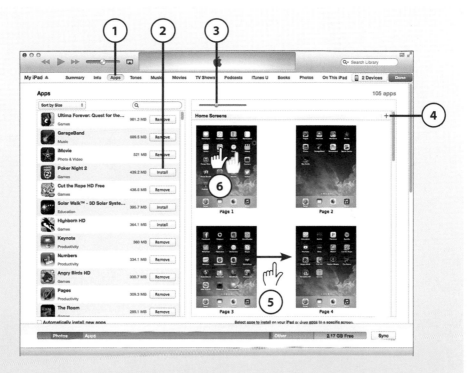

1. Click the Apps button of your iPad's settings in iTunes.

2. Use the Remove or Install buttons next to each app to remove or install the app, depending on its current state and what you want to do. Install appears next to apps that are currently not on the iPad, and you can click it to install it the next time you sync.

3. Use this slider to adjust the size of the screens so you can see more screens at a time, or make them larger to see the icons more clearly.

4. Click here to add a new screen.

5. You can swap entire pages by dragging them around in this area.

6. Double-click a screen to enlarge it.

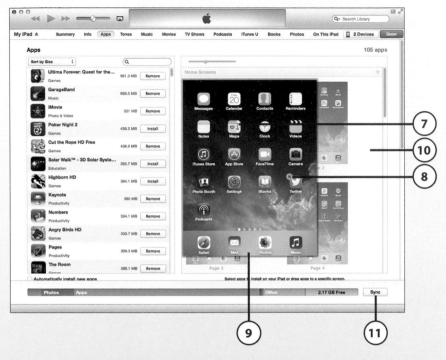

7. Now you can grab icons on this screen and move them around to change their positions. You can also drag them out of this screen. Then the screen will shrink back and allow you to move the icon onto another screen.

8. Move the cursor over an app and an X appears. You can use this to remove the app from your iPad.

Go Ahead—Select More Than One

You can select more than one app icon in iTunes by holding the Shift key and clicking and then drag them around as groups. This makes it easy to rearrange your apps in iTunes, which is the reason many people do it here rather than on the iPad itself.

9. You can also drag apps in and out of the iPad's dock area at the bottom.

10. To shrink a screen back to normal size, click an area outside of the screens.

11. Click the Sync button if you want to apply the changes now.

Syncing Documents

Apps sometimes have documents. For example, Pages is a word processor, so it would naturally have word-processing documents. Documents are stored on your iPad, but you might want to access them on your Mac or PC as well.

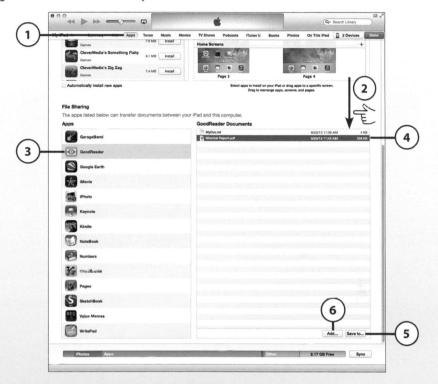

1. Click the Apps button of your iPad's settings in iTunes.

2. Scroll down to the bottom of the Apps page.

3. In the File Sharing section, choose an app.

No File Sharing Section?

The File Sharing section on the Apps screen will only appear if you have at least one app that is capable of sharing files through iTunes. Examples would be Pages, Numbers, Keynote, iMovie, GarageBand, Voice Memos, and GoodReader.

4. Select a document from the right.

5. Click the Save To button to save the document as a file on your computer.

6. Click the Add button to import a file from your computer to your iPad. Each app has its own document space on your iPad. So if you have two PDF readers, and you want the PDF document available to both, you need to add it to each app's documents.

Drag and Drop

You can also use drag and drop to pull documents out of, and import them into, the app's document space.

SYNC WITH ICLOUD

If you are using iCloud and the app supports it, then documents can sync automatically and wirelessly. For instance, if you are using Pages on your Mac with OS X Mountain Lion, and you save a Pages document to iCloud, you will see that document appear in your list of Pages documents on your iPad as well. Both your Mac and your iPad must be using the same iCloud account to enable you to work on the same document, while switching between your Mac and your iPad, with no need to sync in between.

Other apps may not support iCloud, so using iTunes to sync may be your only choice to move documents back and forth. See the section, "Syncing with iCloud," earlier in this chapter to set up iCloud.

Keeping Your iPad Up-to-Date

Apple periodically comes out with updates to iOS. And Apple and other developers come out with updates to apps all the time. Usually all these updates are free and contain useful and important new features. So, there is no reason not to keep your iPad up-to-date. In fact, updates sometimes include important security patches, so you should pay careful attention when an update is available.

To check for iOS and software updates, follow these steps:

1. Tap the Settings icon on the Home screen and then tap General.

2. Tap Software Update.

3. If you have the latest version of iOS, you will see a message like this one. Otherwise, follow the instructions provided to update your iPad.

4. Updating your apps is also important. iOS 7 can do this for you automatically. Make sure you have automatic updates enabled by going to the Settings app and choosing iTunes & App Stores on the left.

5. Under Automatic Downloads, you should have Updates turned on. This means iOS 7 will download app updates in the background. It will actually attempt to do this at times when you are not using your iPad and have a Wi-Fi connection.

6. On the Home screen, find and tap the App Store app. You may also notice a number in a red circle attached to the icon. This tells you how many apps you have that have updates available.

7. Tap the Updates button. This takes you to a screen with a list of all recent app updates.

8. Here you can see a list of all apps that have been updated recently. It also shows a list of changes to these apps.

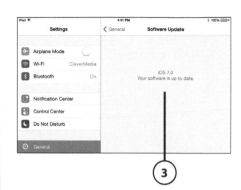

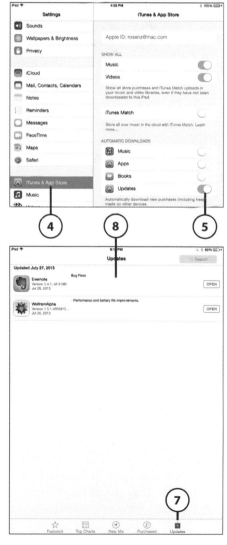

Bandwidth Concerns?

If you often find yourself in a situation where you are worried about Wi-Fi band-width, you may want to turn off automatic updates. For instance, if you pay for a limited Internet connection at home, but have a fast, unlimited connection at work, you can turn off automatic updates and use the Updates section of the App Store app to manually update your apps only while at work.

Sharing with AirDrop

A new way to get files from your iPad to another iOS device is using AirDrop. This technique uses Wi-Fi, but instead of going through a Wi-Fi network, it goes directly from iOS device to iOS device. So the devices don't need to be on the same network—they don't need to be on any Wi-Fi network at all.

AirDrop requires the latest Wi-Fi hardware in your iPad, so it only works with the 4th generation iPad or newer, or an iPad mini. Using AirDrop is pretty simple.

To use AirDrop, follow these steps:

1. To use AirDrop, make sure you have turned it on. Do this by accessing Control Center. See "Using Control Center" in Chapter 1. Make sure that it is set to "Everyone."

2. Let's use the Notes app as an example. You can use any app that can share items, such as the Photos app, Contacts app, and so on. While editing a note, tap the Share button.

3. In addition to sharing options such as Message and Mail, you'll see a list of other AirDrop-compatible devices that are within range. You will see whatever image the user has chosen as a user icon, plus their name. If you do not see your other device, it could be asleep, or have AirDrop disabled, or possibly is not a model that has AirDrop available.

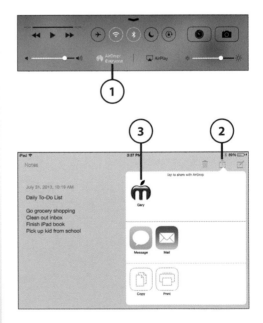

4. After you tap the icon, you see a "Waiting" message below it. In the meantime, the recipient will get an alert asking them to accept the transfer.

For You, Friend

The real power of AirDrop is sending between friends. For instance, if you are standing with your iPad next to a friend with an iPhone 5, you can send her a picture without both of you needing to share a common Wi-Fi network or exchanging email addresses. You just Share, select her for the AirDrop, and she accepts.

Purchase music and
buy or rent videos.

Play your
music.

Listen to Podcasts.

In this chapter, you learn how to use the Music and Video apps to play music and watch video. You also learn how to use iTunes Radio.

→ Playing a Song
→ Building a Playlist
→ Making iTunes Purchases
→ Downloading Podcasts
→ Playing Video
→ Using AirPlay to Play Music and Video on Other Devices
→ Home Sharing
→ Listening to iTunes Radio

Playing Music and Video

The iPad handles playing music as well as any iPod or iPhone ever has, plus it has a big screen for you to use to browse your collection. In Chapter 3, you learned how to sync music to your iPad from your computer. That's one way to get music onto your iPad. You can also use the iTunes app to purchase music, or the iTunes Match service to sync all your music from iCloud.

No matter how you put music on your iPad, you play your music using the Music app.

Playing a Song

So let's start by simply selecting and playing a song with the Music app.

1. Tap the Music icon, which is most likely along the bottom of your Home screen.

2. Tap Songs on the bottom, if it isn't already selected.

3. Tap the name of a song to start it. You can also tap and drag up and down on the screen to scroll through the list, or use the letters on the right to jump to a position in the list.

Music

Playing iTunes Match Music

If you are using iTunes Match, you will see all your music in the list, even songs not currently on your iPad. You can still tap the name of a song to start it. The song will download and play, assuming you are connected to the Internet. You can also tap the iTunes Match (cloud) icon for each song to simply download each song so it is ready to listen to later, even if you are not connected. You would want to do this for some songs if you are going to be away from your Internet connection and plan to listen to music.

Visit www.apple.com/itunes/itunes-match/ to find out more about Apple's iTunes Match service.

4. At the top of the screen, the Play button changes to a Pause button. The red time progress bar to the right begins to move.

5. Use the volume slider at the top to adjust the volume, or use the physical volume controls on the side of your iPad.

6. Tap the Now Playing button at the top to view album artwork for the current song.

7. Tap the repeat button to choose whether to repeat this song over and over again, or repeat the playlist or album you are currently listening to.

8. Tap the Shuffle button to make your iPad play the songs in the album or playlist in a random order.

9. Tap the list button to view the album that contains the song you are currently listening to.

10. Tap the left-facing arrow button at the top left to return to the main Music app interface.

How Else Can I Listen to Music?

You can also listen to music using third-party apps. Some apps access your music collection on your iPad, but the most interesting ones play streaming music from over the Internet. We look at apps, such as Pandora, in Chapter 15. You can also use iTunes Radio to listen to streaming music. We look at that later in this chapter.

11. Tap any of the buttons at the bottom of the screen—Playlists, Songs, Artists, and Albums to sort the list of songs.

12. A list of album artwork is shown. Tap on any album to view the album and the songs in it. Tap a song name to play it.

13. Tap in the Search field at the top of the list to search your songs.

Siri: Playing Music

You can use Siri to play music. Here are some examples:

"Play The Beatles"
"Play Georgia On My Mind"
"Play some blues"
"Play my driving music" (plays the playlist named "driving music")
"Shuffle all songs"
"Skip"
"Pause"

>>>Go Further

CONTROLLING MUSIC PLAYBACK

To control music playback

- Tap and move the red line in the progress bar to move around inside a song.

- Use the Back and Forward buttons that appear on either side of the play/pause button to move from song to song in the list of currently selected songs.

- Press the Pause button at any time to pause the music. Use the same button, which has become a Play button, to restart the music. Many headphones, including the Earpods that Apple sells, have a pause button on the cable that allows you to pause and resume playback and control the volume.

Building a Playlist

Playlists are a way to take the songs you have on your iPad and arrange them in ordered groups. For instance, you can create one to listen to while working, while working out, while trying to go to sleep, or make a party mix for your next get-together.

You can create playlists on your Mac or PC in iTunes, but you can also build actual playlists on your iPad.

1. Tap the Playlists button at the bottom of the main Music app screen.

2. A list of current playlists appears. Tap the New Playlist button.

3. Give the new playlist a name and tap Save.

4. In the expanded list of your music, tap the + buttons next to each song you want to add to the playlist.

5. Tap the Sort buttons at the bottom of the screen to sort through your music.

6. Use the Search field at the top to find songs faster.

7. Tap the Done button when you have selected all the songs you want to add to the playlist.

Genius Playlists

If you turn on the Genius feature in your Mac or PC copy of iTunes, you can use the Genius playlist feature to create playlists. After you click the Atom icon, select a song to use as the start of the Genius playlist. iTunes selects other songs from your collection that are similar and creates a playlist using the name of that song.

8. The playlist will remain on the screen. You can also return to it any time by tapping on the Playlists button at the bottom of the screen and selecting this playlist. If you want to edit the playlist, tap Edit.

9. On the playlist edit screen, remove songs from the playlist by tapping on the red buttons.

10. Tap and drag on the three-line buttons to rearrange the songs.

11. Tap the + button to add more songs to the playlist.

12. Tap Done to exit editing the playlist.

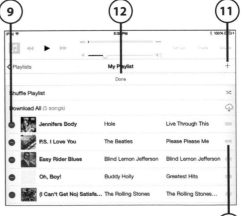

Making iTunes Purchases

You have lots of options when it comes to adding more music to your iPad. You can simply add more music to your iTunes collection on your computer and then sync those songs to your iPad. In that case, you can buy them from iTunes, from another online source, or import them from music CDs.

How Else Can I Get Music?

You can purchase music on your iPad only through the iTunes app. But you can sync music from your computer that you get from any source that doesn't use special copy protection, like CDs you import into iTunes. You can buy online from places such as Amazon.com, eMusic.com, cdbaby.com, or even directly from the websites of some artists.

In addition to syncing music to your iPad from your computer, you can purchase music, movies, TV shows, and audio books directly on your iPad using the iTunes app and using the same account that you use in iTunes on your computer.

1. Tap the iTunes app icon on your Home screen to go to the iTunes store.

2. Use the buttons at the top of the screen to choose which genre of music to view.

3. Swipe left and right to browse more featured albums.

4. Drag the screen up to reveal more lists, such as top albums, top songs, and music videos.

iTunes Store

5. Use the Search field at the top to search for an artist, album, or song by name.

6. Select a suggestion from the list, or tap the Search button on the keyboard to complete the search.

7. Find a song or album you want to buy, and tap its artwork to view more information.

8. If you move down the page by swiping upward, you'll also find ringtones, music videos, movies, and even books that match your search.

Syncing Devices

After you make an iTunes purchase, the music, TV show, or movie you downloaded should transfer to your computer the next time you sync your iPad. From your computer, you can sync your new purchase to any other device you use that uses your iTunes account.

You can also set iTunes on your computer and your other devices to automatically download new purchases. So when you buy on your iPad, you'll get the new music everywhere. On your iPad, that setting is found in Settings, iTunes & App Stores, Automatic Downloads. In iTunes on your computer, it is found in the menu iTunes, Preferences, Store, Automatic Downloads.

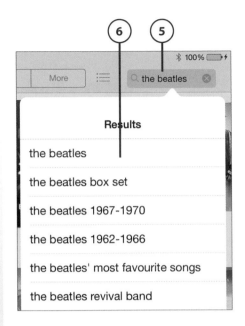

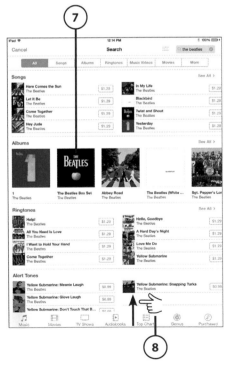

9. Tap a song name to listen to a sample of the song.

10. Tap outside of the album window to close it and return to the previous view.

11. To buy a song, album, or any item in the iTunes music store, tap the price of that item and then tap again on the Buy button.

How About My Home Videos?

If you shoot a home video with a video camera, or iPod touch or iPhone, you can bring that into iTunes on your Mac or PC and sync it to your iPad. They appear as Home Movies in the menu along the top of the Videos app.

What About My DVDs?

If you can import CD music content into iTunes, you'd think you'd be able to import video content from your DVDs. Well, technically it is possible (although not necessarily legal) by using programs like Handbrake (http://handbrake.fr/) for your Mac or PC to import DVD content and then drag the resulting file into iTunes. Then you can sync it with your iPad. These may also show up as Home Movies, since your iPad doesn't recognize them as official movie content.

>>Go Further

BUYING AND RENTING VIDEO

Although buying video is similar to buying music, some significant details are different and worth taking a look at.

Copy Protection   Although music in the iTunes store recently became copy-protection free, videos are a different story altogether. Purchased videos can be played back only on the Apple devices you own that use your iTunes account. You can't burn videos to a DVD, for instance, or watch them on a TV unless it is hooked up to an Apple device. Rentals are even more strict because you can watch them only on the device you rent them on.

Collecting Movies   Thinking of starting a collection of videos by purchasing them from Apple? These videos take up a lot of space on your hard drive. An iPad, even a 128GB version, quickly fills up if you start adding dozens of movies.

Time-Delayed Rentals   Rentals have some strict playback restrictions. After you download a rental, you have 30 days to watch it. After you start watching it, you have only 24 hours to finish it. This means you can load up your iPad in advance with a few movies to watch on an airplane flight or while on vacation.

TV Show Season Passes   You can purchase seasons of TV shows that aren't complete yet. When you do this, you are basically pre-ordering each episode. You get the existing episodes immediately but have to wait for the future episodes. They usually appear the next day after airing on network television.

Multi-Pass   In addition to season passes, you can also get a Multi-Pass, which is for TV shows that broadcast daily. When you purchase a Multi-Pass, you get the most recent episode plus the next 15 episodes when they become available.

HD Versus SD   You can purchase or rent most movies and TV shows in either HD (high definition) or SD (standard definition). Look for the HD/SD button to the right of the buy buttons on movie purchase pages. The difference is the quality of the image, which affects the file size, of course. If you have a slow connection or limited bandwidth, you might want to stick to SD versions of the shows.

iCloud Movies   If you use iCloud, some movies that you purchase (not rent) will appear in your Videos app as well, even if they are not actually on your iPad. You will see a little iCloud icon appear next to them. You can tap that icon to start downloading that movie to your iPad from Apple's servers. This allows you to purchase movies from Apple and not have to worry about where to store them. Simply download them from Apple any time you want to watch. But this only works if the movie studio has given Apple the rights to store and distribute the movie in this manner.

Downloading Podcasts

Podcasts are episodic shows, either audio or video, produced by major networks, small companies, and individuals. You'll find news, information, tutorials, music, comedy, drama, talk shows, and more. There is something covering almost any topic you can think of.

To subscribe to and listen to or watch podcasts, you need to get the Podcasts app from Apple. You can find it in the App Store and add it to your iPad for free. See "Purchasing an App" in Chapter 15 for a step-by-step on how to get a new app.

1. Tap the Podcasts app icon on your Home screen.

2. Tap the My Podcasts button to look at the podcasts you've already downloaded. If you start off by looking at your library, you'll see an equivalent button labeled Store at the bottom left that takes you back to this screen.

3. Use the Search field to search for a podcast by name or keyword.

4. Tap a podcast to get more information about it. You can also swipe right to left to view more in the list.

Podcasts

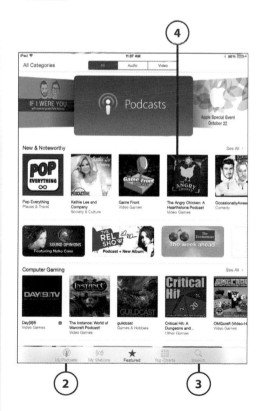

5. Tap Reviews to see what others have to say.

6. Tap the Download button next to a single episode to download just that episode.

7. Tap Subscribe to subscribe to the podcast. This will download the latest episode and also automatically get new episodes as they become available.

8. Using the Library button from step 2, you can go to the list of podcasts and view them by icon or in a list. Tap the list button to see them as a list with each episode shown on the right.

9. Tap the episode to watch or listen to it.

10. Tap the info button to get more details about an episode and to mark it as played without listening. Swipe left to right across an episode to delete it.

11. Tap the settings button to set the sort order and auto-download preferences for the podcast. You would want a current events podcast to put the newest at the top, while a podcast that tells a story or is a learning series would be better suited for oldest on top.

12. Tap Edit to be able to delete podcast episodes from your library.

13. Tap the Edit button at the top left and then use the red buttons next to the podcast names to remove a podcast subscription.

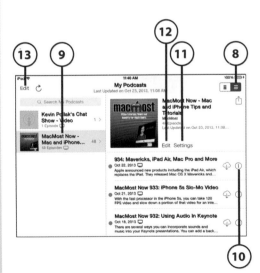

Playing Video

After you have movies, TV shows, and Podcast videos on your iPad, you need to play them using the Videos app.

1. Tap the Videos app icon on your Home screen.

2. The Movies you have on your iPad display by default. Tap TV Shows, Music Videos, or Home Videos to switch lists. If you don't have videos in one or more of these categories, then that button may not appear at all.

3. Tap a movie to view more information about it.

Any Video Alternatives to Apple?

You bet. There is a Netflix app for the iPad that Netflix subscribers can use to stream movies. Amazon also has an Amazon Instant Video app for subscribers to their service. Some companies, such as ABC, have also provided their own apps for viewing their shows on the iPad. You can also view video from any site that has video in standard MP4 formats. The site www.archive.org/details/movies has public domain movies and videos, often in MP4 format. The popular video site http://blip.tv also works well with the iPad.

4. Tap the Play button to start the movie.

Videos

5. After a movie is playing, tap in the middle of the screen to bring up the controls at the top and bottom of the screen.

6. Tap the Done button to exit the movie and return to the movie information screen.

7. Tap the Pause button to pause the movie and then again to resume.

8. Adjust the volume with the volume control.

9. Drag the dot along the line to move to a different section of the movie.

10. Use the Back and Forward buttons to jump between chapters.

11. Use the AirPlay button to send the video stream to another device, such as an Apple TV. See "Using AirPlay to Play Music and Video on Other Devices" later in this chapter.

Changing the Orientation

For most video content, you can rotate your iPad to view in a horizontal orientation and use the Zoom button at the upper right to crop the left and right sides of the video so that it fits vertically on the screen. This is similar to watching a movie on a standard TV.

What Happened to the YouTube App?

In iOS 5 and previous versions of iOS, there was a special YouTube app that enabled you to view YouTube videos. As of iOS 6 this was removed. But a new and improved app has since been released—it just doesn't come preloaded on your iPad. So you can head over to the App Store, search for YouTube, and download the app. See Chapter 16 for more information about the YouTube app.

Using AirPlay to Play Music and Video on Other Devices

In iTunes, with the Video app and many other apps that play music or video, you have the option to send the audio or video stream from your iPad to another device that is connected to the same Wi-Fi network, such as an Apple TV.

You need to enable AirPlay on those devices first. For instance, using the Apple TV (2nd generation models or newer), you need to go into settings on the device and turn on AirPlay. You also need to make sure that the device is using the same Wi-Fi network as your iPad.

1. Look for the AirPlay button in the app you are using. Tap it to bring up a list of available devices.

2. Your iPad will show as the first device. Use this to switch back to playing the media on your iPad if you have switched to something else.

3. Next to each device, you will see either a screen icon or a speaker icon. This tells you whether you can stream video or just audio using that device.

4. Tap on another device, and the music or video currently playing will start to play over that device.

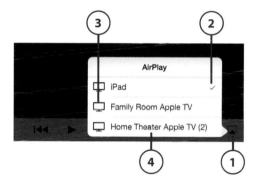

AirPlay Everything

You can also use AirPlay to mirror your iPad's screen with an up-to-date Apple TV 2. In Control Center (see "Using Control Center" in Chapter 1), there is an AirPlay button. Use that to turn on mirroring and send your screen to the Apple TV. Some apps, however, specifically block this. If you simply want to play video from the Videos app or another app that shows video, use the app's AirPlay button, not the Control Center one.

Home Sharing

If you are using iTunes on your Mac or PC, you can play this iTunes content on your iPad if it is on the same local network.

1. In iTunes on your Mac or PC, choose Turn On Home Sharing from the File menu. You are prompted to enter your Apple account ID and password.

2. In the Settings App, tap Music.

3. Enter the same Apple account ID and password used in step 1.

4. In the Music app, tap the More button at the bottom of the screen.

5. Tap Shared, and then choose the name of the library you want to access. The content in your Music app changes to reflect the content in the iTunes library on your Mac or PC. You can now play songs from your computer without having to transfer them to your iPad first.

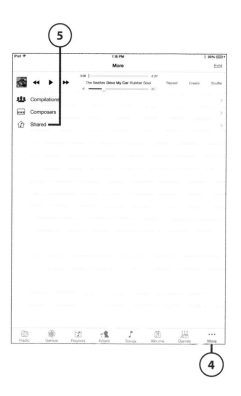

What if My Library Doesn't Appear?

Home Sharing is tricky. It requires that you use the same iTunes account IDs on both your iPad and on your Mac or PC. It also requires that you have the iPad on the same local network as your Mac or PC. In addition, network firewalls and other software may get in the way. It usually works effortlessly, but some users have reported trouble getting Home Sharing to work at all with their particular home network setup.

Listening to iTunes Radio

New in iOS 7 is iTunes Radio. It is very similar to existing services like Pandora and Last.fm. You choose a music genre, artist, or song, and then you hear a continuous stream of songs based on that starting point. That stream is saved as a "station," and you can return to it at any time. Meanwhile, you can create other stations with other starting points and switch between them. The music comes from Apple's servers and includes music you already own, as well as music you don't.

Using iTunes Radio is very easy. You can choose from some sample stations or create your own.

1. Tap the Radio icon at the bottom of the Music app.

2. If this is your first time using iTunes Radio, tap the Start Listening button. Note that you must be signed in to your iCloud account to use iTunes Radio. You can sign in using the Settings app in the iTunes & App Stores section.

3. You can start listening to music right away by tapping one of the Featured Stations at the top.

4. Tap the New Station box to create a station of your own.

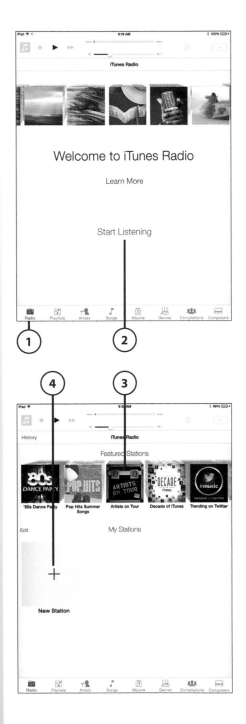

5. Type the name of an artist, genre, or song to search for iTunes content.

6. If you search for an artist, you usually get a "& more" station suggestion at the top. Select that to create a station based on that artist.

7. A song from that artist, or possibly from another artist that is similar, will start playing.

8. You'll now see your station in the My Stations list. You can create more stations and then switch between them by tapping on the icons in this list.

9. Tap the information button for the song that is currently playing.

10. You can purchase the current song from iTunes.

11. You can create a new station from the current artist. You can also do this using the Create button at the top of the Music app while listening to a song you own. So while listening to your favorite playlist, you can tap the Create button and then tap New Station from Song to create an iTunes Radio station and jump to it.

12. You can share your station via text message, email, or other methods. This basically sends information to your friends that lets them create the same iTunes Radio station on their iOS device, or in iTunes on their computer.

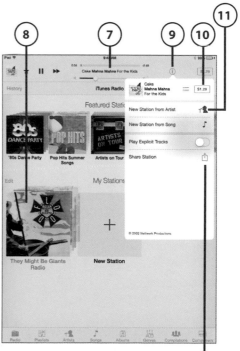

13. Tap the Star button at the top.

14. You can tap Play More Like This to fine-tune your station. This song will be added to the information used to pick which song to play next.

15. Alternatively, you can tap Never Play This Song to stop the song and tell the app to avoid songs like that in the future. By using the Play More Like This and Never Play This Song buttons, you can highly customize your station.

16. Tap the skip button to skip the current song without adding it to the Never Play This Song list for the station.

What About Bandwidth?

iTunes Radio streams music from the Internet. This means it uses bandwidth. If you are using your iPad with a mobile network or have limited bandwidth at home, that is something to be aware of. However, audio streams do not use as much as video streams, so you may be surprised at how little bandwidth an hour or so of music uses compared to watching a few YouTube videos.

And Now a Message from Our Sponsor

iTunes Radio is free, but it also includes commercials. Every so often you'll hear a sponsored message between songs. But if you have an iTunes Match account and are signed into it, as a bonus you get iTunes Radio commercial-free!

Purchase and read books with the iPad's ebook reader.

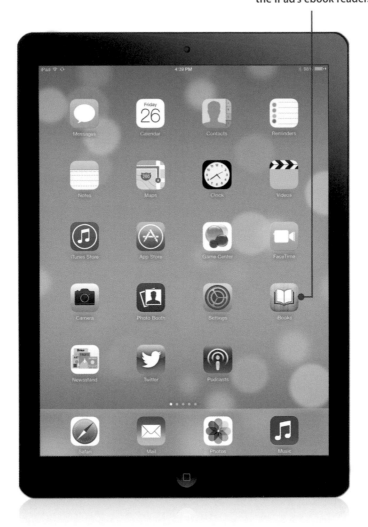

Find out how to purchase books from the iBooks store and how to read them on your iPad.

5

Reading Books

We finally have a better way to enjoy books. As an ebook reader, your iPad can give you access to novels and textbooks alike, storing hundreds inside and allowing you to purchase more right from the device.

A single app, the iBooks app, allows you to both read and purchase new books. You can also download and add books from other sources.

Buying a Book from Apple

The first thing to do with the iBooks app is to get some books! You can buy books using the store in the app. You can also find some free books there.

1. Tap the iBooks app icon to launch iBooks.

2. Tap the Store button to switch to the iBooks store.

iBooks

Don't Want to Purchase from Apple?

You don't necessarily need to buy books from Apple. You can buy from any seller that sends you an ePub or PDF formatted file with no copy protection. After you have the file, just drag and drop it into iTunes. It will add it to your books collection there, ready to be synced to your iPad.

3. Swipe left and right to browse more featured books.

4. Tap the Move button to go to a list of book categories.

5. Tap Top Charts button to see a list of bestsellers.

6. Swipe up to see more featured categories.

7. Use the search field to search for book titles and authors.

8. Tap any book cover to view more information about the book.

9. Tap the price next to a book to purchase it. The price button changes to Buy Book. Tap it again to continue with the purchase.

10. Tap the Get Sample button to download a sample of the book.

Reading a Book

Reading books is a simple process. Following are the basics of reading your downloaded books.

1. Tap the iBooks app icon to launch iBooks.

2. If you are still in the store section of the app, tap Library at the top left to go to your iBooks library. Then, tap a book to open it.

iBooks

Can't Find Your Book?

Did you download a book only to discover that you can't see it in your Library? Try tapping the Collections button at the top of the screen and switching to a different collection. For instance, by default, PDF documents are put in the PDF collection, not in the Books collection.

3. To turn a page, tap and hold anywhere along the right side of the page, and drag to the left. A virtual page turns.

4. Tap and drag from the left to the right or simply tap the left side of the page to turn the page back.

5. To move quickly through pages, tap and drag the small marker at the bottom of the page along the dotted line. Release to jump to a page.

6. Tap the Table of Contents button at the top to view a table of contents.

7. Tap anywhere in the table of contents to jump to that part of the book.

8. Tap the Resume button to return to the page you were previously viewing.

9. Tap the Library button to return to your books. If you return to the book later, you return to the last page you viewed.

Tired of the Special Effects?

If you tire of the page-turning special effect, a quick tap on the right or left side of the screen also turns pages. The effect still shows, but it's quick.

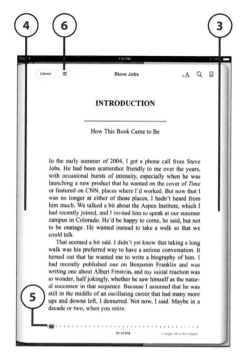

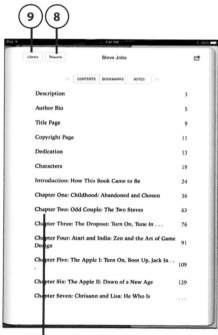

Using Reading Aids

iBooks has a variety of ways you can customize your reading experience. You can change the font size, the font itself, and even turn your iPad on its side to see two pages at one time.

1. While viewing a page in iBooks, tap the display adjustment controls at the top of the screen.

2. Drag the brightness control left or right. Dragging to the left makes the screen dim, which you might use if you're reading in a dark room. Dragging to the right makes it bright, which could make reading easier while outdoors.

3. Tap the smaller "A" button to reduce the size of the text.

4. Tap the larger "A" button to increase the size of the text.

5. Tap the Fonts button to choose from a few font options.

6. Tap the Themes button to select one of three color themes (White, Sepia, or Night). You can also choose to switch to Full Screen to get rid of the book-like border, or switch from flipping pages to vertical scrolling.

7. Turn your iPad on its side to change to a two-page view. (Make sure your orientation lock is not on.)

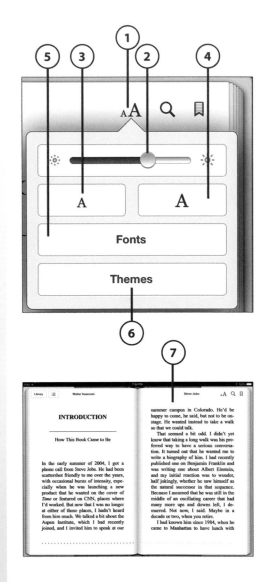

Where Did the Buttons Go?

If you tap in the middle of the screen, the buttons at the top and the dotted line at the bottom disappear. You can still turn the pages; you just don't have access to these buttons. To see the buttons again, tap in the middle of the screen.

Adding Notes and Highlights

Each time you launch iBooks, your iPad returns you to the page you were last reading. However, you might want to mark a favorite passage or a bit of key information.

1. Go to a page in a book in iBooks.

2. Tap a word and hold your finger there for about a second.

3. Release your finger and you see six choices: Copy, Define, Highlight, Note, Search, and Share.

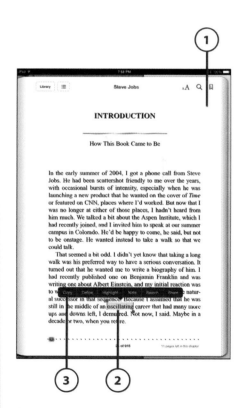

Define and Search

Tapping Define brings up a definition of the word. Tapping Search brings up a list of the locations of the word throughout the text.

Sharing from iBooks

When you choose Share, you can send the excerpt you have selected to someone else using email, a text message, Twitter, or Facebook.

4. Drag the blue dots to enlarge the section of text highlighted.

5. Tap Highlight. Alternatively, you can tap a word and hold for a second and then immediately start dragging to highlight text.

6. The text is now highlighted.

7. Tap the first button to change the type of highlighting. You can choose from various colors or a simple red underline.

8. Tap the second button to remove the highlight completely.

9. Tap Note instead of Highlight to bring up a yellow pad of paper and add a note.

10. Tap in the note to bring up the keyboard and start typing.

11. Tap outside the yellow paper to finish the note. It will then appear as a small yellow sticky note to the right side of the page. Tap it any time you want to view or edit the note. You can delete a note by removing all text in the note.

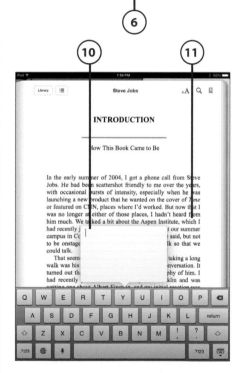

Adding Bookmarks

You can also bookmark a page to easily find it later.

1. Tap the bookmark button at the top of a page to bookmark the page. You can bookmark as many pages as you want in a book.

2. Tap it again to remove the bookmark from the page.

3. Tap the Table of Contents button to go to the table of contents.

4. Tap the Bookmarks button at the top of the table of contents to see a list of all the bookmarks, highlights, and notes you have added to the book.

5. Tap any bookmark, note, or highlight to jump to it.

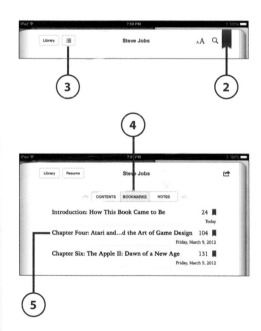

Organizing Your Books

Like to read a lot? You aren't alone. I'm sure many people gather massive collections of ebooks on their iPads. Fortunately, iBooks includes a few great ways to organize your ebooks.

1. Go to your iBooks main page—your Library.

2. Tap the Collections button.

3. Tap a Collection name to jump to that collection. You can think of collections as different bookcases filled with books.

4. Tap New to create a new collection.

5. Tap Edit to delete or re-order collections in the list.

6. Tap the Edit button to enter edit mode.

Books in the Cloud

When you view your Purchased Books collection, you will see all the books you have bought in the past, even if that book is no longer on your iPad because you removed it. These books will have a little iCloud icon in the upper-right corner; when you select one, it will download.

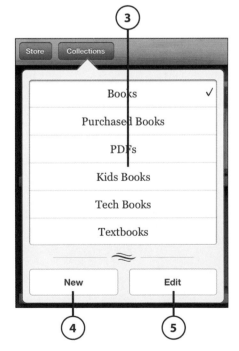

7. Tap one or more books to select them.

8. Tap the Move button to move those books to another collection.

9. Tap the Delete button to delete those books.

10. Tap and hold your finger over a book to drag it to a new position in the library. You can also do this in normal mode or in edit mode.

11. Tap Done to exit edit mode.

12. Tap the List View button.

13. Now you can see a vertical list of your books. Scroll up and down by dragging and flicking.

14. Tap the Titles, Authors, and Categories buttons at the bottom of the screen to change the order of the list.

15. Use the search field to search your library. If you don't see a search field, tap and drag down on the whole list to reveal it. You can also drag down the screen to reveal the search box in the normal icon view of books and type in a search keyword there.

Another Way to Delete

You can also delete books in list view by swiping from left to right across the title of a book. A Delete button appears to the right. Tap it to delete the book.

Using iBooks Alternatives

Copy protection prevents you from taking your ebooks from one platform to the other. Thankfully there are Kindle and Nook apps for the iPad, so you can read the books you purchase from those stores.

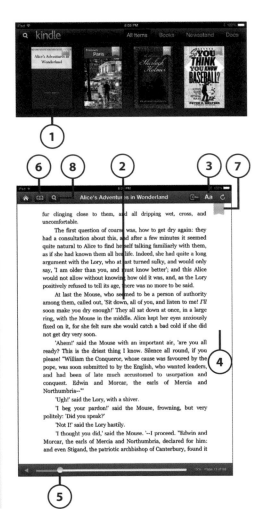

1. When you launch the Kindle app, you see a screen that displays your library. Tap a book to open it.

2. Tap the middle of the page to bring up controls at the top and bottom.

3. Tap the Font button to change the font size, brightness, and background.

4. Tap the right side to flip to the next page.

5. Use the slider at the bottom to quickly move to other pages in the book.

6. The "Go to" button allows you to jump to chapters or specific pages.

7. You can add your own bookmarks just like in iBooks.

8. Tap the Search button to search text in the book.

Cloud Versus Device

The new Kindle app has a Cloud/Device control at the bottom of the screen. Selecting Cloud shows you all the books you have purchased. Selecting Device shows you which books are on your iPad and ready to read. You can tap on a book on the Cloud screen to download it to your device. You can tap on it again after it has been downloaded to read it.

More eBook Alternatives

If you like to buy your books from Barnes & Noble, you can also get the Nook app. This lets you read books that can be purchased in the Nook store. If you own a Nook and have already bought books, you can access those books and load them onto your iPad.

Another App you can get is the Google Play Books app. This works with books purchased in the Google Play store, which is similar to the Amazon Kindle store or the iBookstore. You can choose whether you want to buy from Apple, Amazon, Barnes & Noble, or Google.

Track your
appointments
and events.

Set reminders.

Store and
search
all your
contacts.

Take notes
and create
lists.

In this chapter, we learn how to add and look up contacts and calendar events. We also look at the Notes app.

6

Organizing Your Life

Whether you are a well-connected businessperson or just someone who has lots of friends, you can use the iPad to organize your life with the default Contacts, Calendar, Reminders, and Clock apps. Let's take a close look at some of the things you can do with these apps.

Adding a Contact

If you use Contacts on your Mac or a contact management application on Windows, all your contacts can transfer to your iPad the first time you sync. If you have been using iCloud on your Mac or another iOS device, then your contacts will automatically appear on your iPad when you sign in to iCloud. You can also add new contacts directly on your iPad.

1. Tap the Contacts app icon to launch the app.

2. Press the + button near the top of the screen. A New Contact form and keyboard appear.

3. Type the first name of the contact. No need to use Shift to capitalize the name because that happens automatically.

4. Tap the return key on the keyboard to advance to the next field and type the last name for the contact.

5. To add more information, like a phone number, tap the green + button next to the field name.

Contacts

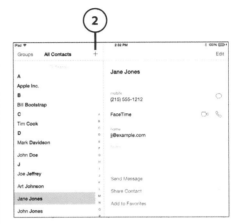

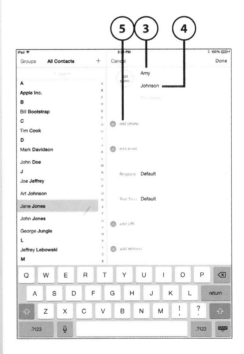

6. Type the phone number.

7. If you ever want to remove some information from the contact, you can use the red – buttons.

8. You can add more than one phone number per contact. Some contacts may have many: home, work, mobile, and so on.

9. Tap Add Photo to add a photo from one of your photo albums.

Don't Worry About Formatting

You don't need to type phone numbers with parentheses or dashes. Your iPad formats the number for you.

10. You can add one or more email addresses to the contact as well. These will be used in your Mail app when you compose a new message. You will only need to type the person's name, or choose them from a list, instead of typing their email address.

11. You can add one or more physical addresses for the contact.

12. You can select a specific ringtone for the contact that is used when they call you via FaceTime. You can also set a specific Text tone.

13. You can swipe up to see more fields. You can even add custom fields and notes to a contact.

14. Tap the Done button to complete the new contact.

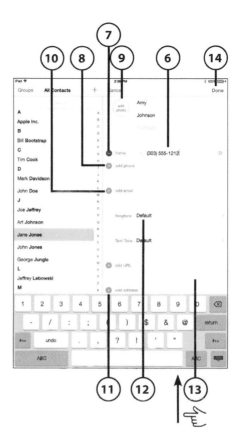

Contacts Sync

Contacts that you add to your iPad sync back to your iCloud account right away, as long as you have a connection. They will then also sync right away to your other iCloud-enabled devices. If you are not using iCloud, they will sync to your computer the next time you connect and sync using iTunes.

Siri: Call Me Ray

You can set a nickname field in a contact. When you do this, and the contact happens to be yours, Siri will call you by that name. You can always tell Siri: "Call me *name*" and it will change your nickname field even if you are not in the Contacts app at the moment.

You can also set relationships in your contacts by saying things like "Debby is my wife."

Searching for a Contact

If you didn't have a lot of friends before, I'm sure you gained quite a few since you got a new iPad. So how do you search though all those contacts to find the one you want?

1. Tap the Contacts app icon to launch the app.

Contacts

2. Tap in the Search field. A keyboard appears at the bottom of the screen.

Other Ways to Find Contacts

You can also drag (or flick to move quickly) through the contact list to find a name. In addition, the list of letters on the left side of the Contacts app enables you to jump right to that letter in your contacts list.

Siri: Show Me

You can also use Siri to find a contact. Try these phrases:

"Show me John Smith."

"Show me my contact."

"Show me my wife."

3. Start typing the name of the person you are looking for. As soon as you start typing, the app starts making a list of contacts that contain the letters you've typed.

4. Keep typing until you narrow down the list of names and spot the one you are looking for.

5. Tap the name to bring up the contact.

6. Tap the Cancel button to dismiss the search.

Working with Contacts

After you have contacts in your iPad, you can do a few things from a contact in the Contacts app.

1. Tap and hold the name to copy it to the clipboard buffer.

2. Tap and hold the phone number to copy it to the clipboard buffer.

3. Tap the message button to send a text message to the user using that phone number. This uses Apple's iMessage system, so it will only work for other Apple users, not those who use mobile carrier's SMS systems.

4. Tap the FaceTime button to start a video chat with the user, providing they are also on an iOS device (or a Mac) and have set up FaceTime. You can start a FaceTime video call, or tap the phone-like button for an audio-only call.

5. Tap the email address to start composing a new email in the Mail app.

6. Tap to the right of Notes to add more information without entering Edit mode.

7. Tap Share Contact to send the contact information via a text message, email, or using AirDrop.

8. Tap Add to Favorites to add this contact to your Favorites group for easier access.

9. Tap Edit to enter Edit mode, which gives you the same basic functionality as entering a new contact.

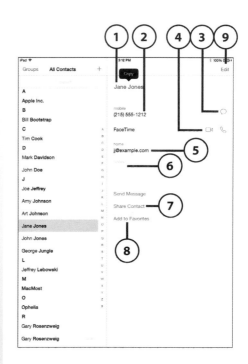

Creating a Calendar Event

Now that you have people in your Contacts app, you need to schedule some things to do with them. Let's look at the Calendar app.

1. Tap the Calendar app icon on the Home screen.

2. Tap the + button at the upper right.

3. Enter a title for the event.

4. Enter a Location for the event, or skip this field.

5. Tap the Starts field to bring up a control for setting the starting time.

6. Tap the Ends field to bring up a control for setting the ending time for the event.

7. If the event covers the entire day, or a series of days, then slide the All-day switch on. The Starts and Ends fields will now be dates only, and won't include a specific time.

8. Tap Repeat to set an event to repeat every day, week, 2 weeks, month, or year.

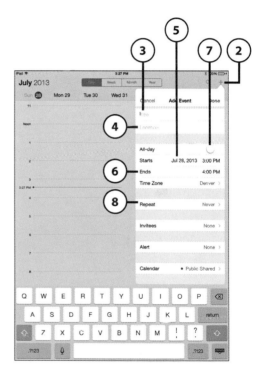

9. Tap Invitees to send an email invitation to another person for this event, if your calendar system allows this. If you and the other person are both using iCloud, they will get a notification of the event and have the option to accept or decline. If they accept, the event will be added to their calendar. You will then be able to look at your event's invitation list in this same location and see if they have accepted or declined.

10. Tap Alert to set the time for a notification alert to appear. This can be at the time of the event, or before the event, such as 5 minutes, 15 minutes, or even as much as a week before.

11. Tap Done to complete the event.

Siri: Creating Events

You can use Siri to create new events even when the Calendar app is not on your screen.

"Schedule a doctor appointment for 3 PM next Wednesday."
"Set up a meeting with John tomorrow at noon."
"Cancel my dentist appointment."

Using Calendar Views

There are three main ways to view your calendar: Day, Week, and Month. Let's take a look at each.

Exploring Day View

The Day view is broken into two halves: the left side shows a timeline from morning until evening. Events are shown as blocks of color in this vertical timeline. The right side shows information for the event selected, if any.

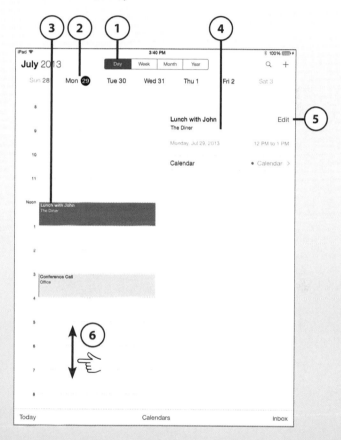

1. Tap Day to enter Day view mode.

2. You can tap any day shown at the top to jump to the list of events for that day. You can also drag left and right here to see previous days and upcoming ones.

3. Tap any event shown to view information about that event.

4. The information appears on the right.

5. You can tap Edit to edit that event and change any aspect of it, or delete it.

6. You can drag up and down to view the entire day.

7. Tap Today to jump to the current day, in case you have moved to another day and want to return quickly.

8. Tap Calendars to select which calendars are shown. This is useful if you have set up multiple calendars in iCloud, or have subscribed to public calendars.

9. Tap Inbox to view any invitations you may have received via email or messages. You can accept or reject them. Accepted invitations will be added to your calendar.

10. Tap + to add a new event.

Exploring Week View

To get a view of all the events for the week, switch to Week view. This gives you seven days across, but less space to preview each event. You can still select and edit events.

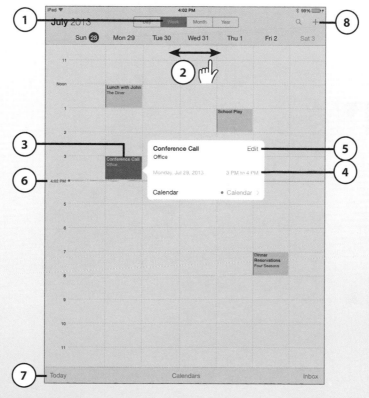

1. Tap Week to go to the Week view.

2. You can move to the previous week or the next by tapping and dragging in any blank part of the calendar. You can also drag vertically to see earlier in the morning or late in the evening.

3. Tap an event to view more information about it.

4. The information appears in a box to the left or right of the event.

5. You can tap Edit to edit the event right here. The familiar editing interface will appear in an expanded box while you remain in the Week view.

6. You can see the current time represented by a red line.

7. Tap Today if you have navigated away from the current week and want to get back.

8. Tap + to add a new event while remaining in Week view.

Exploring Month View

To see the "big picture," you may want to use Month view. This gives you a grid of seven days across and six or more weeks vertically. While this view is similar to a monthly calendar, it doesn't necessarily have to show a single month. It can be used to show any group of six consecutive weeks.

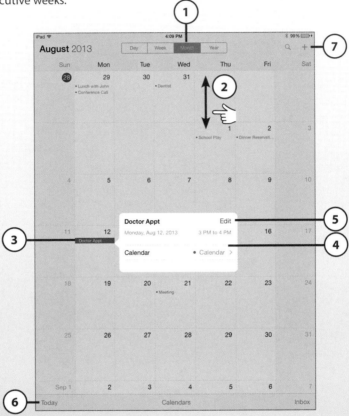

1. Tap Month to enter Month view.

2. While in Month view, you can tap and drag in blank areas to scroll up and down.

3. Tap an event to view more information.

4. The information appears in a box, like in Week view.

5. Tap Edit to edit the information right here in Month view. The editing interface will appear inside an enlarged box.

6. Tap Today to return to the current day if you have scrolled away from it.

7. Tap + to add a new event right here in Month view.

Siri: Checking Your Schedule

You can use Siri to see what events you have coming up.

"What do I have going on tomorrow?"

"What is on my calendar for this week?"

"When is my dentist appointment?"

Year View

There is also a Year view, as you may have already noticed since there is a Year button at the top of the screen. This shows you 12 very small monthly calendars, with colored-in spaces on days where you have events. You can use this view to quickly navigate to an event in a different week or month. Or, you can use it to see when the days fall in the week.

Creating Calendars

You may have noticed in the previous tasks that you can select a calendar when you create an event. You can create multiple calendars to organize your events. For instance, you may want to have one for work and one for home.

1. From any calendar view, tap the Calendars button at the bottom center.

2. You can scroll up and down this list and disable or enable calendars by tapping on the checkmarks. A calendar without a checkmark is hidden and won't appear in your views.

3. You can also view and change information about a calendar, such as changing the color used as a background for events. You can also share calendars with other iCloud users.

4. Tap Edit to go into editing mode.

5. In Editing mode, you can also select calendars to change their color and who they are shared with.

6. Tap Add Calendar to create a new calendar.

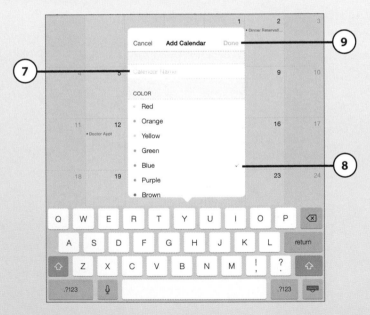

7. Give the new Calendar a name.

8. Set the color for the calendar.

9. Tap Done.

Deleting a Calendar

You can delete a calendar by following the previous steps 1–4 and then selecting a calendar to edit. Scroll to the bottom below the list of colors and choose Delete Calendar.

Default Calendar

Which calendar will be used when you create a new event? The default calendar is a setting you can find in the Settings app, under Mail, Contacts, Calendars, way near the bottom of the list of preferences on the right.

>>>Go Further

SHARING CALENDARS

When you edit a calendar's information, you can also use the Add Person button that appears above the list of colors to share a calendar with a specific iCloud user. Below the colors list you can choose to set the calendar to "public" and then share an Internet link that others can use to subscribe. For instance, you can create a schedule for your softball team and make it public, and then put a link to the calendar on the team's website. Anyone can subscribe to this calendar, but only to view it. By default, others can edit it, but you can turn off Allow Editing by tapping the i button for the calendar, and then View & Edit next to the person's name with whom you are sharing it.

Creating Notes

Another organization app that comes with your iPad is the Notes app. Although this one is much more free-form than a Contacts or Calendar app, it can be useful for keeping quick notes or to-do lists.

1. Tap the Notes icon on your Home screen.

2. Notes opens up the note you were previously working on. To type, tap on the screen where you want the insertion point, and a keyboard appears.

What's in a Name

The filename for a note is just the first line of the note, so get in the habit of putting the title of a note as the first line of text to make finding the note easier.

3. To start a new note, tap the Compose button at the upper right.

4. To view a list of all your notes, and to jump to another note, tap the Notes button.

5. Tap the name of the note you want to switch to.

6. Tap and type in the Search field to find text inside of notes.

7. Turn your iPad to horizontal orientation, and you'll have a permanent list of notes on the left, you don't need to tap Notes as you did in step 4 to see the list.

8. Tap the Trash button at the top-right of the screen to delete notes.

9. Tap the Share button at the top-right of the screen to share the note in a number of ways. For instance, you can start a new email message in the Mail app using the contents of the note, or print the note using AirPrint.

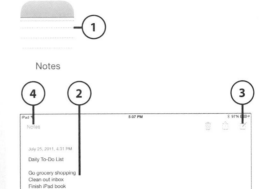

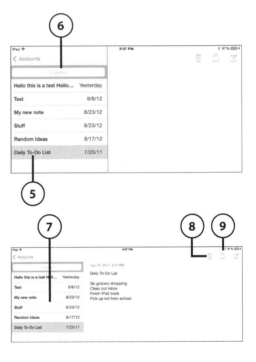

Notes Isn't a Word Processor

You can't actually use Notes for any serious writing. There aren't any styles or formatting choices. You can't even change the display font to make it larger. If you need to use your iPad for writing, consider Pages or a third-party word processing app.

Notes in the Cloud

What happens to notes after you create them can be confusing. Notes usually are attached to cloud services accounts like iCloud in the same way email messages are. If you are using the same cloud account on your Mac, for instance, you should see the notes appear almost instantly on your Mac, synced through iCloud. They will also appear on your other iOS devices.

Setting Reminders

Reminders is a to-do list application available on iPad, iPod touch, iPhone, and Macs running OS X 10.8 Mountain Lion or newer. This app is for creating an ongoing list of tasks you need to accomplish or things you need to remember. These reminders can be similar to calendar events with times and alarms. Or, they can be simple items in a list with no time attached to them.

1. Tap the Reminders icon on your Home screen.

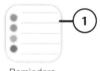

Reminders

2. Select the list you want to add a new Reminder to.

3. Tap in a new line to create a new reminder.

4. Type the reminder and close the keyboard when done.

5. Tap the i button next to the reminder to bring up the Details dialog. If you don't see an i button, then tap any reminder item first.

6. Tap here to edit the reminder.

7. Slide the Remind me on a day switch to on to set a reminder alert.

8. Set a time for the alert to occur.

9. Add a note to the reminder if you want to include more details.

10. Tap outside of the Details box when you are finished editing the reminder.

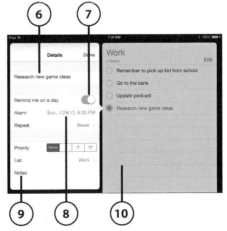

11. Tap the button next to the reminder when you have completed the task. It will remain in the list temporarily.

12. Tap Add List to add a new reminders list.

13. Tap Show Completed to see completed reminders.

14. You can also search for reminders by typing the title or something from the content.

15. Tap Edit to remove reminders.

16. Tap the red button next to a reminder to delete it.

17. Tap and drag the right side of the reminders to re-order them.

18. Tap Done when you are finished deleting and re-ordering the reminders.

19. You can also delete the entire list.

Reminders sync by using the iCloud service from Apple. So, they are automatically backed up and should also appear on your Mac in the Reminders app, if you have OS X 10.8 Mountain Lion or newer. And if you use an iPhone, they should appear there as well.

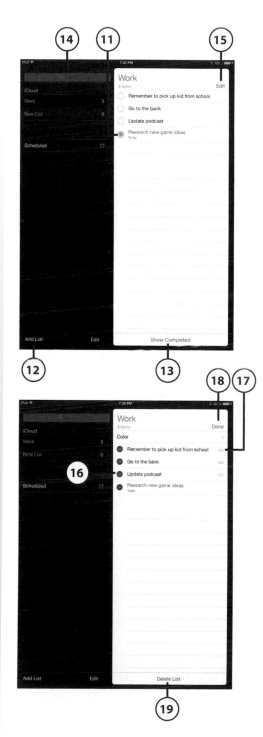

Siri: Remind Me
You can create new reminders using Siri like this:

"Remind me to watch Doctor Who tonight at 8 PM."
"Remind me to pick up milk when I leave work."
"Remind me to check my stocks every day at 9 AM."

Setting Clock Alarms

The advantage of using an alarm rather than a reminder is that an often-recurring alarm, like your morning wake-up call, or a reminder on when to pick up your child at school, won't clutter up your Reminders list or calendar.

1. Tap the Clock app.

2. The main screen shows up to six clocks in any time zone you want. Tap a clock to have it fill the screen.

3. Tap an empty clock to add a new city.

4. Tap Edit to remove or rearrange the clocks.

5. Tap Alarm to view and edit alarms.

Clock

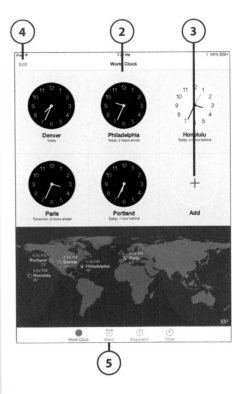

6. To add a new alarm, tap the + button.

7. Select a time for the alarm.

8. Select the days of the week for the alarm. Leaving it set to Never means you just want the alarm to be used once, as you might do if setting an alarm to wake you up early so you can catch a plane the next day. Otherwise, you can select from seven days of the week. So, you can set an alarm for Monday through Friday and leave out the weekend.

9. Tap Label to give the alarm a custom name.

10. Select a sound for the alarm. You can choose from preset sounds or your ringtone collection.

11. Leave the Snooze switch on if you want the ability to use snooze when the alarm goes off.

12. Tap Save to save all your settings and add the alarm.

13. The alarm now appears in the special Clock calendar.

14. You can switch off the alarm, while leaving it in the calendar for future use.

15. Tap Edit on an alarm to edit or delete it.

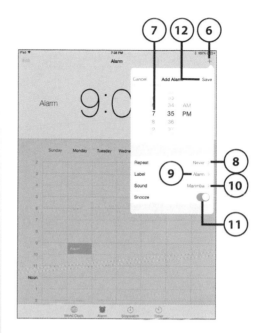

16. The alarm will sound and a message will appear when it is time. Even if your iPad is sleeping, it will wake up.

17. If you've enabled snooze, tapping here will silence the alarm and try again in 9 minutes.

18. To silence the alarm normally, assuming it has sounded while the iPad is asleep and locked, you need to swipe the lock switch. If the iPad was awake when the alarm went off, you simply get a button to tap.

Wake Up!

When you set an alarm, it will sound even if you lower your volume to nothing, mute the sound with the side switch or Control Center, and switch into Do Not Disturb mode. This way, you can't accidentally turn off an alarm just because you wanted to avoid other distractions.

Siri: Create Alarms

You can use Siri to create and delete alarms. Try these phrases:

"Set an alarm for weekdays at 9 AM."
"Create an alarm for tomorrow at 10 AM."
"Cancel my 9 AM alarm."
"Turn on my 9 AM alarm."
"Turn off my 9 AM alarm."

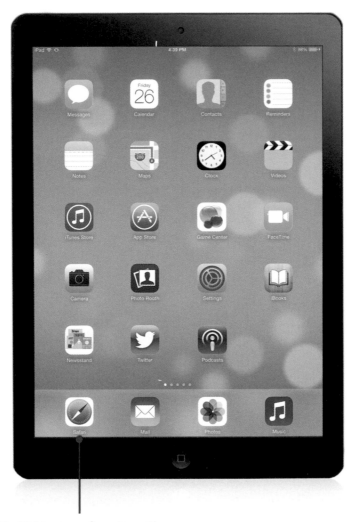

The Web is at your fingertips with
iPad's Safari web browser.

In this chapter, you learn about Safari, the browser built-in to the iPad. You can use it to browse the Web, bookmark web pages, fill in forms, and search the Internet.

Surfing the Web

The iPad is a beautiful web surfing device. Its size is perfect for web pages, and your ability to touch the screen lets you interact with content in a way that even a computer typically cannot.

Browsing to a URL and Searching

Undoubtedly, you know how to get to web pages on a computer using a web browser. You use Safari on your iPad in the same way, but the interface is a little different.

At the top of the Safari browser is a toolbar with just a few buttons. In the middle, the largest interface element is the address field. This is where you can type the address of any web page on the Internet, or enter a search query.

1. Touch the Safari icon on your iPad to launch the browser. It might be located at the bottom of the screen, along with your other most commonly used applications.

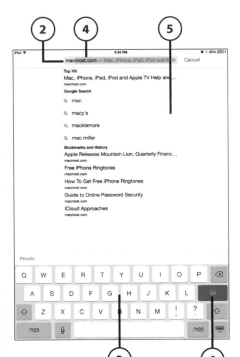

Safari

2. Tap in the field at the top of the screen. This opens up the keyboard at the bottom of the screen. If you were already viewing a web page, the address of that page remains in the address field. Otherwise, it will be blank.

Clear the Slate

To clear the field at any time, tap the X button located inside the field all the way to the right.

3. Start typing a search term or a URL such as apple.com or macmost.com.

4. The area to the right of where you are typing will fill with a complete address and description, trying to predict the URL you want. You can ignore this and keep typing until you have completed the URL. You can then skip to step 6.

5. As you type, suggestions based on previous pages you have visited and past web searches from other users appear. To go directly to one of these pages, tap the page in the list.

6. Tap the Go button on the keyboard when you finish typing. If you typed or selected a URL, you will be taken to that web page.

7. Notice that the address field at the top of the screen shows you the domain name for the website you are visiting, but doesn't display the complete URL of the specific page of that site you are on.

If you typed a search term, or selected a search from the list, the term will remain at the top and you will get a page of search results.

8. Tap on any result to jump to that page.

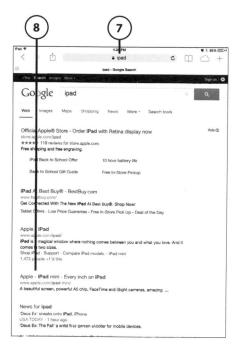

TIPS FOR TYPING A URL

- A URL is a Universal Resource Locator. It can be a website name or a specific page in a website.

- For most websites, you don't need to type the "www." at the beginning. For instance, you can type **www.apple.com** or **apple.com** and both take you to Apple's home page. You never need to type "http://" either, though occasionally you need to type "https://" to specify that you want to go to a secure web page.

- Instead of typing ".com." you can tap and hold the period button on the iPad keyboard. You can select .com, .edu, .org, .us, or .net.

Nothing Special, Please

Some websites present you with a special iPad version of the site. This is not as common as the special iPhone or iPod touch versions that many sites offer. If a website does not look the same on your iPad as it does on your computer, you might want to check to see if a switch is on the web page provided by the site to view the standard web version, instead of a special iPad version. This is especially useful if a site has lumped the iPad together with the iPhone and provided a needlessly simplified version.

Search This Page

Below Google Suggestions in the search suggestions drop-down menu is a list of recent searches and the occurrences of the phrase on the web page you are viewing. Use the latter to find the phrase on the page.

>>>Go Further

TIPS FOR SEARCHING THE WEB

- You can go deeper than just typing some words. For instance, you can put a + in front of a word to require it and a – in front to avoid that word in the results.

- You can use special search terms to look for things such as movie times, weather, flight tracking, and more. See http://www.google.com/landing/searchtips/ for all sorts of things you can do with a Google search.

- Using iPad's Settings app, you can choose the search engine that Safari uses as its default. Tap the Settings icon and choose Safari on the left, and then look for the Search Engine setting. You can choose Bing or Yahoo! instead of Google, for instance.

- Using Google, you can search for much more than text on web pages. Look at the top of the search results, and you see links such as Images, Videos, Maps, News, and Shopping. Tap "more" and you can also search for things such as Blogs and Books.

- To explore the search results without moving away from the page listing the results, tap and hold over a link to see a button that enables you to open a link in a new tab, leaving the results open in the current tab.

- You can use many search settings with Google. These are not specific to the iPad but work on your computer as well when performing searches. Tap Google's settings button (looks like a small gear) and then the Search Settings link in the upper-right corner of the search results page to choose a language, filters, and other settings. Set up a Google account (same as a Gmail account) and log in to save these search preferences and use them between different devices.

Siri: Search the Web

You can use Siri to search the web, even if you are not currently looking at the Safari screen. Sometimes Siri will also answer general questions by suggesting a web search:

"Search the web for iPad tutorials."
"Search for local plumbers."
"Search for MacMost.com."
"Search Wikipedia for Paris."
"Show me some websites about geology."
"Google Denver news."
"Search for iPad tutorials on MacMost.com."

Viewing Web Pages

Whether you typed in a URL or searched for a web page, after you have one open on your iPad screen, you can control what you view in several ways. You need to know these techniques to view the complete contents of a web page and navigate among web pages.

1. Navigate to any web page using either of the two techniques in the previous step-by-step instructions. When you arrive at the page, only the domain name shows at the top.

2. When you are viewing a page, you can touch and drag the page up and down with your finger. As you do so, notice the bar on the right side that gives you an indication of how much of the complete web page you are viewing at one time.

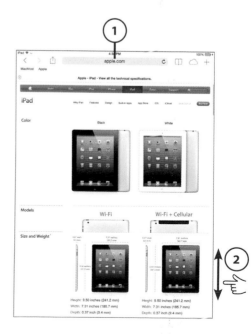

Flick It

If you release your finger from the iPad screen to stop scrolling while dragging, the screen will continue to scroll with a decelerating affect and then come to a stop quickly.

3. To zoom in on an area in the page, touch the screen with two fingers and move your fingers apart. This is called an unpinch. You can also move them closer together (pinch) to zoom back out. A double-tap restores the page to normal scaling. This works well on websites made for desktop computers, but mobile sites usually are set to already fit the screen at optimal resolution.

4. You can also double-tap images and paragraphs of text to zoom in to those elements in the web page. A second double-tap zooms back out.

5. While zoomed in, you can also touch and drag left and right to view different parts of the web page. You see a bar at the bottom of the screen when you do this, just like the bar on the right side in step 2.

6. To move to another web page from a link in the current web page, just tap the link. Links are usually an underlined or colored piece of text; however, they can also be pictures or button-like images.

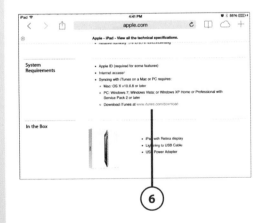

It's Not All Good

Where's the Link?

Unfortunately, it isn't always easy to figure out which words on a page are links. Years ago, these were all blue and underlined. But today, links can be any color and may not be underlined.

On the iPad, it is even more difficult to figure out which words are links. This is because many web pages highlight links when the cursor moves over the word. But with the touch interface of the iPad, there is no cursor.

Bookmarks, History, and Reading List

You can always visit a web page by typing its address in the field at the top of Safari. But the app also has a way for you to get to your most frequently visited sites easily, find a page you recently visited, or save a page to read later.

Using Bookmarks and Favorites

Bookmarks allow you to save the web pages you visit most often and then access them with just a few taps. Favorites are bookmarks that appear at the top of the Safari browser for easier access.

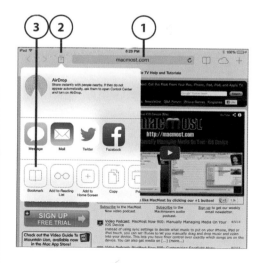

1. Use Safari to navigate to any web page.

2. Tap the Share button at the top of the screen.

3. Tap Bookmark.

4. Edit the title of the bookmark. The official title of the web page is prefilled, but you can use the keyboard to change it. You can tap the X to clear the text and start fresh.

5. Tap Location to place the bookmark in a bookmarks folder.

6. You can choose to place the bookmark in Favorites, so it will appear at the top of the Safari window where you can easily find it.

7. Or you can put it in Bookmarks, where you can select it from the Bookmarks menu.

8. Tap Save to finish creating the bookmark.

9. To use a bookmark, first tap the Bookmarks button.

10. Find the bookmark in the list and tap it to go to that web page.

11. If you put the bookmark in Favorites, or another folder, you have to tap that folder name first to dig down to find the bookmark.

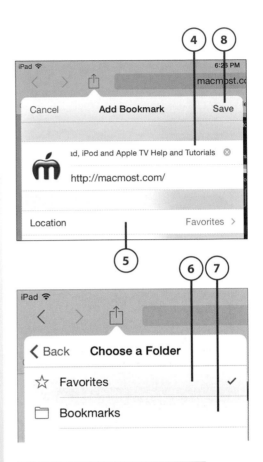

TIPS FOR BOOKMARKING WEBSITES

- The titles of web pages are often long and descriptive. It is a good idea to shorten the title to something you can easily recognize, especially if it is a web page that you plan to visit often.

- Only save the most important bookmarks to the Favorites folder. These always show up at the top of your Safari screen unless you have disabled Favorites in the Settings app under Safari. If use shorter names for these bookmarks, you can fit more onto the Favorites bar.

- To create folders inside the Bookmarks folder, tap the Bookmarks button at the top of the Safari screen. Then choose the Bookmarks button at the top. At the bottom of that menu, tap Edit and then tap New Folder.

- You can create folders of bookmarks under Favorites. These appear as their own pop-up menu when you tap them, giving you direct access to a subset of your bookmarks.

- Favorites also appear when you close all tabs in Safari, or start a new tab by tapping the + button. Instead of a blank page, you get a screen full of icons, one for each Favorite you have added. This makes these "blank" web pages a good launch point for Web surfing.

Using History

Safari keeps track of which web pages you have visited. You can use this history to find a page you went to earlier today, yesterday, or even several days back.

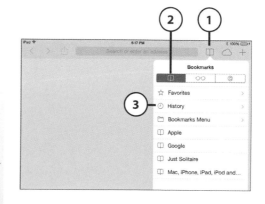

1. After using Safari to view several pages, tap the Bookmarks button at the top of the screen.

2. Tap the first tab at the top of this menu to view your bookmarks and history folders.

3. You may already be viewing your history at this point. If the top of this menu reads History instead of Bookmarks, then you are. Otherwise, tap the History item to go into your history.

4. Tap any item in the list to jump to that web page.

5. Previous pages you have visited are broken into groups by date.

6. You can clear your browsing history by tapping the Clear button.

History/Bookmarks

Safari treats both history and bookmarks the same. They are both just lists of web pages. Think of your history as a bookmark list of every site you have visited recently.

Deleting Your Bookmarks

Adding and using bookmarks is just the start. You eventually need to delete ones you don't use. Some might link to missing or obsolete pages, or some you simply no longer use. There are two ways to delete a bookmark. The results of the two methods are the same; however, you might find the second method gives you a little more control.

Delete a Single Bookmark

The first method uses the Bookmarks list to locate and delete a single bookmark.

1. Tap the Bookmarks button at the top of the Safari screen.

2. Navigate to the Bookmarks section of that menu.

3. Tap Edit.

4. Tap the red button next to a bookmark.

5. Tap the Delete button to remove the bookmark. The bookmark is instantly deleted.

6. Tap Done when you finish deleting bookmarks.

Sync Your Bookmarks

If you are using iCloud, your bookmarks should sync between all your iOS and Mac devices. Safari on your computer gives you greater control over moving and deleting bookmarks. So just do your wholesale editing on your computer and those changes should be reflected in your iPad's bookmarks as well.

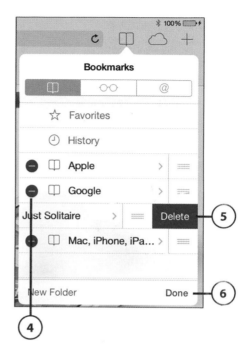

Creating Home Screen Bookmarks

If a web page is somewhat important, you might want to create a bookmark for it. If it is extremely important and you need to go to it often, you might want to make sure that bookmark is saved to your Bookmarks Bar so that it is easily accessible.

However, if a web page is even more important to you than that, you can save it as an icon on your iPad's Home screen.

1. Use Safari to navigate to any web page.

2. Tap the Share button at the top of the screen.

3. Tap Add to Home Screen. Note that the icon shown here will change to use the icon for that website or to a small screen capture of the site.

Managing Home Screen Bookmarks

You can arrange and delete Home screen bookmarks just like icons that represent apps. See "Arranging Apps on Your iPad" in Chapter 15 for details.

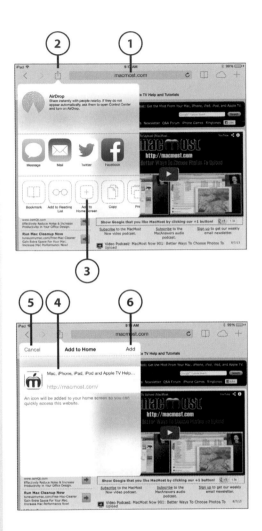

4. You can now edit the name of the page. Most web page titles are too long to display under an icon on the Home screen of the iPad, so edit the name down to as short a title as possible.

5. You can tap Cancel to leave this interface without sending the bookmark to the Home screen.

6. Tap Add to complete adding the icon to the Home screen.

7. Press the Home button to return to your Home screen.

8. Look for the new icon on your Home screen that represents this bookmark. You may need to swipe through the pages of your Home screens to find it. Then, you can move it to any page or into a folder. The icon acts just like the app icons on your Home screen. See "Arranging Apps on Your iPad" in Chapter 14.

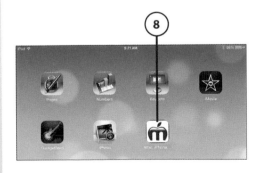

Website Icons

The icon for this type of bookmark can come from one of two sources. Web page owners can provide a special iPhone/iPad icon that would be used whenever someone tries to bookmark her page.

However, if no such icon has been provided, your iPad will take a screen shot of the web page and shrink it down to make an icon.

Building a Reading List

Your reading list is similar to bookmarks. You can add a page to your reading list to remember to return to that page later. When you do, it will be removed from the Unread section of your reading list, but still appear in the All section.

In addition, pages you add to your reading list are downloaded to your iPad so that you can read them later while not connected to the Internet.

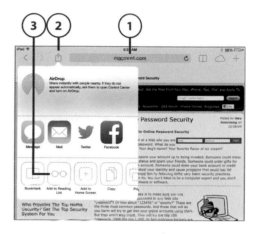

1. Find an article you want to read later.

2. Tap the Share button.

3. Tap Add to Reading List.

4. To see your reading list, tap the Bookmarks button.

5. Tap the Reading List button.

6. Tap any item to view the page. Even if you are not connected to the Internet, the page will show because Safari stored the content when you added the page to the Reading List.

7. At the bottom you see either Show All or Show Unread. This lets you switch between the two lists. Show All shows everything in your Reading List. Show Unread does not show items you have already opened from the Reading List.

Reading List Syncing

The Reading List also syncs across your iOS devices and Macs using iCloud. So you can add it on your Mac and then see it appear in your Reading List on your iPad.

Shared Links

In addition to Bookmarks and Reading List, there is a third button that looks like an @ symbol that appears only if you are signed into social media networks like Twitter or Facebook in the Settings app. Here you find shared links. Recently shared links from those networks appear in this list.

Filling in Web Forms

The Web isn't a one-way street. Often you need to interact with web pages, filling in forms or text fields. Doing this on the iPad is similar to doing it on a computer, but with a few key differences.

The keyboard shares screen space with the web page, so when you tap on a field, you bring up the keyboard at the bottom of the screen.

Also pull-down menus behave differently. On the iPad, you get a special menu showing you all the options.

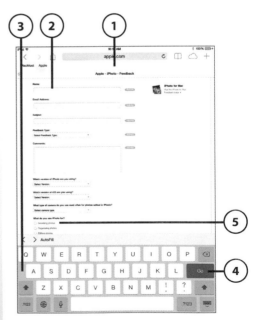

1. Use Safari to navigate to a web page with a form. For demonstration purposes, try one of the pages at http://apple.com/feedback/.

2. To type in a text field, tap that field.

3. The keyboard appears at the bottom of the screen. Use it to type text into the field.

4. Tap the Go button when you finish filling in all the required fields.

5. To select a check box or radio button, tap it just as you would click on it on your computer using the mouse.

6. To select an item in a pull-down menu, tap the menu.

7. The special iPad pull-down menu reacts like any other iPad interface. You can tap an item to select it. You can touch and drag up and down to view more selections if the list is long.

8. A check mark appears next to the currently selected item. Tap that item or any other one to select it and dismiss the menu.

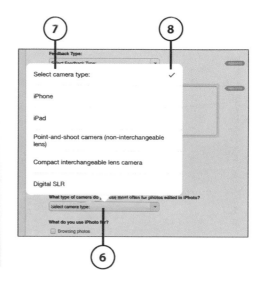

Special Menus

Some websites may use special menus that they build from scratch, rather than these default HTML menus. When this is the case, you get a menu that looks exactly like the one you get when viewing the web page on a computer. If the web page is well coded, it should work fine on the iPad, though it might be slightly more difficult to make a selection.

TIPS FOR FILLING IN FORMS

- You can use the AutoFill button just above the keyboard to fill in your name, address, and other contact info instead of typing on the keyboard. To enable AutoFill, go into your iPad Settings and look for the Passwords & AutoFill preferences under Safari. Also make sure your own information is correct and complete in your card in the Contacts application.

- To move between fields in a form, use the flat left and right arrow buttons just above the keyboard that move to the Previous or Next field. You can quickly fill in an entire form this way without having to tap on the web page to select the next item.

Opening Multiple Web Pages with Tabs

Safari on the iPad enables you to open multiple web pages at the same time. You can view only one at a time, but you can hold your place on a page while you look at something on another page.

1. Instead of tapping on a link, tap down and hold your finger there until a contextual menu pops up above your finger.

2. Tap Open in New Tab.

3. Alternatively, you can tap the + button at the top of the screen to open a new tab that shows icons linking to the websites you have put in your Favorites.

4. You see two tabs at the top of the screen now. The one on the right is in front of the one on the left and represents the page you are looking at below.

5. You can switch tabs by tapping on the other tab; that tab now appears front of the one on the right, and the screen area below shows that page.

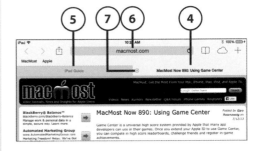

6. When you enter a new web address, search, or use a bookmark, it changes the page of the current tab, but doesn't affect the other tab.

7. You can close the current tab by tapping the X button to the left of the tab's name.

iCloud Tabs

If you have iCloud set up on multiple iOS devices and/or Macs running Mountain Lion, you may see a cloud icon in the Safari toolbar next to the Bookmarks button. Tap that and you will see tabs that are currently open on those other devices. You can select one item to open that page. This means you can surf on your Mac for a while, and then switch to the iPad and easily find the pages you were just looking at on your Mac.

Copying Text from a Web Page

You can select text from web pages to copy and paste into your own documents or email messages.

1. Use Safari to navigate to a web page.

2. Tap and hold over a piece of text. You don't need to be exact because you can adjust the selection later. The word Copy appears above the selected area that is highlighted in light blue.

3. You can tap and drag one of the four blue dots to change the selection area. When your selection gets small enough, it changes to only two blue dots indicating the first and last character of the selection.

4. Tap outside the selection at any time to cancel the selection.

5. Tap the Copy button over the selection to copy the text.

6. You can now go to another application such as Mail or Pages and tap in a text area to choose Paste and paste the text into the area. You can also do this in a form on a page in Safari, such as a web-based email form.

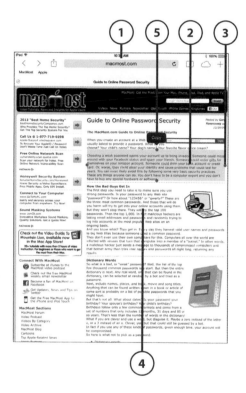

What Does That Mean?

If you select only a single word in Safari, or just tap and hold any word in the text of a web page, you get the menu with Copy as an option as well as a second option: Define. Use this to get a quick definition of a word in a little window that overlays the web page.

Copying Images from Web Pages

Along with copying and pasting text from Safari, you can copy images and save them to your photo collection.

1. Use Safari to navigate to a web page that has an image you want to save.

2. Tap and hold your finger on that image until the contextual menu appears.

3. The menu shows you the title of the image and some options. If the image is also a link to another web page, you might see options to Open that page here as well.

4. Select Copy to copy the image to the Clipboard. You can then go to a program such as Mail or Pages and paste that image into the document you are composing.

5. Alternatively, you can tap Save Image and put a copy of the image in your Camera Roll. This may be a good option because many apps use the Camera Roll to allow you to import, edit, share, and do other things to images.

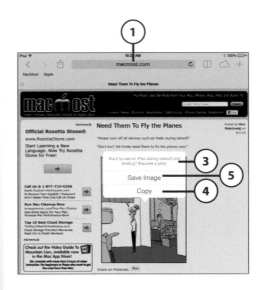

Viewing Articles with Safari Reader

Web pages on the iPad can be vibrant and pretty. But sometimes the website tries to cram so much text and other junk onto a page that it can be painful to read. You can clear away all the clutter to reveal the text of a news article or blog post using the Reader feature.

1. Look for the Reader button in the address field. It will only appear on some news articles and blog posts. Tap it to enter the Reader mode.

2. In Reader mode, only the text and inline images of the article appear.

3. Tap Reader again to return to the regular view of the page.

Reader Font Size

Previous versions of Reader have allowed you to change the font size at the top of the page. You can still change the font size, but not as easily, and not just for Reader. In the Settings app, go to General, TextSize. You can drag a slider there to increase the font size used by Safari's Reader feature. This will affect other apps as well, such as Mail and Notes.

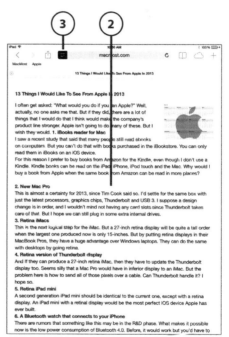

Saving Time with AutoFill

When you go to websites and fill out forms, it can be annoying to type out basic information like your name and address, or your user ID and password. Furthermore, if you have to type your password every time you visit a site, or even on a daily or weekly basis, this encourages you to use simple, easy-to-guess passwords so you don't have to type long complex strings of characters.

The Keychain function built into Safari allows you to automatically fill in forms and login prompts. After you enter your information the first time, you never have to do it again for that website.

Setting Up AutoFill

To set up AutoFill in Safari, start by going to the Settings app.

1. Tap Safari in the Settings app.

2. Tap Passwords & AutoFill.

3. Slide the Use Contact Info switch on, if it's not. Now any time you go to a web page with a form that asks for basics like name, address, or telephone number, AutoFill uses your contact information in the Contacts app to fill those fields automatically.

4. Tap My Info to tell Safari which contact in the Contacts app is you.

5. Slide the Names and Passwords switch on to have Safari remember user IDs and passwords when you log on to websites. As you will see in the next section, Safari prompts you each time you enter a new User ID and Password so you can decide the passwords that are saved.

6. After you have visited some sites and saved some passwords, you can access the list of saved passwords by tapping Saved Passwords.

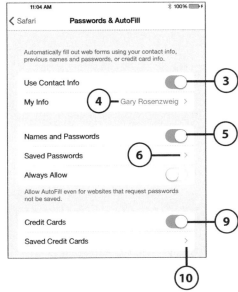

7. Tap on any entry to view the ID, password, and the website it belongs to.

8. You can enter Edit mode to delete entries.

9. Safari can also remember credit card information. Slide the Credit Cards switch to on for this information to be saved.

10. Tap Saved Credit Cards to see a list of your saved credit cards and to add new ones. When you add a credit card, include your name, the card number, the expiration date, and a short description. However, the security code for the card is not saved. Most websites will ask you for this even after Safari has auto-filled in the information it has saved.

SAFETY AND SECURITY

If you add your passwords and credit card information for Safari to automatically fill in, isn't that incredibly insecure? Well, it is if you have not set a passcode for your iPad. The Settings app recommends this when you turn these options on.

You should set a passcode under Settings, General, Passcode Lock. Then, you should set the Require Passcode option to Immediately so as soon as you lock your iPad by closing the Smart Cover or pressing the sleep button, the passcode is required to use it.

Even with the security enabled, using a simple passcode like 1234 or letting it sit around unlocked still presents a problem. You don't need to use AutoFill on every website. You could use it for unimportant sites like games and forums, and avoid using it for bank accounts and social media sites.

The advantage to using AutoFill for passwords is that you can use a long, random password for an account rather than a short, memorable one. It is more likely that your account will be broken into remotely when you use a short, common password than someone stealing your iPad and using it to gain access to that website. And even if they do, you can simply change your important passwords if your iPad is stolen.

Using AutoFill

After you have AutoFill set up, using it is relatively simple. You can use it with a form that asks for basic contact information, or for a login form. The process is the same. Let's look at using it with a simple login form.

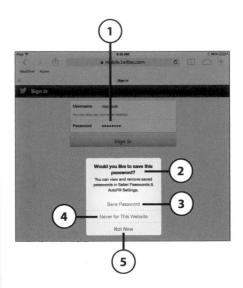

1. Enter an ID or password at a website.

2. If AutoFill is enabled, you may be prompted by Safari to save the password.

3. Tap Save Password to save the user ID and password.

4. Alternatively, you can tell Safari that you don't want to save the password for this site, and not to ask again.

5. You can also skip this for now. This is useful if you have multiple logons for a site and don't want to save the one you are using at this moment.

6. Log out and then return to the same website.

7. You'll notice that the ID and password are already filled in. The fields turn yellow to show that AutoFill has been used to fill them in.

8. Tap the button used by the site to complete the login.

9. On some websites, the information might not fill in automatically. You can try tapping the AutoFill Password button to force it.

Changing Passwords

So what happens if you change passwords for a site? Simply use the keyboard to erase and retype the password when logging into that site the next time. AutoFill will prompt you, asking if you want to save the new password, replacing the old one in its database.

It's Not All Good

AutoFill Not Working?

AutoFill works because forms use typical names for fields: id, password, name, firstname, lastname, zip, and so on. If a website wants to get creative, or intentionally block AutoFill functions of browsers, then the site may obfuscate the names of fields to make it impossible for AutoFill to tell which field is which.

Therefore, some websites might not work with AutoFill, while others do. This may be intentional, depending on the sites you visit.

Send and receive
messages from other iOS
and Mac users.

Keep up with
your friends on
Twitter.

Send and receive email from your ISP or a
variety of popular email services.

Next, we look at how to configure and use the Mail program on your iPad to correspond using email and how to use the Messaging and Twitter apps to send and receive messages.

8

Communicating with Email, Messaging, and Twitter

Now that you have an iPad with a battery that seems to last forever, you have no excuse for not replying to emails. You need to be comfortable using the built-in Mail app that enables you to connect with your home or work email using standard protocols such as POP and IMAP. You can even connect with more proprietary systems such as AOL, Exchange, and Yahoo! You can also send messages to your friends using Apple's iMessage system or Twitter.

Configuring Your iPad for Email

It's easy to set up your email if you use one of the popular email services like iCloud, Gmail, Yahoo, AOL, or Microsoft. But if you use another kind of service, such as the email given to you by your local ISP, you need to collect some information to set things up. Here is a list of information you need to set up your iPad for a basic email account

- Email Address
- Account Type (POP or IMAP)
- Incoming Mail Server Address
- Incoming Mail User ID
- Incoming Mail Password
- Outgoing Mail Server Address
- Outgoing Mail User ID
- Outgoing Mail Password

>>>Go Further

IMAP VERSUS POP

POP (Post Office Protocol) fetches and removes email from a server. The server acts as a temporary holding place for email. It is difficult to use POP if you receive email using both your iPad and a computer. You need to either deal with some email going to one device and some to another, or set up one device to not remove email from the server so that the other device can also retrieve it.

IMAP (Internet Message Access Protocol) makes the server the place where all messages are stored, and your iPad and computer simply display what is on the server. It is more ideal in situations where you have multiple devices getting email from the same account.

Popular email services like iCloud and Gmail use an IMAP-like system so you can easily manage your email from both your iPad and your desktop computer—and even your phone.

If you wonder why you shouldn't skip all the setup and just use webmail on your iPad, it's because you can't use emailing features in other apps—such as emailing web page links or emailing photos—if you don't configure the email settings.

If you are using iCloud, Gmail, or any of the other services listed on the Add Account screen, all you need to do is enter your email address and password. Your iPad will set up the account from those two pieces of information. But if you are using another type of email account, you need to enter several details about your account.

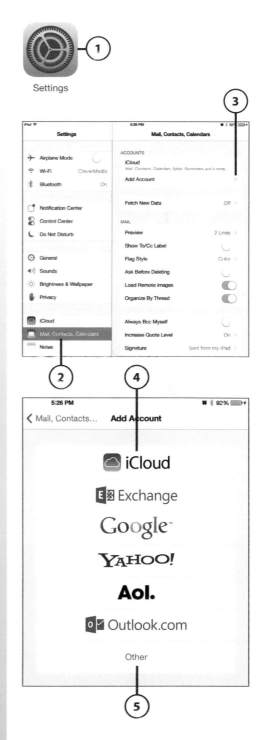

Settings

1. Tap the Settings icon on your Home screen.

2. Tap Mail, Contacts, Calendars.

3. Tap Add Account.

4. If you have an iCloud, Microsoft Exchange, Gmail, Yahoo! Mail, AOL, or Hotmail account, tap the corresponding button. From there, simply enter your user ID and password information, and your iPad figures out the rest. You can skip the rest of the steps!

5. Tap Other if you have a traditional POP or IMAP account from work, your Internet providers, or a traditional hosting company.

6. Tap Add Mail Account.

7. Tap in the Name field and enter your name.

8. Tap in the Address field and enter your email address.

9. Tap in the Password field and enter your password.

10. The Description field should automatically fill with a copy of your email address. Keep it or use another description for the account.

11. Tap Next.

12. Tap IMAP or POP as the email account type.

13. Tap in the Incoming Mail Server, Host Name field and enter your email host's address.

14. Tap in the Incoming Mail Server, User Name field and enter your user name.

15. Tap in the Incoming Mail Server, Password field and enter your password.

16. Repeat the previous three steps for Outgoing Mail Server.

17. Tap Next, and the verification process, which can take up to a minute, begins.

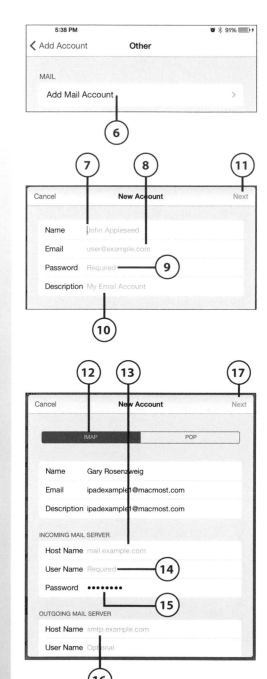

What if the Settings Won't Verify?

If your settings fail to verify, you need to double-check all the information you entered. When something is wrong, it often comes down to a single character being mistyped in one of these fields. For instance, some email systems expect yourname+example.com as the user ID if your email address is yourname@example.com. Be careful you don't miss little things like that.

Reading Your Email

You use the Mail app to read your email, which is much easier to navigate and type with your iPad turned horizontally. Let's start by reading some email.

Mail

1. Tap the Mail app icon on the Home screen.

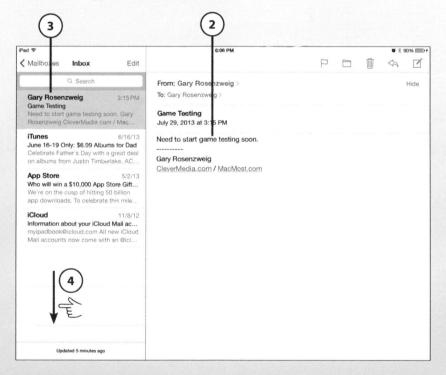

2. On the left, you see a list of incoming mail. On the right, you see the selected message.

3. Tap a message in the list to view it.

4. If you want to check for new mail, drag the list of messages down and release. It will spring back up and ask the server to see if there are new messages.

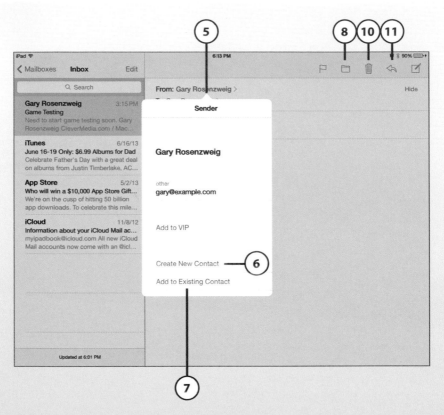

5. Tap the name or email address of the sender.

6. Tap Create New Contact to add the sender to your contacts.

7. Tap Add to Existing Contact to add the email address to a contact you already have in your Contacts app.

8. Tap the Folder button at the top of the message.

9. Tap a folder to move the current message to that folder.

10. Tap the Trash button at the top of the message to send the message directly to the Trash folder.

11. Tap the arrow button at the top of the message to reply or forward the message.

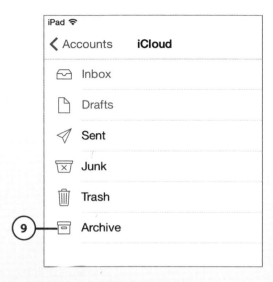

Multiple Inboxes

If you have more than one email account, you can choose to look at each inbox individually or a single unified inbox that includes messages from all accounts. Just tap the Mailboxes button at the upper-left corner of the screen and choose All Inboxes. You can also choose to look at the inbox of a single account, or dig down into any folder of an account.

How Do You Create Folders?

For most email accounts—particularly IMAP, Gmail, and iCloud accounts—you can create folders using the Mail app. Use the back arrow at the upper-left corner of Mail and back out to the list of inboxes and accounts. Choose an account. Then tap the Edit button, and you'll see a New Mailbox button at the bottom of the screen.

VIPs

You can make a contact a VIP when you select the sender's name in an incoming email. Then, their messages will continue to appear in your inbox as normal, but they will also appear in the VIP inbox. So if you get a lot of email and want to occasionally focus only on a few very important people instead of everyone, choose your VIP inbox rather than your inbox.

If you are using VIPs with your iCloud email accounts, you'll see the same VIPs for your Mac and other iOS devices using that iCloud account.

Composing a New Message

Whether you compose a new message or reply to one you received, the process is similar. Let's take a look at composing one from scratch.

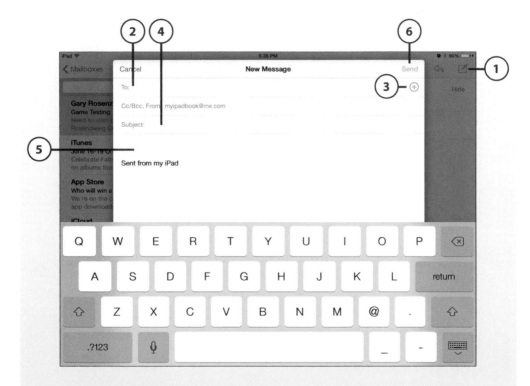

1. In the Mail app, tap the Compose button.

2. Enter a To: address.

3. Alternatively, tap the + button to bring up a list of contacts, and choose from there.

4. Tap in the Subject field and type a subject for the email.

Siri: Sending Email

You can use Siri to send email by asking it to "send an email to" and the name of the recipient. It will ask you for a subject and a body to the message, and then display it. You can choose to send it or cancel.

---

5. Tap below the subject field in the body of the email, and type your message.

6. Tap the Send button.

Including Images

You can copy and paste inside a Mail message just like you can inside of any text entry area on your iPad. But you can also paste in images! Just copy an image from any source—Photos app, Safari, and so on. Then tap in the message body and select Paste. You can paste in more than one image as well.

Creating a Signature

You can create a signature that appears below your messages automatically. You do this in the Settings app.

1. In the Settings app, choose Mail, Contacts, Calendars.

2. Tap Signature, which is way down in the list on the right.

3. If you have more than one email account set up, you can choose to have one signature for all accounts or a different signature for each account.

4. Type a signature in one of the signature text fields. You don't need to do anything to save the signature. You can tap the Home button on your iPad to exit Settings if you like.

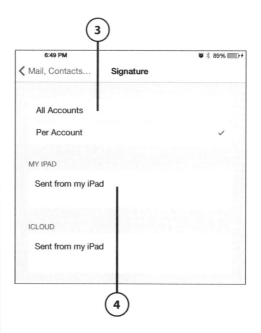

Case-By-Case Signatures

You can have only one signature, even if you have multiple email accounts on your iPad. But the signature is placed in the editable area of the message composition field, so you can edit it like the rest of your message.

Deleting and Moving Messages

While viewing a message, you can simply tap the Trash Can icon and move it to the trash. You can also move a group of messages to a folder or the trash.

1. In the Mail app, go to any mailbox and any subfolder, such as your Inbox.

2. Tap the Edit button.

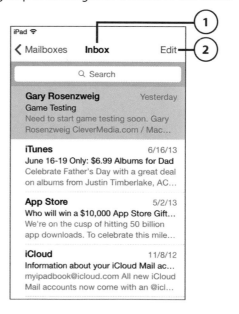

3. Tap the circles next to each message to select them.

4. They will be added to the middle of the screen in a neat stack.

5. Tap the Trash button to delete the selected messages.

6. Tap the Move button, and the left side of the screen changes to a list of folders. You can select one to move all the messages to that folder.

7. Tap the Cancel button to exit without deleting or moving any messages.

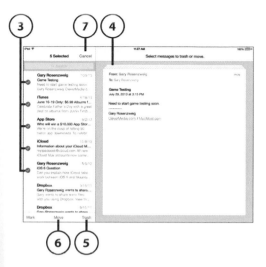

Where's the Trash?

If you are just deleting the single message that you happen to be viewing, you can tap the trashcan icon at the top. But sometimes that icon isn't there. Instead, you may see an icon that looks like a file box. This is an Archive button. Some email services, like Gmail, insist that you archive your email instead of deleting it. To facilitate this, they provide a nearly infinite amount of storage space, so you might as well use that Archive button.

What About Spam?

Your iPad has no built-in spam filter. Fortunately, most email servers filter out spam at the server level. Using a raw POP or IMAP account from an ISP might mean you don't have any server-side spam filtering, unfortunately. But using an account at a service such as Gmail means that you get spam filtering on the server and junk mail automatically goes to the Junk folder, not your Inbox.

Searching Email

You can also search your messages using the Mail app.

1. In the Mail app, from a mailbox view, tap in the Search field.

2. Type a search term.

3. Select a message to view from the search results.

4. Tap the keyboard hide key at the bottom right to hide the keyboard.

5. Tap Cancel to exit the search and return to the mailbox you were previously viewing.

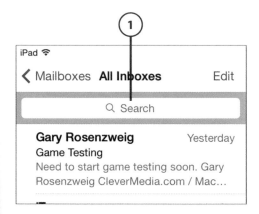

Search What?

Searches work on From, To, Subject fields and the body of the message. However, this only works on messages stored on your iPad. If you are using a server-based email solution, such as IMAP, iCloud, Gmail, and so on, you may not get all the results you expect.

Configuring How Email Is Received

You have more settings for email beyond the basic account setup. You can decide how you want to receive email, using either push delivery (iCloud, IMAP, and Microsoft Exchange) or fetch delivery (all other email accounts).

1. Go to the Settings app and tap on Mail, Contacts, Calendars.

2. Tap Fetch New Data.

3. Turn on Push to use push email reception, if you use email accounts that can send email via push. Push means that the email servers alert your iPad when new mail arrives, instead of waiting for your iPad to check for new mail every so often.

4. Otherwise, select how often you want your iPad to go out to the server and fetch email.

5. Tap one of your email accounts to customize the settings for that particular account.

6. For each account you can set your preferences to Fetch, Manual, or Push if available for that email account.

Push Settings

The two choices for most email accounts are Fetch and Manual. If you have a push account, such as iCloud, you have three choices: Push, Fetch, and Manual. You can switch a Push account to Fetch or Manual if you prefer. You might want to use Manual if you are concerned about bandwidth, like when traveling internationally and only want to check email when using Wi-Fi.

Siri: Checking Email

You can ask Siri for a quick list of new email messages by saying "check my email." You'll get a list from within the Siri interface, and you can tap on a message to read it in the Mail app.

More Email Settings

You can change even more email settings in the Settings app. Let's take a look at some of them.

1. Tap Preview to choose how many lines of message preview to show when stacking messages up in the list view.

2. Turn Show To/Cc Label on to view "To" or "Cc" in each email listed so that you know if you were the primary recipient or someone who was just copied on an email to someone else.

3. Turn Ask Before Deleting on to require a confirmation when you tap the trash can button in Mail.

4. Turn Load Remote Images off so that images referenced in an mail, but stored on a remote server, are not shown in the message body.

5. To group replies to a message under the original message, select Organize By Thread. This is handy when you subscribe to email discussion lists.

6. Turn Always Bcc Myself on if you want to get a copy of every email you send so that later you can move your copies of emails to your Sent folder on your computer. This might be a good idea if you are using an older email system. Modern email systems like iCloud and Gmail should save your sent messages to the server just like other messages.

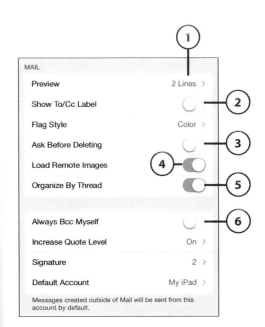

7. Choose whether to indent the quoted text from the original email when replying to a message.

8. Tap Default Account to determine which account is used to send email by default if you have more than one account set up on your iPad.

9. In most apps from which you send emails, you can type a message and also change the account you use to send the email. To do this, tap on the email address shown next to From: and you get a list of all your accounts, including alternate email addresses for each account.

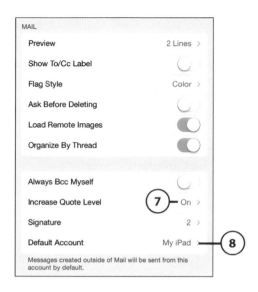

MAIL	
Preview	2 Lines >
Show To/Cc Label	
Flag Style	Color >
Ask Before Deleting	
Load Remote Images	
Organize By Thread	
Always Bcc Myself	
Increase Quote Level	**7** On >
Signature	2 >
Default Account	My iPad > **8**

Messages created outside of Mail will be sent from this account by default.

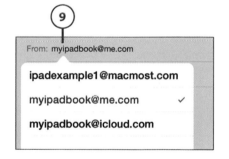

9

From: myipadbook@me.com

ipadexample1@macmost.com

myipadbook@me.com ✓

myipadbook@icloud.com

Why Not Show Remote Images?

The main reason to not show remote images is bandwidth. If you get an email that has 15 images referenced in it, you need to download a lot of data, and it takes a while for that email to show up completely. However, remote images are often used as ways to indicate whether you have opened and looked at messages. So, turning this off might break some statistics and receipt functionality expected from the sender.

Siri: Sending Email

You can use Siri to send email through a series of responses. First, activate Siri and say something like "Send an email to John." You are asked for the subject of the message. After dictating that, you are asked for the message text. Then, you are shown the message to review it. You are then asked "Ready to send it?" If you respond "yes," Siri sends the email. Otherwise, respond "no" to cancel.

Setting Up Messaging

Even though your iPad isn't a phone, you can send text messages. The catch is that you can only message others who are also using Apple's iMessage system. This would include anyone using iOS 5 or newer with an iPad, iPhone, or iPod touch, as long as they have signed up for the free service. Mac users can also send messages with the iMessage system.

1. Launch the Messages app.

2. If this is your first time, you need to enter your Apple ID and password. Otherwise, you can go to step 3.

3. Tap Sign In.

Messages

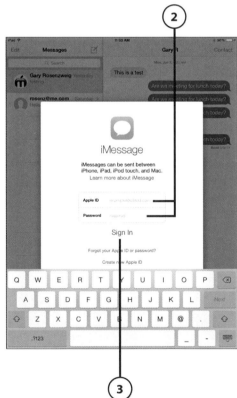

4. You can further customize how you send and receive messages in the Settings app. Go to the Settings app and choose Messages.

5. If you turn this option on, when someone sends you a message they will also get an indication when you have viewed the message. This can save you from having to send simple "OK" messages in response.

6. You can use any valid email address that you own for Messages, even if it is not the same as your Apple ID email address. You can control which email addresses can be used to find you, adding more and removing others.

7. Apple's iMessage system can include a subject line along with the message, though most people don't use this.

8. Tap Block to add email addresses to block so individuals cannot send you messages.

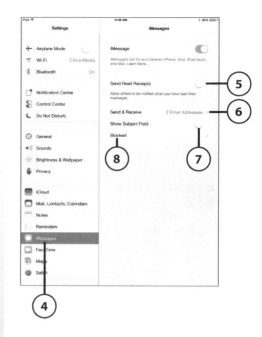

Conversing with Messages

After you have set up an account with Messages, you can quickly and easily send messages to others. The next time you launch Messages, you will be taken directly to the main screen.

1. Tap the New Message button at the top of the screen.

2. In a new message, tap in the To field and enter the email address of the recipient. Note that they should already be signed up for iMessage or you will not be able to send them anything. Some iPhone users may use their phone number as their iMessage ID instead of, or in addition to, their email address. As long as the phone number is tied to an iMessage account, you can still converse with them using Messages on your iPad.

3. Tap the text field above the keyboard to type your message.

4. If you want to include a picture with your message, tap the camera button. This allows you to choose a picture from your photo library, or take a new one with your iPad's camera.

5. Tap Send to send your message.

6. You will see the conversation as a series of talk bubbles. Yours will appear on the right.

7. When your friend responds, you will see their talk bubbles as well.

8. A list of conversations appears on the left. You can have many going on at the same time, or use this list to look at old conversations.

9. Tap the Compose button to start a new conversation.

10. Tap Edit to access buttons to delete old conversations.

11. Tap on the Contact button to do various tasks such as adding them to your contacts, or starting a FaceTime video chat.

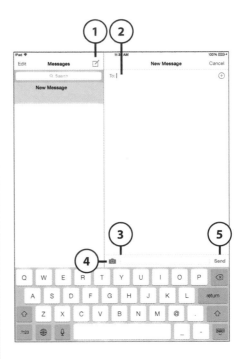

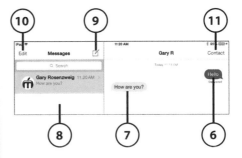

12. Tap and hold on any message to bring up more options.

13. Use the More button to bring up options like selecting and deleting individual messages in the conversation.

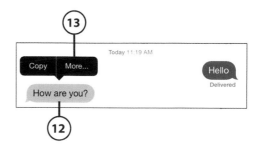

Siri: Sending Messages

You can use Siri to send messages. Simply tell Siri something like "Send a text message to Gary" and Siri will respond by asking you what you want to say in your message. You can review the message before it is sent for a truly hands-free operation. When you get a message, you can also ask Siri to "Read me that message" and you can listen to the message without ever glancing at your iPad's screen.

Setting Up Twitter

Another way to message is to use the popular service Twitter. But instead of a private conversation, Twitter is all about telling the world what you are up to. If you already have a Twitter account, you can use the official Twitter app that comes with your iPad. Otherwise, you can set up a new account.

1. If you don't already have it, install the Twitter app by going to Settings and tapping Twitter on the left side. Launch the Twitter app from the Home screen.

Twitter

2. If you already have an account, tap Sign In.

3. If you need to create a Twitter account, you can do so here by tapping Sign Up. Then enter the required information for a new account.

4. Enter your Twitter Username and Password.

5. Tap Sign In.

Following People on Twitter

Even if you don't tweet much yourself, you can have fun with Twitter by following others. You can even learn things and stay informed. The key is to figure out who you want to follow and then add them.

1. With the Twitter app open, tap the Search button.

2. Type in the name or Twitter handle of the person you want to follow. You can also use terms that describe them, like which website or company they are associated with.

3. Tap the profile that matches your search, and then use the picture to help identify the right person.

4. Tap the Follow button to add them to the list of people you follow.

Who to Follow?

This depends on what you want from Twitter. If you just want to know what your friends are up to, then only follow your friends. If you want to hear what celebrities have to say, then search for some of your favorites. You can also search for professional and industry experts to learn more and stay informed. And don't limit your search to people. Local and worldwide news publications and organizations also have Twitter feeds.

How to Tweet

Thinking about adding your voice to the conversation? You can send a tweet easily with the Twitter app.

1. With the Twitter app open, tap the Compose button.

2. Enter the text of your tweet. It must be 140 characters or less.

3. You can add a photo or video to your tweet. This will upload the image to the service you have selected in your Twitter account and put a link to the file in the tweet.

4. You can add your GPS location to the tweet.

5. Tap Tweet.

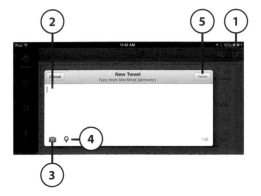

Siri: Tweeting

You can send a tweet with Siri simply by asking it to "send a tweet." You will then be prompted to speak the message. Like with sending email, you can review and confirm the message before it is sent.

Take pictures with
the iPad's cameras.

Edit your photos
using iPhoto.

Browse your photos on the iPad's
brilliant screen.

In this chapter, we use the Camera app to take photos, the Photos app to view your pictures and create slideshows, and the iPhoto app to edit photos and create journals.

→ Taking and Editing Photos
→ Using Photo Booth
→ Browsing Your Photos
→ Sharing Photos
→ Using Photo Stream
→ Viewing Photo Collections
→ Viewing Albums
→ Creating Albums
→ Creating a Slideshow
→ Capturing the Screen
→ Deleting Photos
→ Adjusting Photos in iPhoto
→ Using Brushed Effects with Photos in iPhoto
→ Applying Special Effects to Photos in iPhoto
→ Creating Online Journals with iPhoto

9

Taking and Editing Photos

In addition to replacing books, the iPad replaces photo albums. You can literally carry thousands of photos with you on your iPad. Plus, your iPad's screen is a beautiful way to display these photos.

To access photos on your iPad, you first must sync them from your computer. Then you can use the Photos app to browse and view your photos.

With the iPad's cameras, you can also take photos with your iPad. You can view those in the Photos app as well.

Taking and Editing Photos

The 2nd and 3rd generation iPads include two cameras that you can use to take photos. The primary app for doing this is the Camera app.

Camera

1. Tap the Camera app icon on the home screen. This brings up the Camera app, and you should immediately see the image from the camera.

2. The camera app has three modes: Video, Photo, and Square. The first one is for movie filming mode, and the others take rectangular and square photographs. To switch between modes, tap and drag up and down where you see Video, Photo, and Square. The three words will move vertically while the yellow dot remains in the same place. The option with the yellow dot is the mode you are currently using.

3. Tap the button at the top right switch between front and rear cameras.

4. Tap anywhere on the image to specify that you want to use that portion of the image to determine the exposure for the photo.

5. After you have tapped on the image, and if you are using the rear-facing camera, you can zoom in. To do that, use your fingers to pinch apart. After you do so, you will see a zoom slider at the bottom of the screen. Drag it to the right to increase the zoom.

6. Tap the HDR button to turn on High Dynamic Range Imaging.

7. Tap the large camera button at the right side of the screen to take the picture.

8. Tap the button at the lower right to go to the Camera Roll and see the pictures you have taken.

High Dynamic What?

High Dynamic Range Imaging is a process where two pictures are taken in quick succession, each using a different exposure. Then the two images are combined. For instance, if you are taking a picture of a person with a bright sky behind them, one picture will do better with the person, and the other with the sky. Combining the two images gives you a picture that shows them both better than a single shot would.

When you use HDR, be sure to hold your iPad steady so each shot captures the same image. They will be taken a fraction of a second apart. So, HDR does not work well with moving objects or a moving camera.

9. If you don't see buttons at the top and bottom of the photo, tap the middle of the image from the Camera Roll to bring up controls on the top and bottom of the screen.

10. Use the thumbnails at the bottom to flip through images you have taken that are in your Camera Roll. Or just swipe left and right through the thumbnails to flip through your photos.

11. Tap Camera Roll to exit viewing this one image and jump to an icon view of all of your Camera Roll photos.

12. Tap Done to exit this screen and return to take more pictures.

13. Tap the Trash icon to delete the photo.

14. Tap the Share icon to send the photo to someone else via message, email, AirDrop and a variety of other methods depending on which apps you have installed. This is also where you can copy the image so you can paste it into an email or another app.

15. Tap Edit to adjust the photo.

16. Tap Rotate to rotate the image 90 degrees counterclockwise.

17. Tap Enhance to have the app examine the brightness and contrast in the photo and try to bring out the best image.

18. Tap Filters to access a choice of several filters to apply to the photo, such as Mono, Noir, Fade, Chrome, Transfer, and Instant.

19. Tap Red-Eye, and then tap red eyes in the photo and they are automatically corrected.

20. Tap Crop to crop the image and get rid of unwanted things at the edges or to focus on a specific object in the photo.

21. You can tap Revert to Original at any time to throw away all the edits you might have made with the options in steps 16 to 20. You can try different adjustments without permanently committing to them. You can also tap Undo to throw away only the very last adjustment you made.

22. You can also tap the Cancel button to throw away changes and return to the previous screen.

23. If you want to make the changes stay with the photo, you can tap the Save button.

>>>Go Further

IT'S HIP TO BE SQUARE

The square format of the Camera app comes from a trend to post square images online. Social media icons are square, and square images often look better in online posts. The popularity of the Instagram photo sharing service is another reason we see a lot of square photos.

Square format works great for things like faces or objects where landscape or portrait photos have wasted space on the sides or top and bottom. Photographers can debate the merits of both formats. Some think that landscape photos look good when the subject is off to one side and the background is at the center of the image, whereas square photos look good when the subject is right at the center.

Using Photo Booth

In addition to the basic picture-taking functionality of the Camera app, you can also use the included Photo Booth app to take more creative shots using one of eight special filters.

1. Launch the Photo Booth app.

2. You'll start by seeing all the filters you can choose from. Tap one of the filters to select it.

Photo Booth

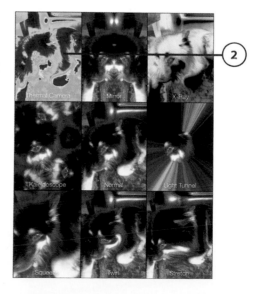

3. Now you'll see just that one filter. In addition, you have some buttons. Tap on the button at the bottom right to switch between the front and rear cameras.

4. Tap the button at the bottom left to return to the 9-filter preview.

5. Tap the camera button at the bottom to take a picture.

6. Some filters also allow you to tap the live video image to adjust the filter. For instance, the Light Tunnel filter enables you to set the position of the center of the tunnel.

7. All you do with Photo Booth is take photos. Then they are sent right to your Camera Roll. See the next section to learn how to browse your photos in the Camera Roll.

A Kind of Flash
When you take a picture with the camera on the front of the iPad, you get a kind of flash effect from the screen. It simply turns all white for a second. This helps in low light situations.

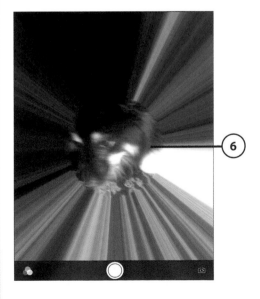

Browsing Your Photos

After you have synced to your Mac or PC, you should have some photos on your iPad, provided you have set some to sync in either iPhoto or iTunes. Then you can browse them with the Photos app.

Photos

1. Tap on the Photos app icon to launch it.

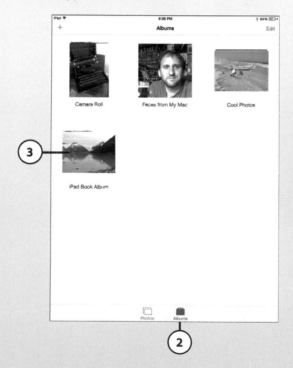

2. Tap to view your photos by photo collections or albums. For this example, we'll use albums. These are both just different ways of sorting the photos on your iPad.

3. Tap an album to view the photos in it.

4. Tap a photo to view it. For most photos, you might want to rotate the iPad to its horizontal orientation for wide-screen viewing.

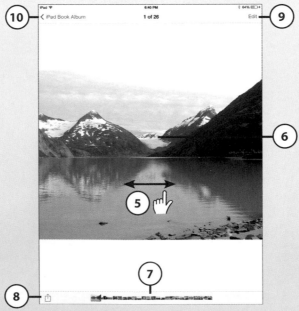

5. To move to the next or previous photo, drag left or right.

6. To bring up controls at the top and bottom of a photo, if they are not already present, tap in the center of the screen.

7. You can tap and run your finger over the small thumbnails at the bottom of the screen to move through that album's photos.

8. Tap the Share button to copy the photo, or send it to a friend or another app.

9. Tap Edit to adjust the photo, the same way you did in the task "Taking and Editing Photos" earlier in this chapter, steps 16 to 23.

10. Tap the name of the album at the top of the screen to return to the list of photos.

ZOOM AND ROTATE

>>Go Further

Here are a few tips on how to navigate your photos as you view them:

- Pinch or unpinch with two fingers to zoom out and in.

- Double-tap a photo to zoom back out to normal size.

- While a photo is at normal size, double-tap to zoom it to make it fit on the screen with the edges cropped.

- If you pinch in far enough, the picture closes, and you return to the browsing mode.

Sharing Photos

There are many ways you can share photos from the Photos app.

1. While viewing a single image in the Photos app, or in the Camera app right after taking a new photo, tap the Share button in the lower-left corner.

2. The image is selected, but you can also select other images in the album by swiping to the left and right and tapping the checkmark circle at the bottom of each image. This way you can share a set of photos instead of just one.

3. If any other iOS devices using AirDrop are nearby, you will see them in this area and can tap their icon to send the photo via AirDrop.

4. Tap the Message button to send a text message that includes the selected image(s) using iMessage to another person. See "Setting Up Messaging" in Chapter 8.

5. Tap Mail to send the current photo in an email message.

6. After you tap Mail, a message composition screen appears and starts a new message. The photo is attached to the message.

7. If you are using iCloud's Photo Stream feature, you can send the photo to Photo Stream—even if it is not a photo you have taken with the iPad's camera, such as a photo taken with your iPhone. We'll look at using Photo Stream in the next section.

8. You can also send (tweet) the photo using your Twitter account. Tap the Twitter button and a small Twitter composition dialog appears, which allows you to add a message to go along with the photo.

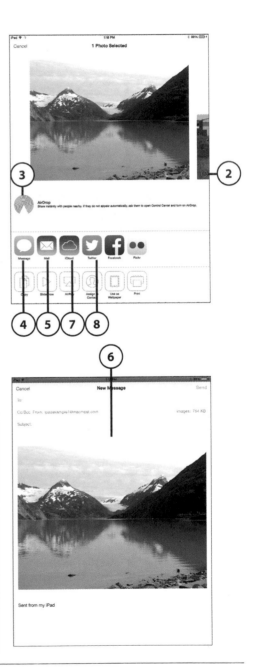

It's Not the Original Image

If you sync a photo from your computer to your iPad, and then email it to people, they actually receive a reduced image, not the original. iPad albums contain reduced images to save space. If you want to send the original, email it from your computer.

9. Likewise, tap the Facebook button to post the photo, along with a message, to your Facebook wall.

10. If you use Flickr, tap the Flickr button to post the image to your Flickr account. Go to the Flickr section of the Settings app to configure your Flickr account first.

11. Tap Copy to copy the photo to your clipboard. Putting the photo on the clipboard enables you to paste it into documents or email messages in other apps.

12. Tap Slideshow to start a slideshow with the selected pictures. It can display on the iPad's screen, or you can select to view it on an AirPlay device like an Apple TV on the same network.

13. You can also show a single photo on a TV using an Apple TV. This only appears if you are using AirPlay on your network.

14. Tap Assign to Contact to display a list of all your contacts so that you can add the photo to the contact's thumbnail image.

15. Tap Use as Wallpaper to assign the image to either the Lock Screen background or the Home Screen background, or both.

16. Tap Print to send the photo to your networked printer. See "Printing from Your iPad" in Chapter 18.

You can share your photos in many ways, and it is likely that more will be added in the future. What you can use depends on what you have set up on your iPad. For instance, if you have Messaging and Twitter set up, you can use the Message and Tweet buttons to share using those services.

Using Photo Stream

Photo Stream is a feature of iCloud that can do two things: First, it can automatically upload new photos you take on your iPad to iCloud. Then these photos will sync to your other iOS devices and your Mac using iPhoto. This can essentially replace syncing your iPad to your computer to transfer your photos.

A second feature of Photo Stream is the ability to create online photo galleries that your friends and family can view. This also happens wirelessly using iCloud.

Setting Up Photo Stream

To use these Photo Stream features, you first need to enable Photo Stream in the Settings app.

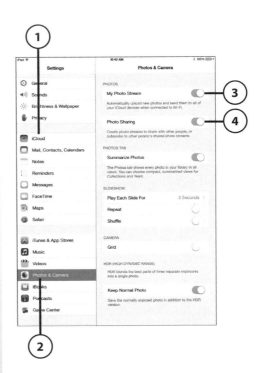

1. In the Settings app, first go to the iCloud settings and make sure you are signed in to your iCloud account. See "Syncing Using iCloud" in Chapter 3.

2. Once again in the Settings app, tap Photos & Camera.

3. Turn on My Photo Stream, which automatically saves the photos you take to iCloud.

4. Turn on Photo Sharing, which enables you to create online photo galleries.

After you have Photo Stream enabled, each photo you take with your iPad will be placed in an album titled for the current month. These albums will also appear, with their photos, on your other iOS devices and in iPhoto on a Mac, if you have one. Of course, your iPad must be connected to the Internet for this to happen.

Photo Stream in iPhoto

If you are a Mac user, you can set up Photo Stream in iPhoto on your Mac as well. Go to iPhoto, Preferences, Photo Stream and turn it on. Turn on My Photo Stream and Automatic Import. You will see Photo Stream show up in the left sidebar. When you take a picture on your iPad, it will upload to Photo Stream as long as you have an Internet connection. Then it will appear in the Photo Stream section of iPhoto on your Mac a minute later.

Sharing Photos with Photo Stream

After you have turned on Photo Sharing in Settings, you can create shared streams that others can view in a web browser.

1. In the Photos app, tap Shared at the bottom.

2. Tap New Shared Stream.

3. Enter a name for the stream and tap Next.

4. Enter contact names or email addresses of people who will be able to see the photo stream. You will be able to modify this later to add more. Tap Create when you are done.

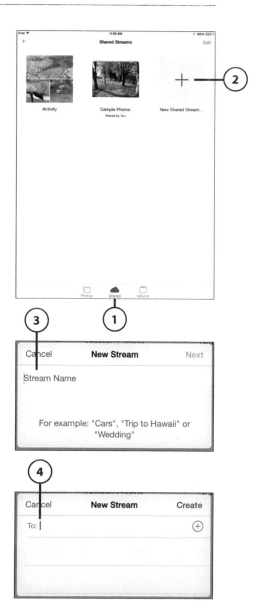

5. You now see your list of shared photo streams again. Tap the new one to enter it.

6. There are no photos here yet, so tap the + button to add one.

7. Select photos you want to add.

8. Tap Done.

9. Enter a message to accompany the posting of these new photos. The message will become the description for the photos when viewed.

10. Tap Post.

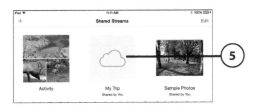

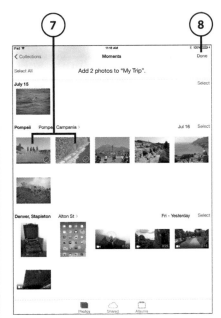

11. You are returned to the stream and can see the photos have been added.

12. Tap People for more shared photo stream settings.

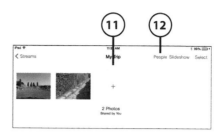

13. You can always remove people from the shared list by tapping the name and then choosing Remove Subscriber from the options presented.

14. You can invite new people.

15. If Subscribers Can Post is turned on, the people on your list can upload photos from their iOS devices and iPhoto to this stream.

16. You can also enable Public Website to make the whole photo stream public. You will get a public URL that you can share with people or post to your blog or social media networks. Anyone can view the photos using that link.

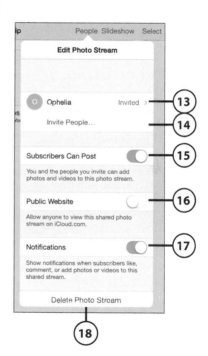

17. Shared photo streams allow likes and comments to photos. Leave Notifications on if you want to get a notification on your iPad when someone interacts with your stream.

18. Delete Photo Stream is the option that enables you to delete the entire stream. This is handy if your photo stream was only meant to be a temporary way for family and friends to see what was going on during a trip or event.

Photo Stream, Interrupted

So what happens when you take a new picture but Photo Stream can't connect to the Internet at that moment? Or, you choose to share a photo and there is no connection?

Like a typical cloud service, you can perform all the steps, and your iPad will simply complete the upload next time it has a connection.

Viewing Photo Collections

When you use the Photos app, you can view your photos in several ways. One way if by collections. Collections are groups created by the Photos app from the information stored in your photos, such as time and location of the photo. You don't create collections; you just leave that up to iOS. In the next section, we look at viewing based on albums, which are groups you define.

1. The top level of the collections hierarchy is Years. Go to the Photos app and tap Photos at the bottom. If you do not see Years as the title at the top, use the button at the top left to move up the hierarchy to Years.

2. Your photos are then divided up into years. Every year that has enough photos will show, and years that have only a few photos will be grouped with other years. For instance, you may see 2008-2010 as a group.

3. Each year shows a list of locations. Tap this list, not the photo thumbnails, to jump to the map view.

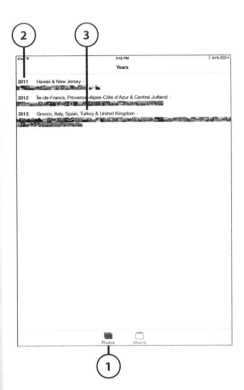

4. A map appears with groups of photos over various locations. If you only use a camera that does not have GPS capability, then you may not see any. The scale of the map will change depending on where your photos for that year were located. Tap Years to return to the previous screen without working with the map.

5. Tap a collection of photos over a location to go to that set of photos.

6. Now you are viewing the photos in that collection. You can tap the year button at the top to jump back up to the map.

7. Tap Slideshow to start an automatic slideshow with all the photos.

8. Tap Select to be able to select multiple photos from this collection for sharing.

9. Tap a photo to view it full screen.

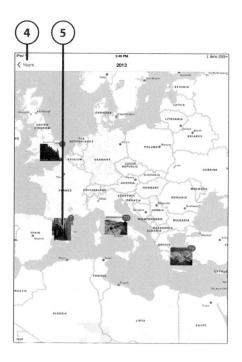

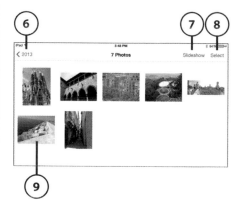

10. When viewing photos, you may want to turn your iPad to horizontal orientation—most pictures are wider than they are taller.

11. Use the thumbnails at the bottom to select another photo from the collection, or simply swipe left or right from the center of the screen to move between photos.

12. Tap Edit to edit the photo from here. See the task "Taking and Editing Photos" earlier in this chapter, steps 15 to 23.

13. You can share the photo, using the same controls from the "Sharing Photos" task earlier in this chapter.

14. To return to the collection, tap the button at the top left. Tap in that area twice more to return all the way back to the list of photos by Years that we started with in step 1.

15. On the Years screen, tap and hold over any tiny thumbnail to see a larger version of it appear above your finger. Then you can move your finger around the screen to view larger versions of other thumbnails.

16. Tapping any thumbnail, as opposed to tapping the list of place names, takes you to a different screen.

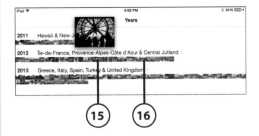

17. This screen shows collections of photos in smaller selections of time, called "Moments." Tap any thumbnail to jump into a collection.

18. You can tap any photo to view it full screen, just like in step 9.

19. You can drag up and down to look at other Moments. You can also do this on the Collections screen.

20. If you want to quickly share the entire set of photos that comprise one Moment, tap the Share button.

21. You can return to the previous screen by tapping Collections in the upper left corner.

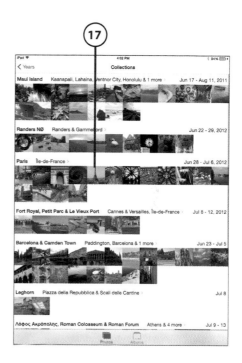

Collections Are Not for Organizing

When given a collection, such as a collection of photos, our instinct is to organize it. That's what albums are for. Collections can be frustrating for some, as you do not have many options to organize the photos. They are simply grouped based on the data in the photos, which was added when the photo was taken.

If the time or location of a photo is wrong, there is no way to change it in the Photos app. There are some third-party apps in the app store that can do this, and you can also do this in iPhoto on your Mac.

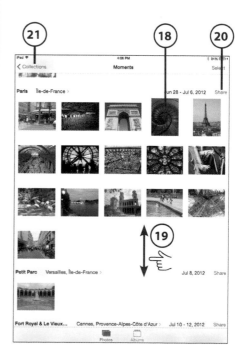

Viewing Albums

Using the Photos button at the bottom of the Photos app is a great way to find the photos you want to view. But, if you would rather organize your photos yourself, you can do so by creating albums.

Albums can be made in iPhoto or Aperture on your Mac, Photoshop Albums or Photoshop Elements on Windows, or by using file system folders on Mac and windows. When you sync to your iPad, you'll see these albums using the steps that follow.

1. In the Photos app, tap the Albums button.

2. Tap on an album to expand it to see all the photos.

3. Tap any photo to view it.

4. Tap the album name to return from viewing the photo, and then tap the Albums button on the next screen to return to the list of albums.

Getting Back to the Album

After you finish digging down into an album, you can go back to the list of albums by tapping the Albums button, or a similarly named button, at the top left. But you can also pinch in all photos to group them in the middle of the screen and then release to move back to the albums list.

Faces Too

iPhoto and Aperture on the Mac have the ability to find faces in your photos. If you use this feature and you sync your photos to your iPad, you will also have an option to view groups of photos that correspond to those faces. You can even select faces to sync to your iPad in iTunes on your Mac.

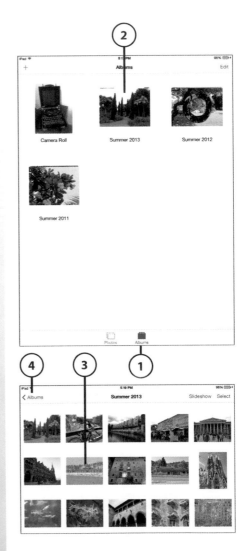

Creating Albums

Syncing with iTunes isn't the only way to organize your photos into albums. You can create new albums right on your iPad. The process involves naming a new album and then selecting the photos to appear in the album.

1. In the Photos app, tap Albums at the bottom to view your albums.

2. Tap the + button to create a new album.

3. Enter a name for the album.

4. Tap Save.

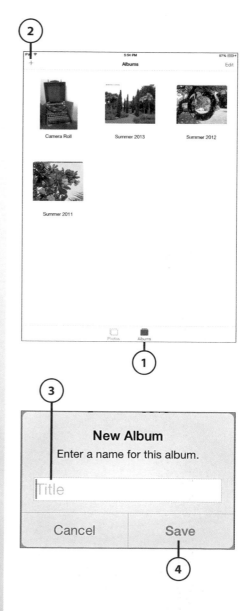

5. Now you can start adding some photos to this empty album. You will see all your photos appear in the Moments view, just as they did in step 17 of the task "Viewing Photo Collections," earlier in this chapter.

6. Tap and drag vertically to flip through your photos to locate the ones you want to include in this new album.

7. If you prefer Albums view, you can tap Albums to switch to that view.

8. You can also tap Collections to move up to Collections view.

9. Tap a single photo to add it to the album. Tap again to undo the selection.

10. You can also select an entire collection.

11. When you have added all the photos you want to the album, tap Done. You can always add more by viewing that album, tapping the Select button at the top, and then tapping the Add button at the top.

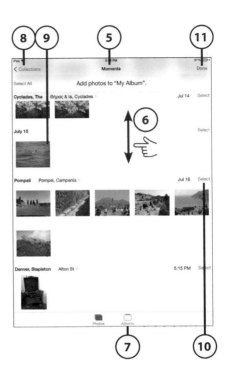

Creating a Slideshow

Another way to look at your photos is as a slideshow with music and transitions. You can quickly and easily create a slideshow with any group of photos in the Photos app that shows a Slideshow button at the top—for example, an album synced to, or that you created on, your iPad.

1. In the Photos app, tap Albums.

2. Tap an album to select it.

3. Tap the Slideshow button at the top of the album.

4. Tap Transition to select a transition that you want to appear between images. There are several to choose from.

5. Slide the Play Music button on or off. If you toggle it on, you will be able to select a song from your iTunes collection.

6. Tap Start Slideshow.

Stopping a Slideshow

Tap on the screen anywhere to stop a slideshow.

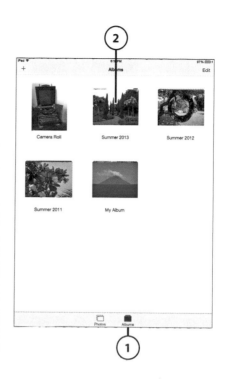

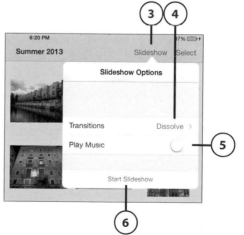

Capturing the Screen

You can capture the entire iPad screen and send it to your Photos app. This feature is useful if you want to save what you see to an image for later.

1. Make sure the screen shows what you want to capture. Try the Home screen, as an example.

2. Press and hold the Wake/Sleep button and Home button at the same time. The screen flashes and you hear a camera shutter sound, unless you have the volume turned down.

3. Go to the Photos app.

4. Tap on the Camera Roll album. The last image in this album should be your new screen capture. Tap it to open it.

5. Tap the last image in your Camera Roll, which should be the screenshot you just took.

6. The example is a vertical capture of the Home screen, so it might be confusing to look at. Turn your iPad horizontally.

7. Tap the Share icon to email the photo or copy it to use in another application. Or you can leave the photo in your Camera Roll album for future use.

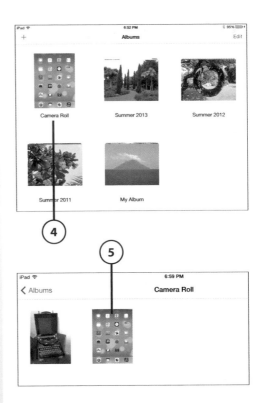

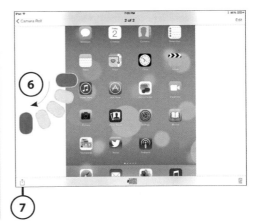

Deleting Photos

You can only delete photos from the Camera Roll album (sometimes referred to as the "Saved Photos" album) and your Photo Stream.

1. In the Photos app, tap Albums.

2. Tap on Camera Roll.

3. Tap a photo to view it.

4. Tap the Trash Can button.

5. Tap Delete Photo.

6. Alternatively, you can go back to step 3 and then tap the Select button.

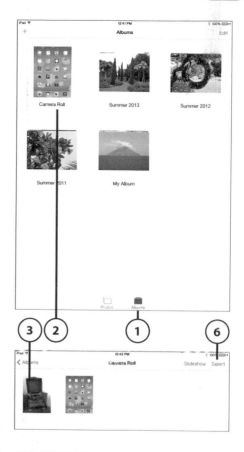

7. Tap multiple photos to select them.

8. Tap the trashcan button, and then tap the Delete Selected Photos button that appears.

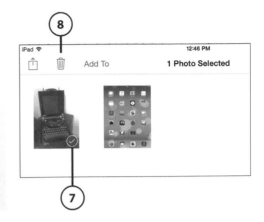

So How Can I Delete Other Photos?

The Camera Roll album is special; it contains photos created on your iPad. The rest of the albums are just copies of photos synced from your computer. You can't delete them from your iPad any more than you can delete music synced to your iPad.

To delete these photos, go back to iPhoto on your computer, and remove them from any albums that you have set to sync to your iPad. Also, go into iTunes on your computer, and make sure the photo syncing options there—such as to sync Last 12 Months—won't copy that photo.

If you think of your photos like you think of your music, understanding which photos are synced and why makes more sense.

Adjusting Photos in iPhoto

Although the Photos app gives you the ability to make basic adjustments to your pictures, the iPhoto app goes much further. iPhoto does not come preloaded with the iOS—you need to add it from the App Store. Then, you can use the iPhoto app to apply a variety of filters, adjustments, and special effects to your photos.

1. After you download iPhoto, tap its icon to run it.

iPhoto

2. First, you need to select a photo to edit. Tap Albums to view your photos grouped into the same albums as in the Photos app.

3. You can view the photos you have taken with your iPad's camera in the Camera Roll. You can also see photos you have created in other apps here.

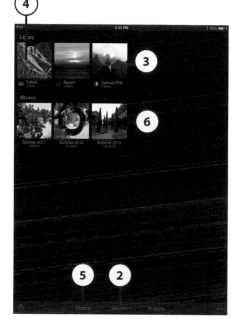

4. If you have already edited a photo, you will see the Edited album. This contains all altered photos. You can go here to continue to work on them.

5. Tap Photos to see one long list of all the photos on your iPad.

6. Tap an album to dig into that album's photos.

7. You will see one of the photos from the album in the center of the screen. This is the photo you are currently editing.

8. Tap the Thumbnail Grid button to see the rest of the photos in the album at the bottom so that you can switch between them.

9. Tap any photo to switch to it. Alternatively, you can swipe left or right to move between photos.

10. Tap the Help button to bring up labels for all of buttons and controls in iPhoto.

11. Try the Auto-enhance button if you want to let your iPad figure out how to adjust the brightness, contrast, and other alterations that should improve the look of the picture.

12. Tap the Exposure button to reveal the brightness and contrast controls.

13. Drag the brightness control left or right to adjust the general brightness of the photo.

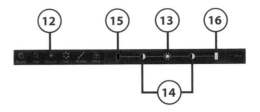

14. Drag the contrast controls left or right to adjust the contrast.

15. Drag the shadows control to adjust the exposure for the dark areas of the photo.

16. Drag the highlights control to adjust the exposure for the light areas of the photo.

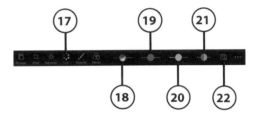

17. Tap the Color adjustments button.

18. Drag the Saturation control left and right to saturate or desaturate the image. The first enhances the color in your photo, and the second removes color, bringing it closer to black and white.

19. Adjust the blue tones in the picture.

20. Adjust the green tones in the picture.

21. Adjust the skin tones in the picture.

22. Tap to bring up manual controls for white balance and to adjust the image for specific lighting conditions. These include sun, cloudy, flash, shade, incandescent, fluorescent, or underwater.

Cropping, Straightening, and Rotating

In addition to color effects and adjustments, you can also crop and rotate your pictures. The Crop & Straighten button is at the bottom-left corner and enables you to trim the edges down and straighten the image. To rotate an image 90 degrees, tap the Browse icon at the bottom-left. Using two finger, tap and spin the image in the direction you want it to rotate.

Using Brushed Effects on Photos in iPhoto

There are also adjustments that you can make on parts of a photo rather than the entire image.

1. Tap the Brushes button.

2. Select a brush to use.

3. Use your finger to manually brush the area you want the effect applied to. For instance, you can desaturate everything in this photo except the flower.

4. Tap the undo button to revert to how the image was before you tried the brush. Using the undo button, you can try a variety of brushes and other effects knowing that you can undo the change easily.

5. Tap the Show Original button if you want to quickly compare your changes to the original photo without undoing the changes.

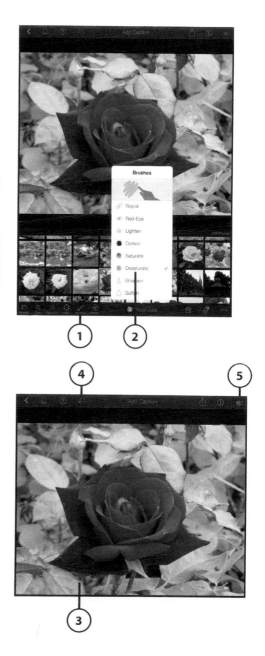

Applying Special Effects to Photos in iPhoto

You can also apply a variety of filters to your entire photo.

1. Tap the Effects button.

2. Select one of the effects sets.

3. All of the effects in the category you chose appear at the bottom of the screen.Tap one and try it with the current image.

4. Use undo to revert back to the original image before trying another one.

5. Tap the Show All Effects button to choose from a different category of effects.

Ordering Prints with iPhoto

If you want printed copies of some of your photos, you can order some from right within iPhoto on your iPad. You pay for the service with your iTunes account, just like buying music or apps.

1. While viewing photos in an album, tap the Share button.

2. Tap Order Prints.

3. If you had previously selected several photos, you can simply use the Selected button to jump to step 7. If the album you are viewing is 100 photos or less, you can tap the All button to order copies of every photo in the album.

4. To select photos to order at this stage, simply tap Choose Photos.

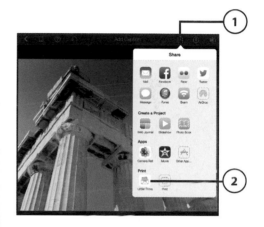

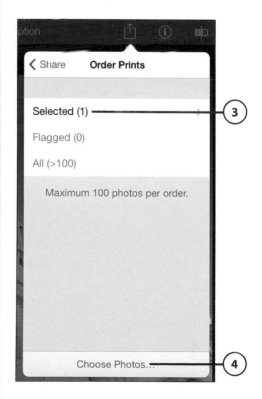

5. Tap on photos to select them. You see a checkmark on each photo you select.

6. Tap Next.

7. Choose a photo sizing option. Each sizing option has further options to choose from.

8. Review your photos and then tap the price to order them. You will be prompted for an address and then you will finish on a final confirmation screen before the order is complete.

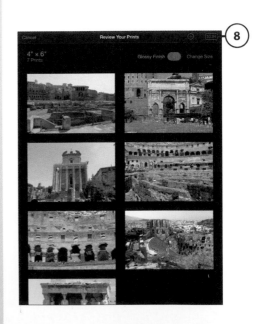

Making Photo Books with iPhoto

An alternative to individual prints is to create a book with your photos. If your plan is to put the photos into an album anyway, this saves you the time and gives you some interesting and creative options.

1. While viewing photos in an album, tap the Share button.

2. Tap Photo Book.

3. You can select photos just as you did in the previous task. Or, just tap All to use all the photos in the album.

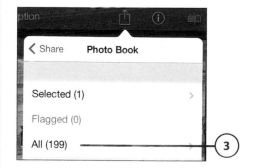

4. Tap in the name field to type a name for your book and choose a size.

5. Select a basic book theme.

6. Tap Create Photo Book.

7. iPhoto automatically creates and populates a book with your selected photos. When it is done, tap Show to view the book.

8. You can scroll through the pages of the book, or double-tap a page to view it closer.

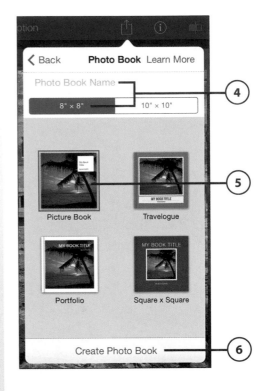

9. Tap any photo for options to edit it, replace it, or remove it.

10. You can also drag a photo from the unused photos list at the bottom and replace any photo on the pages. You can also drag a photo to another photo on the pages to swap them.

11. Tap the Page button at the top.

12. You can now change the layout style of the left or right page.

13. You can also change the background pattern.

14. If you like, you can insert a new page or spread of two pages.

15. Tap the back button to view the whole book again.

16. Tap the options button to review the book's options and make changes.

17. The price of the book will vary depending on the number of pages you have. Tap the price to begin the process of ordering the book, just like ordering prints from the previous task.

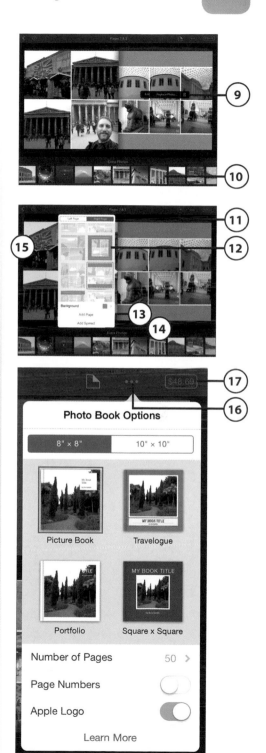

Record video with your
iPad's two cameras.

Make video calls
with FaceTime.

Put together movies from your video
clips and photos.

In this chapter, we use the Camera, Photo Booth, and iMovie apps to shoot and edit video with your iPad. We'll also use the FaceTime app to make a video call.

Recording Video

You can record video using either of the two cameras on your iPad. The primary app for doing this is the Camera app.

In addition, you can edit video with the iMovie app. This app, which you can purchase from Apple in the App Store, lets you combine clips and add transitions, titles, and audio.

The cameras on your iPad can also be used to video chat with someone on another iPad, an iPhone, iPod Touch, or a Mac using the FaceTime app.

Shooting Video

If you simply want to record something that is happening using the cameras, you can do it with the Camera app.

Camera

1. Launch the Camera app. Also, turn your iPad sideways so you are shooting horizontal video, like you are used to seeing on TV and in movies. Your iPad can shoot in both vertical and horizontal orientations, but horizontal is better for playback on most screens.

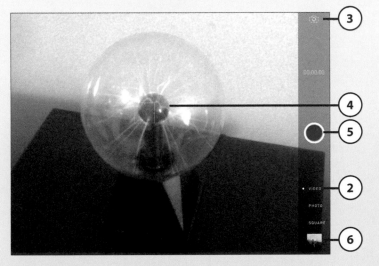

2. Switch the camera mode to video by tapping this area and sliding the words "Video, Photo and Square" so that "Video" is next to the yellow dot.

3. If needed, you can toggle between the rear and front cameras. Remember that the rear camera is much better quality than the front camera, so use the rear one whenever possible.

4. Optionally, tap in the image to set the best point for the exposure setting.

5. Tap the record button to start recording. While you are recording, the red dot will flash and the length of the recording will show on the right side above the button. Tap the same button to stop recording.

6. Tap the image in the lower-right corner to view your video when you are done.

7. You are now in the Camera Roll, the same place as you were in "Taking and Editing Photos," in Chapter 9. But the interface looks different when you have a video instead of a still photo. Tap the play button to watch the video.

8. Tap the Share button to email the video, send via a text message, or upload it directly to a service like YouTube, Facebook, or Vimeo. You can also stream it to an AirPlay device on your network such as an Apple TV.

9. Tap the trashcan to delete the video.

10. When you are done viewing your video, tap Done to shoot another.

It's Not All Good

Emailing Compresses the Video

Video with the rear camera is shot at 1280x720 on the iPad 2 and 1920x1080 on newer iPads. But when you email a video, it's usually compressed to a much smaller size. This is good because you won't be sending a massive video file, using your bandwidth and the bandwidth of the recipient. But don't use email to save your videos to your computer. Instead, sync and transfer, as you would do with photos.

Trimming Video Clips

While viewing a video in the Camera Roll, you can also trim it to cut some unneeded footage from the start and end of the video.

1. You can get to the Camera Roll by either using the Photos app or the Camera app. For instance, launch the Camera app and immediately tap the thumbnail in the lower right on the screen.

2. If you are viewing a video, you will see a timeline of sorts at the top of the screen.

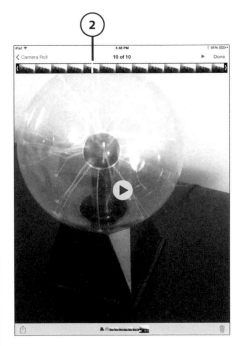

3. Drag the left side of the timeline to the right to trim from the start of the video.

4. Drag the right side of the timeline to the left to trim from the end of the video.

5. Tap the Trim button.

6. Tap Trim Original to replace the video with the trimmed version.

7. Tap Save as New Clip to keep the original, and also save your trimmed version as a separate clip.

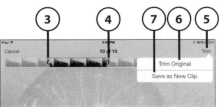

Combining Clips in iMovie

The trimming functionality of the Camera and Photos apps gives you the basic ability to edit a video clip, but you can go a lot further if you purchase the iMovie app from Apple. Although not a full-featured editor like you might have on your computer, you can combine clips, add titles and transitions, and produce a short video from your clips.

iMovie

1. Launch the iMovie app. Turn your iPad to look at the screen horizontally. iMovie is a little easier to use in that orientation.

2. Tap the + button.

3. Tap Movie.

4. Tap Simple.

5. Tap Create Movie.

6. You can add a video to your project by tapping on a clip on the right, and then tapping the down arrow to place it in the timeline at the bottom.

7. You can also record new video clips using the camera button at the bottom.

8. Continue to add more clips. Each one will be appended to the end of the project.

9. The line indicates the current position of the video.

10. The preview area shows you the image at the current position.

11. You can drag the project timeline left and right to scroll through it.

12. You can pinch in and out to shrink or enlarge the timeline.

13. Press play to play the video in the preview area. If the line is at the end of the video, it will jump back to the start of the video first.

14. Tap and hold a clip until it "pops" off the timeline, and you can drag it to a different part of the project timeline.

15. Tap the back button when you are done editing. There is no need to "save" your project—the current state of the project is always saved.

16. Tap the name of the project to edit the name.

17. Tap the play button to view the finished project.

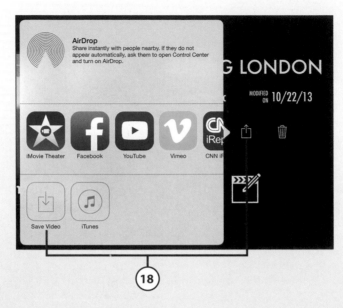

18. Tap the Share button to save the video to your Camera Roll, export it to iTunes the next time you sync, or upload to one of the listed Internet video sites.

Best Way to Share with Friends?

While it may seem to be a good idea to simply email a video to your friends, remember that video files are usually very large. Even if you have the bandwidth to upload them, your friends need the bandwidth to download them. Some may have restrictions on how large email attachments can be.

So, the video sharing options in iMovie are better for all concerned. You can upload to your Facebook or YouTube account and even set the video to "private" or "unlisted." Then just let a few friends know about it with the link in an email instead of a huge file attachment.

Editing Transitions in iMovie

Between each clip in your iMovie project is a transition. You can choose between a direct cut (no transition), a cross-dissolve transition, or a special theme transition. But first, you must select a theme.

1. Open up the project you created in the previous task.

2. Tap the settings button at the lower right to select a theme.

3. Flip through the themes and choose one.

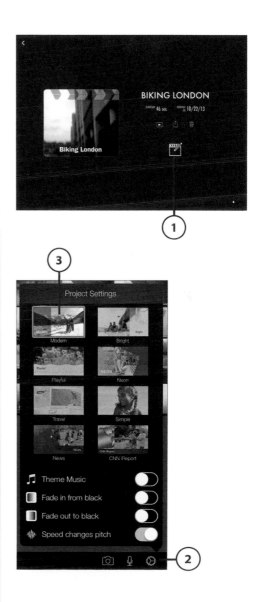

4. Double-tap one of the transition buttons that appear between each clip. This should bring up the Transition Settings menu along the bottom of the screen.

5. Choose None if you want one clip to start right after the other.

6. Choose Cross Dissolve if you want one clip to fade into the other.

7. Choose Theme to use the special theme transition. These vary depending on which theme you choose.

8. The slide transition moves the next clip over the current one.

9. The wipe transition wipes and replaces one clip with the other starting at one edge.

10. This transition will fade out to black and then fade in the next clip.

11. Choose a duration for the transition.

12. Tap the triangles below the transition button to expand into a precision editor.

13. Move the transition area to select how you want the two clips to overlap during the transition. To make it easier to move the yellow bars, you may want to pinch out to zoom in for a closer look at the area.

14. Tap the triangles to leave the precision edit mode.

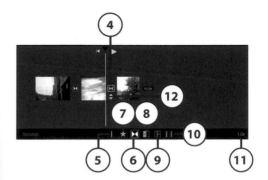

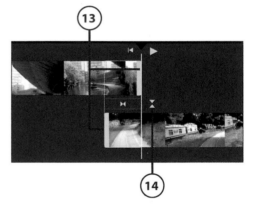

Adding Photos to Your Video in iMovie

You can also add photos from your Camera Roll or any album on your iPad. You can just use a series of photos in a video, or mix photos and video clips.

1. Continuing with the previous example, scroll the timeline all the way to the left.
2. Tap the photos button.
3. Tap the name of the album that contains your photo.

4. Tap the photo you want to use.
5. It now appears in the timeline at the current position. Tap it to select it.

Go Further

GETTING CREATIVE WITH PICTURES

You can even create a video without any photos. For example, you could use one of the drawing programs mentioned in Chapter 16, such as SketchBook Pro, Brushes, ArtStudio, or Adobe Ideas, to create images with text and drawings on them. Create a series to illustrate an idea or story. Then bring them together as a series of pictures in an iMovie project. Add music and a voice over to make something very interesting.

6. Tap and drag the yellow bars to change the duration of the photo in the timeline. It starts with a default of 5 seconds. But, for example, you could increase it to 10 seconds.

7. Tap the Start button that appears in the preview area. Then adjust the photo by pinching zooming and dragging to get it just as you like. For instance, pinch in so the photo fits into the frame.

8. Tap the End button to set the end position for the picture. For instance, unpinch to zoom in on a specific area.

9. Tap Done when you finish adjusting both the start and end positions.

10. Slide the timeline back and forth to preview how the movement in the picture will work.

You can continue to add pictures just as you would add video clips. Add as many as you like. You can even create a slideshow of just photos without ever shooting a single second of video footage.

Adding Video Titles in iMovie

You can also add titles that overlay clips or photos in iMovie. Like the transitions, the style of the titles depends on the theme you are using.

1. Continue with the example we have been building. Tap on a clip to select it and then tap Title at the bottom of the screen.

2. Tap the title style button.

3. Select a title style. As you do so, a preview appears in the preview area.

4. Tap in the text field area in the preview to bring up the keyboard, and enter text.

5. Some title types show a map or have a space where the location is displayed. Tap Location to enter a name for the location.

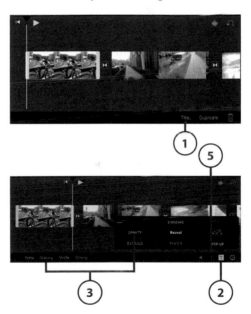

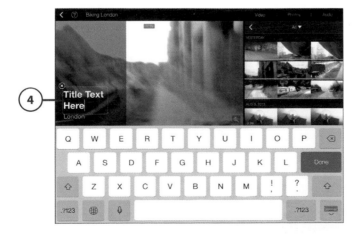

MUSIC AND VOICEOVERS

You can also do a lot with the audio in iMovie. You can add any song from your iPad's iTunes collection to the video as the background track. There are also a number of theme music tracks included that you can use.

You can also add from a collection of sound effects the same way. However, sound effects can appear at any point in your movie, whereas music covers the entire span of the video.

You can also record a voiceover so you can narrate your video. This means you can have four audio tracks: the audio attached to the video, background music, sound effects, and a voiceover.

To learn how to use all the additional features of iMovie, look for the help button at the bottom-left corner of the projects screen. This brings up complete documentation for the app.

Setting Up FaceTime

Another major use of the video cameras is FaceTime. This is Apple's video calling service. You can make video phone calls between any devices that have FaceTime, including recent iPhones, iPod touches, iPads, and Macs. As the number of people with FaceTime increases, this app will become more useful.

All that's required to make a FaceTime call is a free account. You can use your existing Apple ID or create a new one. You can also assign alternate email addresses to be used as FaceTime "phone numbers" that people can use to contact you via FaceTime.

1. Launch the Settings app.

Settings

2. Tap FaceTime on the left.

3. Turn on FaceTime if it isn't already.

4. An Apple ID is needed for FaceTime even if you don't plan to use that same email address with FaceTime calls. If you haven't used FaceTime before, you will be prompted to enter your Apple ID and password.

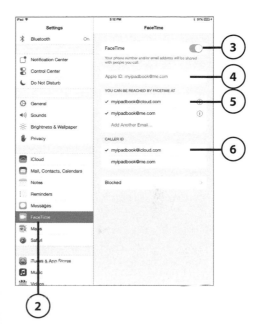

5. This list contains email addresses others can use to reach you via a FaceTime call. By default, your Apple ID email address will be here. But you can add another one and even remove your Apple ID email address if you never want to use that for FaceTime.

6. The Caller ID represents your default email address used to place FaceTime calls. It is what others will see when you call them. You'll see this if you have two or more email addresses assigned to your Apple ID account.

By using different email addresses for different iOS devices, you can more easily specify which device you are calling. For instance, if you and your spouse both have iPhones, and you share an iPad, you can give the iPad a different email address (maybe a free email account). That way you can specify which device you want to call.

Remember that you still need to be connected to the Internet with a Wi-Fi connection. At this time, mobile carriers do not support FaceTime over their 3G or 4G networks, although there are rumors they might in the near future, possibly for an extra charge.

Placing Video Calls with FaceTime

After you have your account set up in FaceTime, you can place and receive calls.

1. Launch the FaceTime app.

2. Select a contact from your list. If your contact list isn't showing, tap the Contacts button at the bottom right of the screen.

3. Alternatively, you can add a new contact. You need to know either their iPhone phone number or the email address they used when creating their FaceTime account.

4. Tap the FaceTime button to initiate a FaceTime call. You'll also notice a second button to the right of it that allows you to place an audio-only FaceTime call. However, this feature only works if both parties have the latest versions of FaceTime, such as the version that comes with iOS 7.

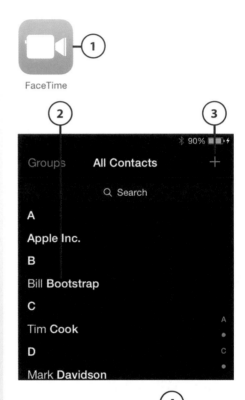

FaceTime

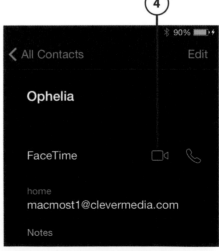

5. Wait while the call is placed. You'll hear a ringing. You can tap the End button to cancel the call.

6. After the other party has answered the call, you can see both her image filling the whole screen and your image in the upper right. You can drag your image to any of the four corners.

7. Tap the mute button to mute your microphone.

8. Tap the switch cameras button to show the view from the rear camera.

9. Tap End to finish the call.

Two-Way Street

In order for you to place a FaceTime call, of course, the recipient also needs to have FaceTime set up. If you try to place a call and they do not have FaceTime, you'll get a message telling you so. It may be that they have simply not given you the correct email address to use for them for FaceTime calls.

Receiving Video Calls with FaceTime

After you have a FaceTime account, you can receive calls as well. Make sure you have set up FaceTime by following the steps in the "Setting Up FaceTime" task earlier in this chapter. Then it is a matter of just waiting to receive a call from a friend.

1. If you aren't currently using your iPad, it will ring using the ringtone you choose in Settings, Sounds. When you pick up your iPad, you'll see something similar to the lock screen, but with a live feed from your camera (so you can see if you look good enough to video chat) and the caller's name at the top.

2. Slide the Slide to Answer button to the right to wake up your iPad and go immediately into the call. If you are using your iPad at the time the call comes in, FaceTime launches and you get a screen with two buttons. The screen will still show your camera's image and the name of the caller.

3. You also have the option to dismiss the call. You can do this by simply pressing the wake/sleep button at the top of your iPad. Or, you can tap the Remind Me button, which will dismiss the call and set a reminder for one hour later so you can call the person back.

4. You can also tap the Message button to dismiss the call and send a polite text message to the caller.

5. You can choose a message from the list.

6. Or, you can tap Custom to type a message.

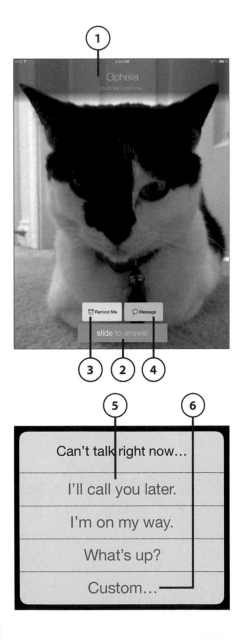

7. After the conversation starts, you can mute your microphone.

8. You can switch to the rear camera.

9. Tap End to end the call.

Ring Ring

Remember that you can set your ringtone in the Settings app under Sounds. You can even set the volume for rings to be unaffected by the volume controls on the side of your iPad. That way you don't miss a call because you left the volume turned down.

SO WHAT IF IT DOESN'T WORK?

>>>Go Further

FaceTime is set up to be simple. It just works. Except when it doesn't. There are no network settings to fiddle with. So the problem usually lies in the Wi-Fi router at either end of the call. If someone has security on their modem or Wi-Fi router, then it could be interfering with the call. See this document at Apple's site for some FaceTime troubleshooting tips:

http://support.apple.com/kb/HT4319.

Write and design
complex
documents.

In this chapter, we begin to get work done on the iPad by using Pages to create and format documents.

11

Writing with Pages

So far, we've mostly been looking at ways to consume media—music, video, books, photos, and so on. The next three chapters deal with the iWork suite of applications: Pages, Numbers, and Keynote.

We start with Pages, the word processor, which you can use for a fair amount of layout and design. Pages is not one of the iPad's built-in apps. You need to download it from the App Store.

Creating a New Document

Let's start off simple. The most basic use of Pages is to create a new document and enter some text.

1. Tap the Pages app icon on the Home screen.

Pages

2. If this is the first time you have run Pages, you will go through a series of screens welcoming you to Pages and asking if you want to set up iCloud as the storage space for Pages documents. Finally, it will ask if you want to create a new document or learn more about using Pages.

iCloud for iWork

Pages, Numbers, and Keynote can store their files on Apple's iCloud service rather than on your iPad. This is the default behavior as long as you have iCloud configured on your iPad and have allowed these three apps to use it. Using just an iPad means you won't notice much of a difference. You can take comfort, however, in knowing that they are being backed up on Apple servers as you work. And if you have a second iCloud device, like an iPhone or a Mac, you will see these documents there as well. For instance, Pages documents saved to iCloud from Pages on your iPad will appear in Pages for Mac. You can also access them at the iCloud website. See "Syncing Using iCloud" in Chapter 3.

3. If this isn't the first time you have run Pages, tap the + button at the top-left corner of the screen to start a new document.

4. Tap Create Document.

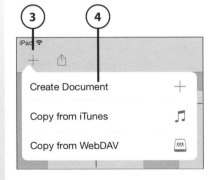

5. The template choices display. You can scroll vertically to see more. Tap the Blank template to go into the main editing view.

6. Type some sample text in the document just to get the feel for entering text.

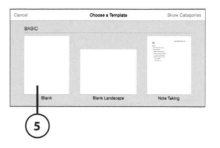

5

7. Return to your documents list by tapping Documents.

8. You can now see all your documents. Tap a document to open it.

7

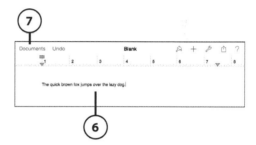

9. Tap Edit to move into Edit mode where you can delete or duplicate any selected document.

6

A Real Keyboard

If you plan on using Pages on your iPad often, you might want to invest in a physical keyboard for your iPad. You can use the Apple Wireless keyboard or almost any Bluetooth keyboard. Apple also has a version of the iPad dock that includes a keyboard. See Chapter 18, "iPad Accessories," for details.

9

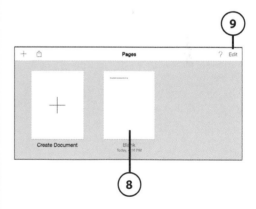

8

Styling Text

Now let's learn how to style text. You can change the font, style, and size.

1. In an open document, double-tap a word to select it.

2. Drag the blue dots to select the area you want to style.

3. Use the toolbar buttons to format your text as bold, italic, or underline. This toolbar appears above the keyboard when you are typing or have text selected.

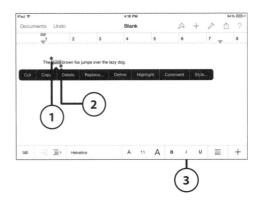

Undo Mistakes

At the top of the Pages screen, there is an Undo button. Use that to undo the last action you took—whether it is typing some text or changing styles. You can use Undo multiple times to go back several steps.

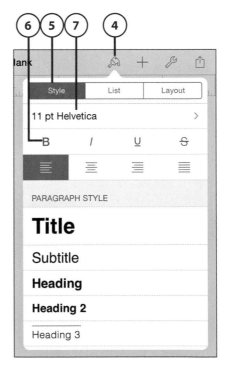

4. Tap the paintbrush button to bring up the Style/List/Layout menu.

5. Tap Style.

6. Tap the B, *I*, and U buttons to format text. Tap the buttons a second time if you want to change the style back to plain text. The fourth button, S, styles the text as strikethrough.

7. Tap the size and name of the font.

8. Set the font size, color, and type. Tap on the top and bottom halves of the font size indicator to increase and decrease the font size.

9. Tap the Color button to get a selection of colors.

10. Tap a color or swipe to the left to look at the page containing grayscale options. If you start with grayscale options, then swipe to the right to get to the colors.

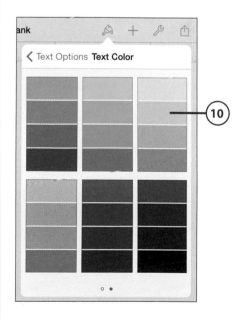

11. The black color tile has a check mark in it to indicate that it is the current color of the text. Swipe right to get back to the first page of colors and choose a different color, such as red.

12. Tap Text Options to return to the Text Options menu.

13. Tap Font.

14. Drag up and down in the list of fonts to view them all.

15. Tap a font to change the selected text to it.

16. Tap the brown info button if it appears to the right of a font to view variations for that font.

17. Tap outside of the menu to dismiss it and return to editing.

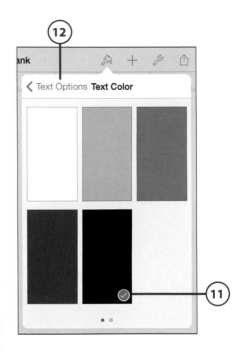

Printing Pages

You can print a document from Pages, Numbers, or Keynote if you have one of the printers compatible with Apple's AirPrint technology built into your iPad. Tap the tool button (it looks like a wrench in the upper-right corner) and then tap Share and Print. You'll be prompted to select a printer, page range, and number of copies. See "Printing from Your iPad" in Chapter 18.

Paragraph Styles

There are many preset styles that apply to an entire paragraph, such as Title, Subtitle, Heading 1, Body, and so on. Select one of these to apply that preset style to the entire paragraph, not just the selected text.

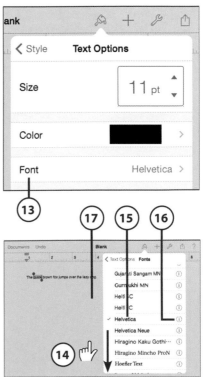

Reusing Styles

So, what if you define the font, style, and size for something in Pages, and you want to use it again with another section of text? Just copy and paste the style from one piece of text to others.

1. Select some text.

2. Tap Style.

3. Tap Copy Style.

4. Select a piece of text to which you want to paste that style.

5. Repeat step 2 to show the Copy Style and Paste Style button, and then tap Paste Style.

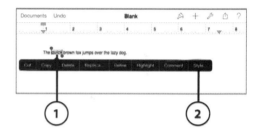

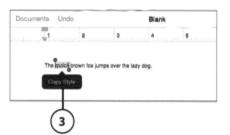

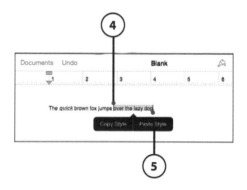

Formatting Text

The next step is to learn how to format and align text, which you do mostly through the toolbars above the keyboard.

1. Continue to work with the sample document, or start a new one and add some text.

2. Tap in the text so that the cursor is somewhere in the paragraph you want to format.

3. Tap the alignment button at the right end of the toolbar.

4. Tap the center alignment button in the menu. You can use the left, right, or justify buttons in the same set to align the text differently.

5. Tap at the end of the line to place the cursor there.

6. Tap the return key on the onscreen keyboard to go to the next line.

7. Type some sample text, just a word or two.

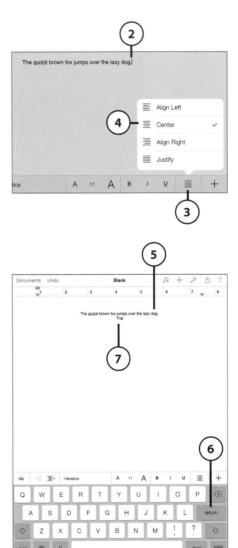

8. Tap the alignment button again.

9. Tap Align Left in the pop-up menu.

10. Tap after a word, and then tap Tab to insert a tab.

11. Type another sample word. We haven't added any tab stops to the document yet, so the position just defaults to the next inch.

12. Tap in the ruler around the 2-inch marker to insert a tab stop, which moves the second word over to match this tab stop's horizontal position. You can tap and drag existing tab stops to reposition them.

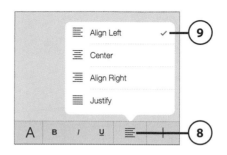

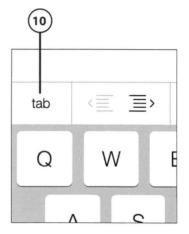

More Tab Options

If you like tabs, you'll be happy to know you can make centered tabs, right tabs, and dotted tabs as you would on a desktop word processor. Just double-tap a tab in the ruler, and it changes to the next type. To remove a tab, just tap and drag it down and out of the ruler.

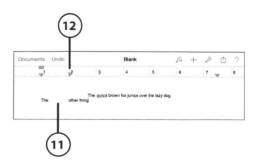

Creating Lists

You can easily create lists in Pages, just like in a normal word processor.

1. Create a new document in Pages using the Blank template.

2. Type a word that could be the first item in a list. Don't tap return.

3. Tap the paintbrush button on the toolbar.

4. Tap List.

5. Tap the Bullet option to turn the text you just typed into the first item in a bulleted list.

6. Use the on-screen keyboard to tap return and type several more lines. Tapping return always creates a new line in the list. Tapping return a second time ends the list formatting.

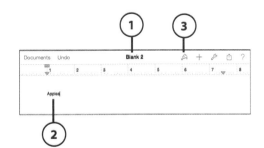

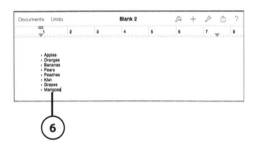

7. Select the entire list.

8. Tap the paintbrush button.

9. Tap Numbered to change the list to a numbered list.

10. Tap one line of the list.

11. Tap paintbrush again.

12. Tap the right arrow in the List menu to indent the line and create a sublist. You can create sublists as you type or by selecting lines and using the arrow buttons to format after you type.

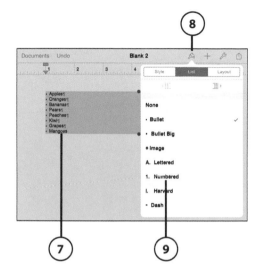

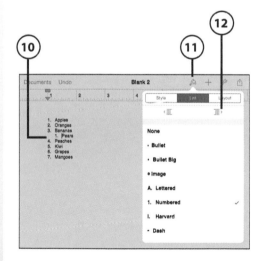

Column Layouts

Pages lets you go beyond boring one-column layouts. You can even change the number of columns for each paragraph.

1. Start a new document and fill it with text—perhaps copy and paste text from a website article. If you open a document, tap inside it so you are editing the document and you can see the keyboard at the bottom.

2. Tap the paintbrush button.

3. Tap Layout.

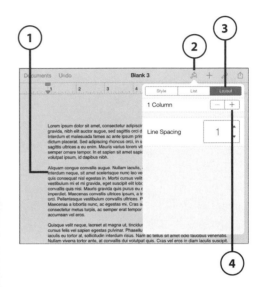

Line Spacing

The Layout menu includes a Line Spacing setting. You can change the line spacing in one-quarter line increments. A change affects the text in the paragraph where the cursor is located or the text in all selected paragraphs.

4. Tap + next to Columns. This adds a column and the entire document changes to a 2-column layout. Continue tapping the + button to add more columns.

5. Tap – to reduce the number of columns until you are back to a 1-column layout.

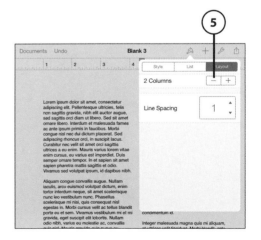

Using Different Column Formats

You can select just one paragraph and apply a two-column layout to it while leaving the rest of your document in one-column layout. Be aware, though, that switching between one column and multiple columns in the same document can yield unpredictable results, so proceed with caution.

Inserting Images

You can place images into your Pages documents. You can even wrap text around the images.

1. Open a new document and fill it with text.

2. Place the cursor somewhere in the text, such as at the beginning of the third paragraph.

3. Tap the + button.

4. Tap Media button.

5. Select a photo from a photo album.

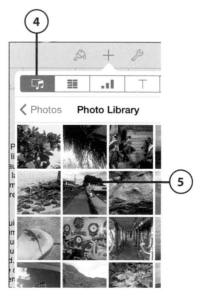

6. The photo appears in the document at the location of the cursor. Tap it to close the menu.

7. You can tap on the image and use Cut, Copy, Delete, and Comment on the photo when it is selected. You can remove the image with the Delete button.

8. Drag the blue dots around the photo to resize it.

9. While resizing, measurements appear next to the photo.

10. Tap the paintbrush button to bring up the Style, Image, and Arrange menu.

11. Tap Arrange to see options for flipping a photo, moving it in front of or behind other items on the page. Tap Image to see options for editing the mask of the photo.

12. Tap Edit Mask.

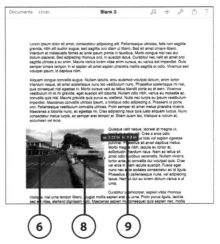

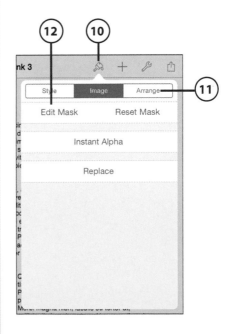

13. Drag the slider to resize the photo. The photo changes size, but the size of the object remains the same, which enables you to put the focus on a particular portion of the photo by moving the photo around inside the space. Tap Done to finish.

14. Tap the Paintbrush icon and tap Arrange. Tap Wrap. Use the Wrap menu to designate how the text wraps around the photo and whether the photo should stay put on the page or move along as you insert text before it.

15. Tap Arrange at the top left to move back to the main formatting menu. Tap Style.

16. Choose the type of border that you want to appear around the photo. There are six basic styles to choose from. In addition, you can tap Style Options and choose your own border and effects.

Rearranging Images

After you place an image in your document, you can drag it around and resize it as much as you want. Pages automatically snaps the edges of the image to the margins and center lines of the page as you drag it around.

Importing Clipart

I've found that the best way to get clip art onto your iPad and into Pages is to drag it into iPhoto. Then, I create a ClipArt event to store the files in. I then sync my iPad, making sure that the ClipArt event is set to sync. You can also do this with a folder if you aren't using iPhoto or are on Windows.

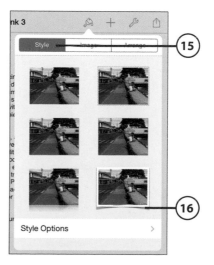

Using Shapes in Documents

In addition to using clip art, you can also use some basic shapes in Pages. Inserting shapes works in the same basic manner.

1. Create a new document and add some text.

2. Tap the + button to bring up the Media/Tables/Charts/Text Box/Shapes menu.

3. Tap the Shapes button. Swipe to the left to see shapes with color options.

4. Tap a shape, such as the rounded rectangle. It is placed in the middle of the text.

5. Tap the shape in the text to dismiss the menu.

6. Use the blue dots to resize the shape.

7. Tap and drag in the middle of the shape to move it around in the document.

8. Double-tap in the shape to enter text into the shape.

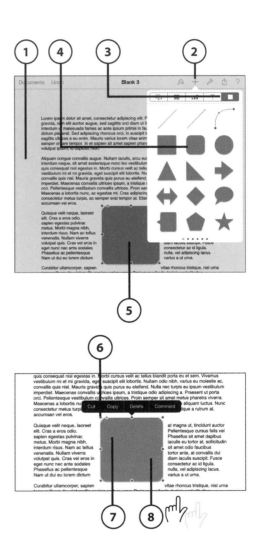

LOTS OF CHOICES

The shape choices are a line, an arrow, a bezier curve, and then the shapes you can more easily see.

If you drag to the left, you can look through six pages of shape variations. These are the same shapes but with different borders, shading, or just outlines.

After you select a shape and add it to a document, you can always select it and tap the paintbrush button to change its style to one of the other five. You can also tap the Style button, and then choose Style Options to specify unique fills, borders, and effects for the shapes.

Creating Tables

Tables are a step up from using lists or tabs to format data in your documents. You can choose from several different types of tables, and entering data into them is relatively easy.

1. Start a new document.

2. Tap the + button.

3. Tap Tables. There are four different table options. In addition, you can swipe left and right in the menu to reveal six color variations.

4. Tap the first table to insert it.

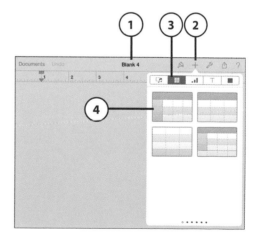

5. Tap the double line button to the right of the table or below the table to adjust the number of columns and rows.

6. Double-tap in a cell to enter text.

7. Tap the paintbrush button to bring up the Table/Headers/Cell menu.

8. Tap Table to choose from six table styles.

9. Tap Table Options to go to a menu that gives you even more control over the borders and background colors of the table. Tap Table in the upper left corner when done.

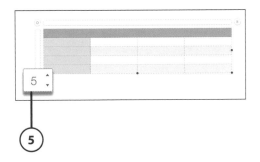

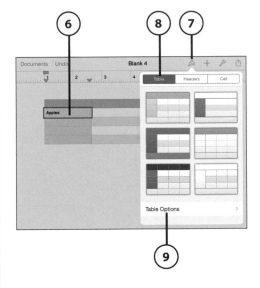

10. Tap Headers to change the number of rows used as a header and the number of columns as well. You can even add footer rows. These all show up as different colors according to the style of table.

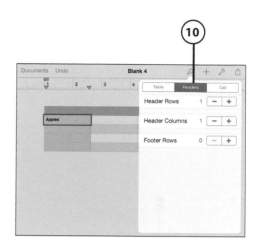

Moving Tables

When the table is selected and you see bars at the top and left and a circle at the top-left corner, you can drag the table around the document by grabbing it at any location and dragging.

Creating Charts

Charts are another way to express numbers visually. Pages supports nine different kinds of charts.

1. Create a blank document.

2. Tap the + button.

3. Tap Charts. You can look through six pages of chart styles, but the basics of each set of charts is the same.

4. Tap a chart to select it and insert that type of chart in the middle of your document.

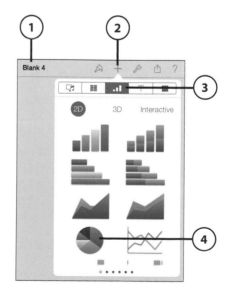

5. After selecting the chart, tap the Edit Data button.

6. Alter the existing data to create your own chart by tapping the field and typing.

7. When you finish entering data, tap Done.

8. When you return to the main document view, select the chart and tap the paintbrush button.

9. From the Chart menu, select a color scheme for the chart. You can also switch between 2D and 3D versions of each style.

10. Tap Chart Options. Use the Chart Options menu to change a variety of properties of the chart.

11. For 3D charts, you can tap and drag in the middle of a chart to adjust its 3D angle.

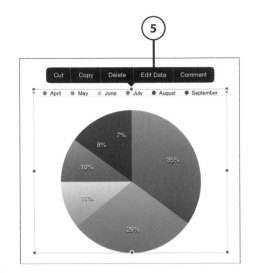

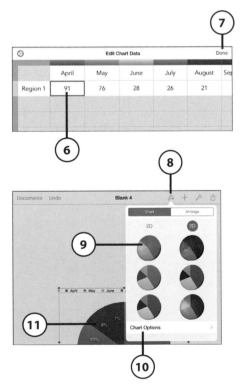

Document Setup

You can change a variety of your document's properties in Pages.

1. Open a document or create a new one.

2. Tap the Wrench button.

3. Choose Document Setup.

4. Drag the arrows at the four edges of the page to adjust the width and height of the page.

5. Tap in the header to add text to the header.

6. While typing in the header, tap in one of the three spaces (left, center, right) and you'll see a toolbar where you can select Page Numbers to have the page number automatically placed in that part of the header.

Add Background Images

One thing you can do with Document Setup that is not obvious is to add background objects that appear under every page. You can tap the + button and add photos, tables, charts, and shapes to the main page area. The image you add appears behind the text. You can even add text that appears on every page by just inserting a text box and adding text to it.

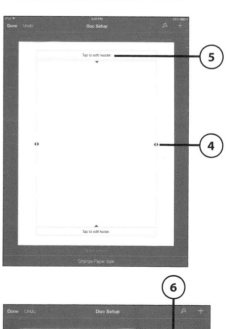

7. Tap the footer to add text to the footer.

8. Tap the button along the bottom of the screen to change the paper size.

Create a Background

You can color the entire background by creating a square box and stretching it to fill the page. Then add a shaded or textured background to it as a color in the shape's Style Options. You can also place a picture over the entire background.

Sharing and Printing Documents

Thanks to iCloud, sharing documents with Pages, Numbers, and Keynote among your own devices is very easy. Any document you create on any device will simply be available to the others. But you can also share your document with another person by emailing it, printing it, or sending it to a network server.

1. Tap the tools button.

2. Tap Print to send the document to a network AirPrint printer.

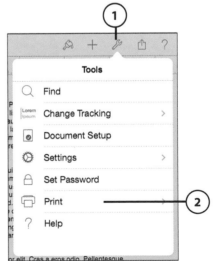

3. Tap the Share button.

4. Tap Send a Copy.

5. Tap AirDrop to send to another nearby iPad. (This option will not appear if no iPad or iPhone with AirDrop is available near you.)

6. Tap Mail to send an email with the document as an attachment.

7. Choose iTunes to place a copy of the document in a location of your iPad where you can see and transfer it using iTunes the next time you sync with your computer.

8. Choose WebDAV this to send the document to an Internet file transfer service.

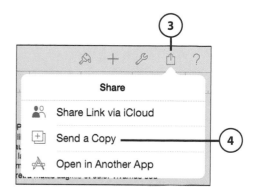

Pages Does Word

You can put more than just Pages documents into the iTunes list to import. Pages can also take Microsoft Word .doc and even .docx files.

Pages Is Not Pages

The Pages on your iPad and the Pages on your Mac are not the same. You can do a lot more with Pages on your Mac. So, sometimes you might receive a Document Import Warning message telling you what didn't work as you import your file to your iPad.

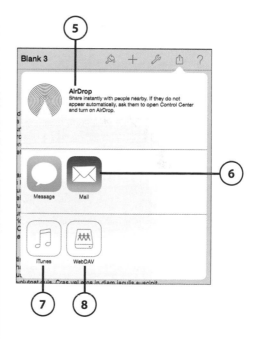

Design and enter data
into spreadsheets.

With Numbers you can create data spreadsheets, perform calculations, and create forms and charts.

- → Creating a New Spreadsheet
- → Totaling Columns
- → Averaging Columns
- → Performing Calculations
- → Formatting Tables
- → Creating Forms
- → Creating Charts
- → Using Multiple Tables

Spreadsheets with Numbers

Numbers is a versatile program that enables you to create the most boring table of numbers ever (feel free to try for the world record on that one) or an elegant chart that illustrates a point like no paragraph of text ever could.

Creating a New Spreadsheet

The way you manage documents in Numbers is exactly the same as you do in Pages, so if you need a refresher, refer to Chapter 11, "Writing with Pages." Let's jump right in to creating a simple spreadsheet.

1. Tap the Numbers icon on your Home screen to start.

2. Tap + and then Create Spreadsheet to see all the template choices.

3. Tap Blank to choose the most basic template.

Numbers Terminology

A grid of numbers is called a *table*. A page of tables, often just a single table taking up the whole page, is a *sheet*. You can have multiple sheets in a document, all represented by tabs. The first tab in this case represents "Sheet 1." Tap the + to add a new sheet.

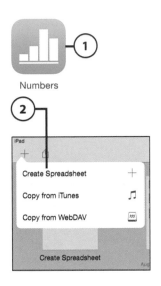

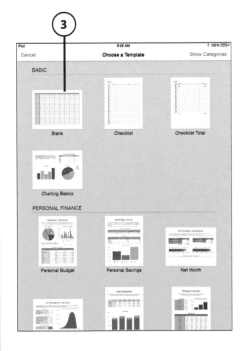

4. Tap in one of the cells to select the sheet. An outline appears around the cell.

5. Double-tap the cell this time. An on-screen keypad appears.

6. Use the keypad to type a number. The number appears in both the cell and a text field above the keypad. Use this text field to edit the text, tapping inside it to reposition the cursor if necessary.

7. Tap the upper next button, the one with the arrow pointing right.

Switching Keyboard Options

The four buttons just above and to the left of the keypad represent number, time, text, and formula formats for cells. If you select the number, you get a keypad to enter a number. If you select the clock, you get a special keypad to enter dates and times. If you select the T, you get a regular keyboard. Finally, if you select the equal sign (=) , you get a keypad and special buttons to enter formulas.

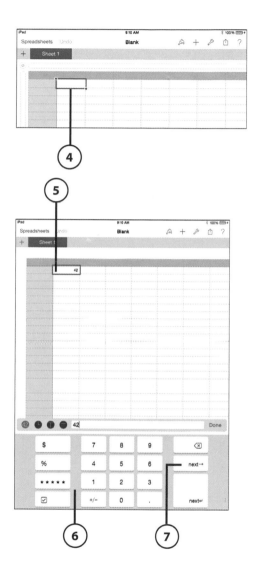

8. The cursor moves to the column in the next cell. Type a number here, too.

9. Tap the next button again and enter a third number.

10. Tap the space just above the first number you entered. The keypad changes to a standard keyboard to type text instead of numbers.

11. Type a label for this first column.

12. Tap in each of the other two column heads to enter titles for them as well.

13. Tap to the left of the first number you entered. Type a row title.

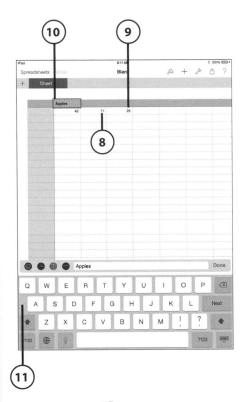

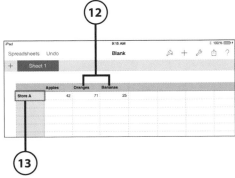

14. Now enter a few more rows of data.

15. Tap the Done button.

16. Tap and drag the circle with two lines in it to the right of the bar above the table. Drag it to the left to remove the unneeded columns.

17. Tap and drag the same circle at the bottom of the vertical bar to the left of the table. Drag it up to remove most of the extra rows, leaving a few for future use.

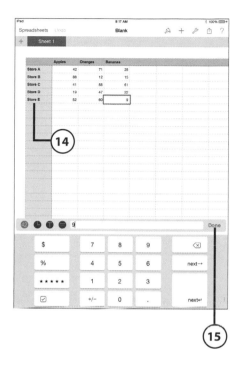

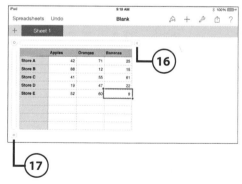

Totaling Columns

One of the most basic formula types is a sum. In the previous example, for instance, you might want to total each column.

1. Start with the result of the previous example. Double-tap in the cell just below the bottom number in the first column.

2. Tap the = button to switch to the formula keypad.

3. Tap the SUM button on the keypad.

4. The formula for the cell appears in the text field.

5. Tap the green check mark button.

6. The result of the formula appears in the cell. Repeat steps 2 through 4 for the other columns in the table.

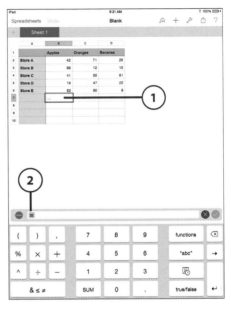

Automatic Updates

If you are not familiar with spreadsheets, the best thing about them is that formulas like this automatically update. So if you change the number of Apples in Store C in the table, the sum in the last row automatically changes to show the new total.

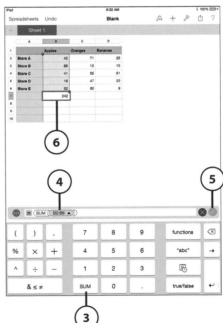

Averaging Columns

We lucked out a bit with the sum function because it has its own button. What about the hundreds of other functions? Let's start with something simple like column averages.

1. Continuing with the example from the previous section, double-tap on the cell below the total of the first column of numbers.

2. Tap the = button to switch to formula mode.

3. Tap the functions button.

4. Tap the Categories tab at the top of the menu, and tap Statistical from the Functions button menu.

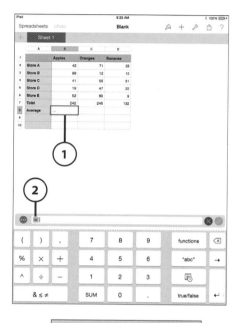

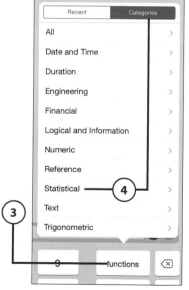

5. Tap AVERAGE from the list of functions.

6. Now you get AVERAGE(value) in the entry field. The light blue means the "value" is selected and ready to be defined.

7. Tap cell B2 (Apples for Store A).

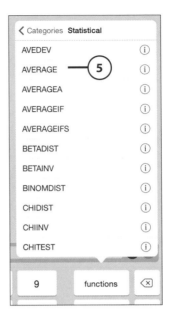

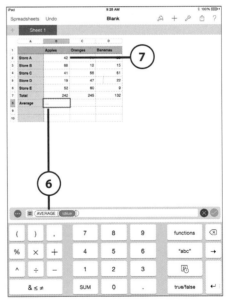

8. Drag the bottom dot to include cells B2 through B6. Don't add the Total row to the average. The entry field should now read AVERAGE(B2:B6).

9. Tap the green check mark button.

10. The average of the column should now be in the cell. Tap it once to see the Cut/Copy/Paste menu.

11. Tap Copy.

12. Tap the cell below the total for the second column of numbers.

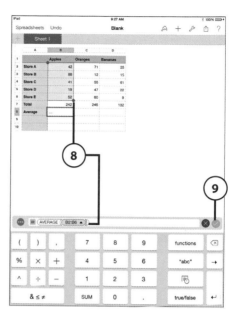

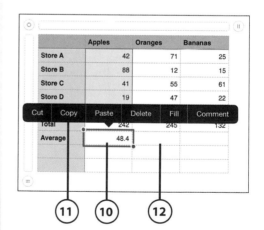

13. Drag the bottom-right dot to expand the area to cover the next cell as well.

14. Tap in the two cells to bring up the Paste option if it isn't already visible.

15. Tap Paste.

16. Tap Paste Formulas.

17. All three columns now show the average for rows 2 through 6. Notice how Numbers is smart enough to understand when you copy and paste a formula from one column to another, that it should look at the same rows but a different column.

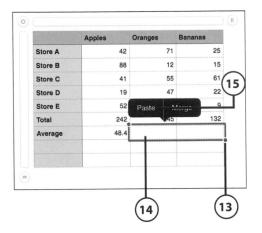

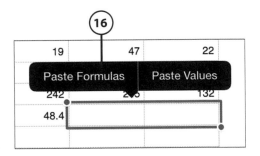

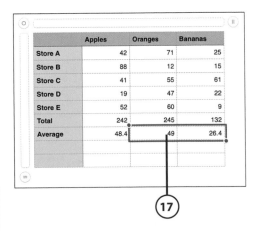

Performing Calculations

So far, we have seen two simple formulas. Let's see what else you can do with one of hundreds of different functions and the standard mathematical symbols.

1. Start with a table like this one. It shows the base and height measurements for three triangles.

2. Double-tap in the third column.

3. Tap the = button to enter a formula.

4. Tap the first number in the first column. "Base Triangle 1" should fill the entry field.

5. Tap the division symbol.

6. Tap the 2.

7. Tap the Multiplication button.

8. Tap the first number in the second column.

9. The entry field now reads "Base Triangle 1 ÷ 2 x Height Triangle 1."

10. Tap the green check mark.

11. You get the result of 10.5, which is half the base of the triangle times its height, or the area of the triangle.

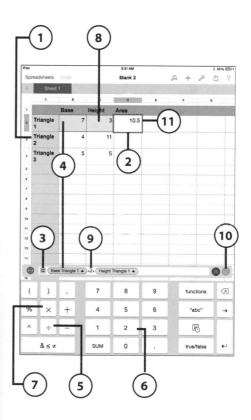

Using Parentheses

Note that a more careful mathematician would rather see it written "(Base Triangle 1 ÷ 2) × Height Triangle 1." By grouping the base divided by 2 inside parentheses, you guarantee the correct result. You can use the parentheses to do that in the formula keypad.

Formatting Tables

Let's move away from calculations to design. You have many formatting options to make your spreadsheets pretty.

Formatting Cells

1. Go back to the original example or something similar.

2. Select the six cells that make up the totals and average.

3. Tap the paintbrush button.

4. Tap Cell to see cell styling, formatting, and coloring choices.

5. Select Fill Color.

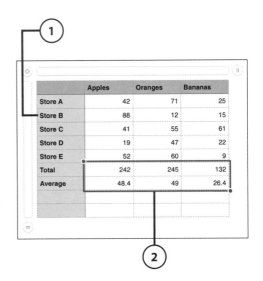

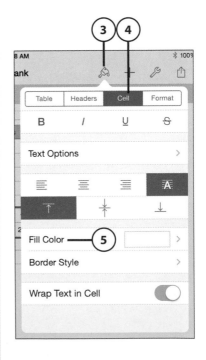

6. Tap the lightest shade of blue. You can also drag to the left to go to the second page of colors, which is actually a set of grays or, drag to the right to get to the colors if you start out with the grays. The second page includes an option to reset the fill to the original style.

7. Tap Cell to go back to the Cell menu.

8. Tap B to make the text bold.

9. Change the selection to include only the row of averages.

10. Tap the paintbrush button again.

11. Tap Text Options.

12. Tap Color.

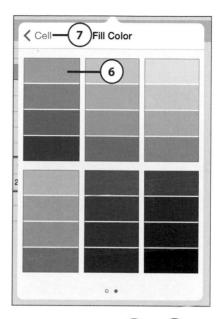

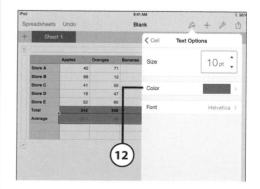

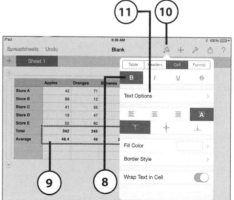

13. Choose the third darkest blue.

14. Tap Text Options and then Cell in the upper left corner to go back to the main menu.

15. Tap Format.

16. Tap the i button to the right of Number.

17. Set the number of decimal places. Try 2.

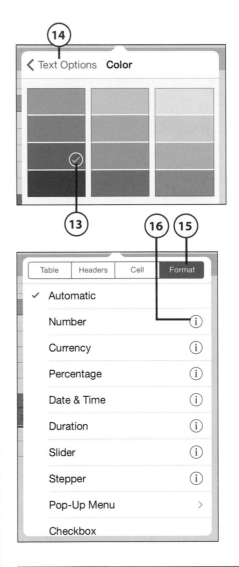

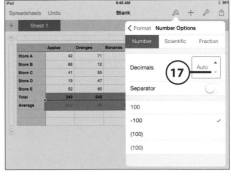

Formatting Whole Tables

Beyond just formatting cells, you can also use many options to change the basic style of your table. Let's explore some of the options.

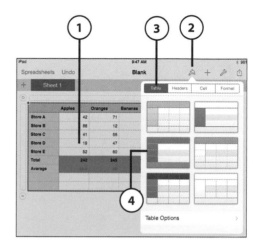

1. Starting with the table from the previous example; tap anywhere in the table to select it.

2. Tap the paintbrush button to bring up the menu.

3. Tap Table.

4. Try a different style, like the greenish one on the left, second down.

5. The new style replaces the formatting we did for the cells, so it is best to find a table style before you customize the cell styles.

6. Tap the Table Options button to explore other table options.

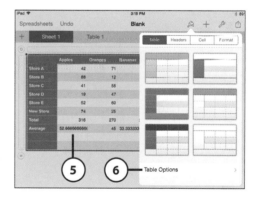

7. Tap the Table Name switch to add or remove the title.

8. Tap the Table Border switch to add or remove a border.

9. Tap the Alternating Rows switch to have the color of the rows alternate.

10. Tap Grid Options for more detailed control of the look of the grid used in the table.

11. Select a font from the list that appears. Tap Table Options in the upper left corner to return to the Table Options menu.

12. Tap Smaller or Larger to change the size of the font.

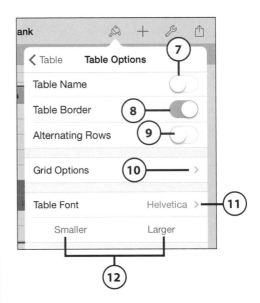

Using Headers and Footers

Let's continue with the previous example to explore headers and footers:

1. Tap the Table button to return to the main formatting menu.

2. Tap the Headers button to adjust the number of header rows and columns and add footer rows.

3. Tap the Footer Rows + button to increase the footer rows to 4.

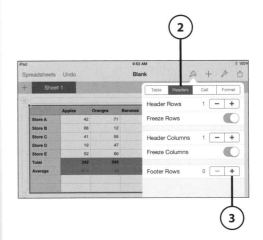

Creating Forms

Forms are an alternative way to enter data in a spreadsheet. A form contains many pages, each page representing a row in a table. Let's continue with the previous example and use it to make a form.

1. Tap the + button in the upper left corner.

2. Tap New Form. Note that in order to get the option to make a form, you need to have at least one column with a value in its header row.

3. Choose a table. We have only one, so the choice is simple. Tap Table 1 to see the first page in the form, which represents the first row of data from our table.

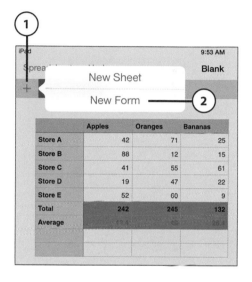

4. Tap the right arrow at the bottom of the screen to move through the five existing rows (pages) of data.

5. Tap the + button at the bottom of the screen to enter a new row of data.

6. Tap at the top of the screen to enter a row heading.

7. Tap in each of the three fields to enter data.

8. Use the next button on the on-screen keypad to move to the next field.

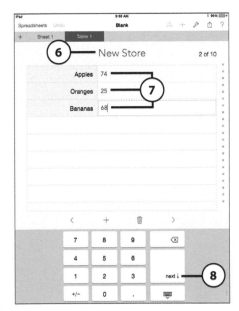

9. When you finish, tap the first tab, Sheet 1, to return to the original spreadsheet. You should see the new data in a new row.

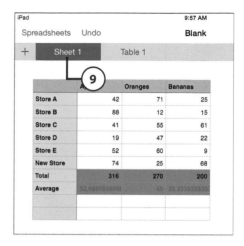

	Apples	Oranges	Bananas
Store A	42	71	25
Store B	88	12	15
Store C	41	55	61
Store D	19	47	22
Store E	52	60	9
New Store	74	25	68
Total	316	270	200
Average	52.6666666666	45	33.333333333

It's Not All Good

Why Didn't the Formulas Update?

Unfortunately, the formulas for the totals and averages in our example did not update to use the new row. They both stuck with rows 2 through 7 of the table and did not expand to use row 8. What went wrong?

Well, first, if we had added a row in the middle of the table, it would have expanded the sum area. So part of our problem is that we added a cell below the sum area.

Second, we created the cell with the sum function in a regular cell. Then we turned it into a footer cell. If we start over by deleting that sum cell and creating it again, Numbers is smart enough to realize that we mean *all* the rows in the column between the header and footer. Instead of =SUM(B2:B7), we would simply get =SUM(B). Then we can add more rows using the form, and the sum would increase properly.

So, delete the formula from B9 and replace it with =SUM(B), and you are in business. Do the same with the other sum and average cells. When you do this, Numbers is smart enough to create the formula for you when you tap the SUM button. The formula is actually stated as =SUM(Apples) because we named the column Apples.

To create your Average row, use the Functions button and select AVERAGE as before, but tap the bar above columns B, C, and D to tell Numbers you want the average of the whole column between the header and footer.

Creating Charts

Representing numbers visually is one of the primary functions of a modern spreadsheet program. With Numbers, you can create bar, line, and pie charts and many variations of each.

1. Create a new blank spreadsheet and then fill it with some basic data to use as an example. Shrink the table to remove unneeded cells.

2. Tap the + button at the top of the screen.

3. Tap the charts button.

4. Page through six different chart color variations. Tap the chart at the top left.

5. You will now be asked to tap the chart and then select data from your spreadsheet.

6. Tap and drag over all the numbers in the body of your table to add all the rows of data to the table.

7. Tap Done.

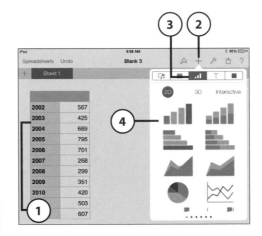

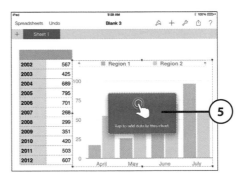

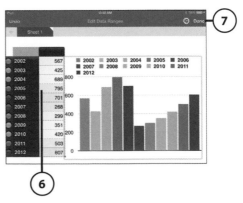

8. Tap and drag the chart and position it on the sheet. You can also use the blue dots to resize it.

9. Tap on the chart to make sure it is selected.

10. Tap the paintbrush button. Notice that you can alter all sorts of properties using the Chart/X Axis/Y Axis and Arrange menu.

11. Tap Chart Options.

12. Tap Chart Type.

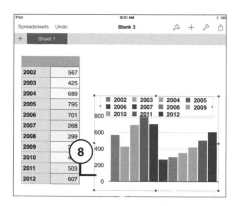

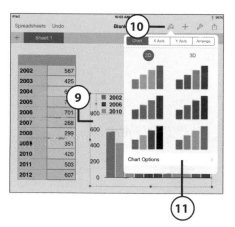

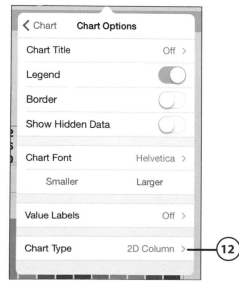

13. Tap 2D Line to change the chart type to a line graph.

14. Tap outside the menu to dismiss it.

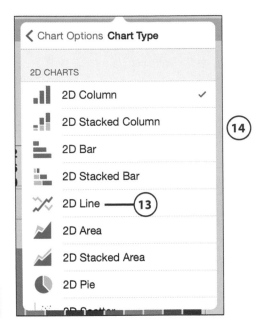

Using Multiple Tables

The primary way Numbers differs from spreadsheet programs such as Excel is that Numbers emphasizes page design. A Numbers sheet is not meant to contain just one grid of numbers. In Numbers, you can use multiple tables.

1. Create a new, blank spreadsheet and fill it with data as in the example image.

2. Shrink the table to remove any unneeded cells.

3. Select the cells in the body.

4. Tap the paintbrush button.

5. Tap Format.

6. Tap Currency.

7. Tap outside the menu to dismiss it.

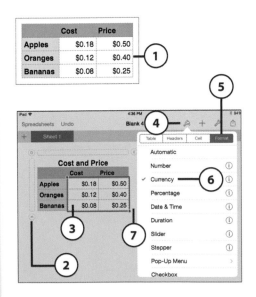

8. Tap the table to select it. Make sure just the table as a whole is selected, not a cell.

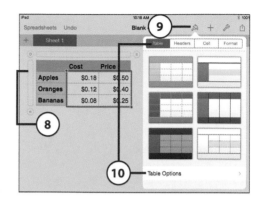

Selecting a Table

It can be difficult to select an entire table without selecting a cell. Tap in a cell to select it. Then tap the circle that appears in the upper-left corner of the table to change your selection to the entire table.

9. Tap the paintbrush button.

10. Tap Table and then tap Table Options.

11. Tap the Table Name switch to give the table a name.

12. Tap outside the menu to dismiss it.

13. Select just the table name and change it.

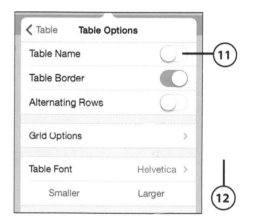

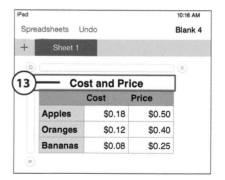

14. Tap the + button.

15. Tap Tables.

16. Select the first table type.

17. Enter the data as shown and shrink the table to remove any unneeded cells.

18. Select the table title and change it.

Clean Up the Formatting

To keep this tutorial short, I left some things out. For instance, you can select the date columns and change the formatting. Obviously each row represents a month. So, you don't need the full date, including the day. You can change the date format of those columns to one that doesn't include the day, only the month and year. Just select those cells and tap the paintbrush button and look under Format. Select Date & Time and tap the blue circle to choose a specific date and time format.

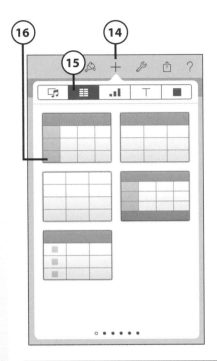

Cost and Price

	Cost	Price
Apples	$0.18	$0.50
Oranges	$0.12	$0.40
Bananas	$0.08	$0.25

Inventory Received

	Apples	Oranges	Bananas
1/1/2013	50	0	0
2/1/2013	50	100	200
3/1/2013	0	200	0
4/1/2013	50	0	200

19. Select the entire second table.

20. Tap the Copy button.

21. Tap outside the table in a new location in the sheet.

22. Tap Paste.

23. Change the title and contents of the new table as shown.

24. Now select the second and third tables and expand them with one extra column each, as shown.

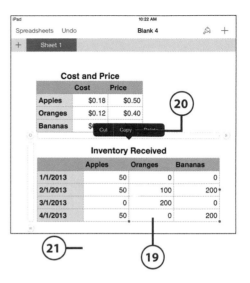

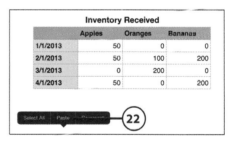

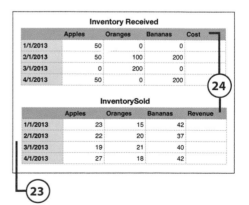

25. Double-tap in the first cell under Cost.

26. Tap on the = button next to the entry field to enter a formula.

27. Tap the Apples cell for the first row.

28. Tap × in the on-screen keyboard, and tap the cost of apples from the Cost and Price table.

29. Tap +.

30. Tap the Oranges cell and then tap × again. Then tap the cost of oranges and again tap +.

31. Tap the Bananas cell. Then tap × and tap the cost of bananas.

32. Tap the part of the formula that reads Cost Apples.

33. Turn on all four preservation switches to prevent the cell reference from changing as we copy and paste. We want the amount of inventory to change with each row, but the price from the other table remains the same.

34. Repeat steps 32 and 33 for the cost of oranges and the cost of bananas in the formula.

35. Tap the green check mark to complete the formula.

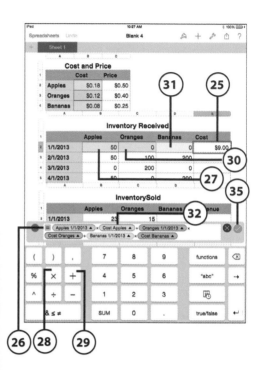

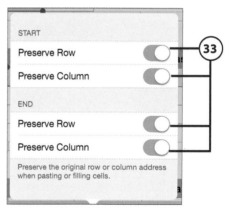

36. Tap the paintbrush button.

37. Change the format of the cell to Currency.

38. Copy that cell and paste it in to the three below it. When prompted, choose to Paste Formulas not Values.

The result is that you have a calculation based on data from two tables. You can complete this spreadsheet for practice, if you want. Create a similar formula for the revenue column of the next table, based on the price of each item and the amount sold.

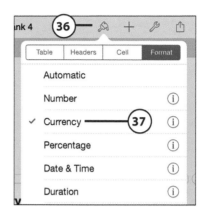

Enhance the Sheet

Another thing you can do is to add more titles, text, and images to the sheet—even shapes and arrows. These not only make the sheet look nice, but can also act as documentation as a reminder of what you need to do each month—or instruct someone else what to do to update the sheet.

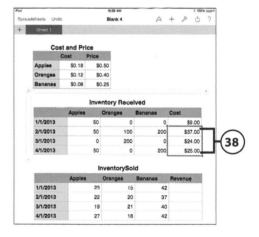

Create and display business
and educational presentations.

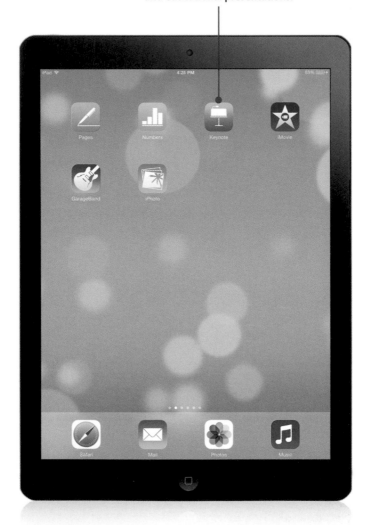

In this chapter, we use Keynote to build and display presentations.

→ Building a Simple Presentation
→ Building Your Own Slide
→ Adding Transitions
→ Organizing Slides
→ Playing Your Presentation
→ Presenting on an External Display

Presentations with Keynote

You can't have a suite of business apps without having a Presentation tool, and Keynote is that tool on the iPad. The basics of using Keynote are the same as for Pages and Numbers. So let's get right to making presentations.

Building a Simple Presentation

Keynote works only in horizontal screen orientation. So after you launch Keynote, turn your iPad on its side. The way you manage documents in Keynote is exactly the same as you do in Pages and Numbers, including the ability to use iCloud to store your documents. If you need a refresher, refer to Chapter 11, "Writing with Pages."

1. Tap the Keynote icon on the Home screen. If this is the first time you are using Keynote, you'll get a series of introduction screens. Continue until you are viewing an empty list of your presentations.

2. Tap the + button to create a new presentation.

3. Tap Create Presentation.

4. Choose a theme. We use Gradient for the task.

5. Double-tap the line of text that reads Double-tap to edit.

6. Type a title using the on-screen keyboard.

7. Double-tap the subtitle area and type a subtitle.

8. Tap the Close Keyboard button.

Keynote

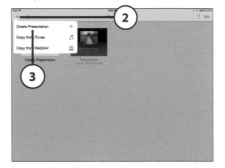

9. Tap the + button at the top of the screen, and then tap the media tab.

10. Choose a photo.

11. Tap on the photo and use the blue dots at the corners and on the sides to resize the photo. Tap and drag in the middle of the photo to position it.

12. Tap the + button at the bottom-left corner to bring up a list of slides.

13. Tap any of the slides templates to add a slide. You now have two slides in your presentation.

>>>Go Further

STARTING NEW PRESENTATIONS

Keynote presentations are made up of slides. The slides in the current presentation are shown at the left of the screen. The selected slide takes up most of the screen. The slides are built from one of many slide templates, which you can modify as needed.

Be aware that there is no way to switch themes or to access the design of another theme after you start a new presentation. If you're used to working with Keynote on a Mac, you might be disappointed by this.

You can copy and paste entire slides between presentation documents, though. So if you want a document that mixes themes, you can achieve it by copying and pasting.

Building Your Own Slide

You can remove items and add your own to any template. You can practice adding your own elements to a slide by using the blank template.

1. Start a new document or continue from the previous example. Tap + to add a new slide.

2. Scroll down in this list and choose the blank slide to the lower right.

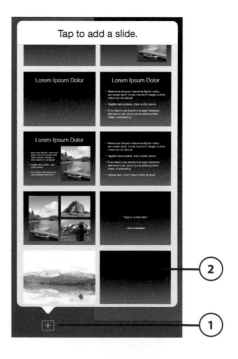

3. Tap the + button at the top to add an element.

4. Tap the media button.

5. Select an album, and then select a photo from that album.

6. With the photo selected, grab one of the blue dots and shrink the image.

7. With the image selected, tap the paintbrush button and then tap Style.

8. Tap the bottom right of the six basic image styles or tap Style Options to customize the look of the photo even more.

Select All

To select all objects, tap a space with no objects. After a short delay, tap there again, and then you can choose Select All.

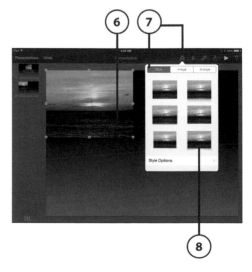

9. Add two more images using steps 3 through 8.

10. To select multiple items, use two fingers. Tap the first image with one finger and hold it. Use a second figure to tap the other two images to add them to the selection. Then drag all three images into a better position.

11. Tap the + button to add another element.

Tables and Charts Anyone?

You can also add tables and charts, even basic shapes, in the same way you would do it in Pages. There are a lot of similarities between using Pages and using Keynote.

12. Tap the text button.

13. Tap the first element, a plain text box.

14. Tap outside the menu to dismiss it.

15. Tap the text box to select it.

16. Drag it to a new position and expand it.

17. Double-tap in the text box to enter some text.

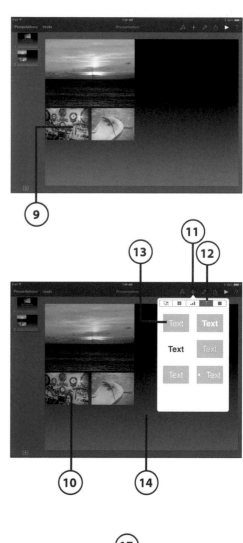

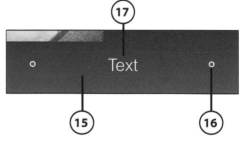

18. Close the keyboard and select the text box. With the text box selected, tap the paintbrush button.

19. Tap Text, and then change the font style and size.

20. Make the text bold by tapping B.

21. Tap outside the menu to dismiss it.

22. Your text is now bold.

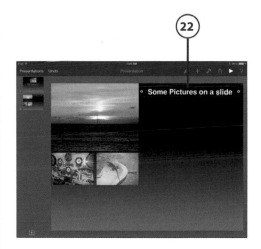

Adding Transitions

Just like other presentation programs, Keynote on iPad has a number of transition options. To practice working with transitions, start with a sample presentation, such as the one we have been working on, or create a new document with some sample slides.

1. Select the first slide on the left and then tap it again.

2. Tap the Transition button that appears.

3. Scroll through the transitions and pick one. Try Cube. The slide animates to show you the transition. It then returns.

4. Tap Options.

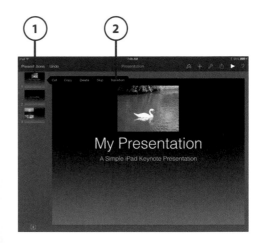

5. Select any options associated with the transition. For example, the Cube transition has a duration setting. If you don't want to change any options, tap elsewhere to dismiss the menu.

6. Tap Done in the upper-right corner of the screen.

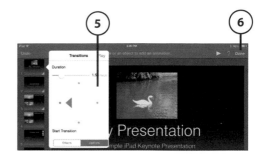

Magic Move

Another type of transition is the Magic Move. This is where objects on one slide are the same as the objects on the next, but they are in different positions. The transition between the slides moves these objects from the first position to the second.

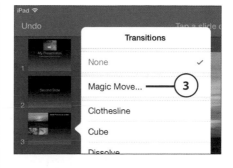

1. Select a slide with several objects on it, such as three images. Tap the Transition button.

2. Tap the transition.

3. Choose Magic Move.

Unique Effects with Magic Move

The great thing about the Magic Move transition is that you can create some unique effects. For instance, in the example, I could bunch all the photos into a tiny space on the first slide and then spread them out in the second slide. The transition would make it seem like the photos are bursting out and falling into place.

4. Tap Yes to duplicate the current slide so that you have two identical slides from which to create the Magic Move transition.

5. Slides 3 and 4 are identical, and slide 4 is the current slide. Move the objects around to reposition them or resize them. The stars indicate which elements are taking part in the magic move.

6. Tap the third frame.

7. Tap the arrow next to Magic Move and then tap play to preview the transition from slide 3 to slide 4. You will need to tap the screen then to proceed from the 3rd slide to the 4th one and see the transition.

8. Tap Done in the upper-right corner of the screen.

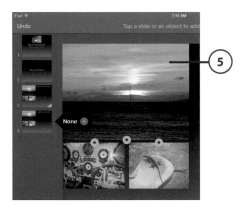

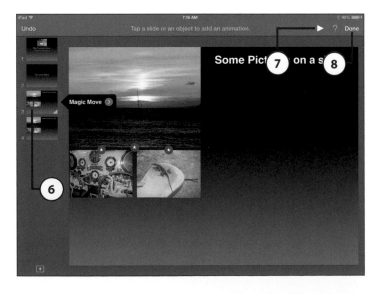

Object Transitions

In addition to the entire screen trans-
forming from one slide to the next,
you can also define how you want
individual elements on the slide to
appear.

1. Start off with a slide that includes
    a title and a bullet list. Tap the
    slide's title text.

2. Tap Animate.

3. Tap the build in button.

4. Tap Blast to see a preview of the
    animation. You can also explore
    the Options, Delivery, and Order
    parts of the menu, but for this
    task we leave those settings
    alone.

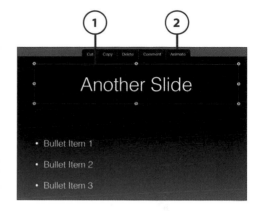

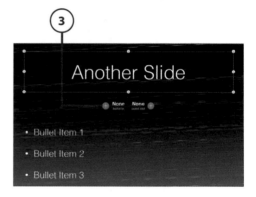

5. Tap the bullet list.

6. Tap build in.

7. Scroll down to Move In and tap it.

8. Tap Delivery.

Don't Build the First Object

A common mistake is to set every object to build, as we have in this example. Because the first object, the title, builds in, it means that nothing appears on the slide at first. You start off blank. Then the title appears and then the bullet items. Sometimes, though, you should start a slide with the title already on it.

9. Tap By Bullet and then tap Done in the upper-right corner of the screen. The effect works by first showing you a blank screen, and then when you tap the screen, the title appears with the Blast transition. Each of your next three taps makes a bullet appear.

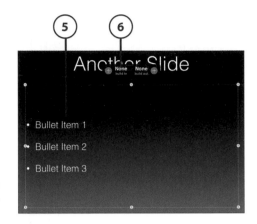

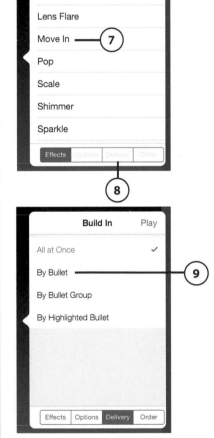

Organizing Slides

As you create presentations on your iPad, you might discover you need to re-order your slides, but that's no problem with Keynote. To practice, use a presentation that has several slides.

1. Create a presentation that includes several slides.

2. Tap and hold the third slide. It grows slightly larger and begins to follow your finger so that you can drag it down into another position.

Grouping Slides

There are two options when you drag a slide and place it back in the list. The first is to place it flush left, where it inserts normally. If you move the slide slightly to the right, though, you are grouping the slide with the one above it. Groups are a great way to put slides that belong together as a single element. That way, you can move them as one unit if you need to. To move them as a group, you close the group by tapping the triangle next to the parent slide. Then move the parent slide around, and all children come with it.

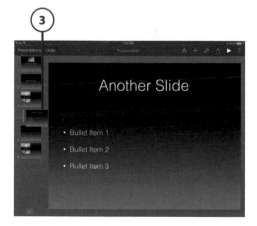

3. Drag slide 4 to the right so it inserts in a group owned by slide 3.

4. Tap the triangle on the left of slide 3 to close the group.

5. Tap slide 5 with your finger and continue to hold.

6. Use your other hand to tap slide 6 and then release your finger. You can now move this group of two slides as one unit.

7. Tap once to select a slide. Then tap a second time after a short delay to bring up a menu.

8. Use Cut, Copy, and Paste as you would while editing text. You can duplicate slides this way.

9. Tap Delete to remove a slide.

10. Tap Skip to mark a slide as one to skip during the presentation. This comes in handy when you want to remove a slide from a presentation temporarily, perhaps while presenting to a specific audience.

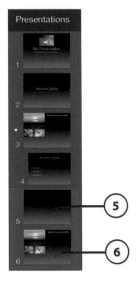

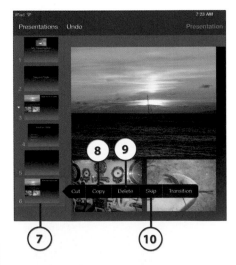

Playing Your Presentation

After you create your presentation, or if you want to preview what you've done, you can play your presentation.

1. With a presentation open in Keynote, tap the Play button.

2. The presentation fills the screen. Tap on the center or right side of the screen to advance to the next slide. You can also tap and drag from left to right.

3. To go back to the previous slide, drag right to left.

4. Tap on the left edge of the screen to bring up a list of slides.

5. Tap one of the items in the list to go directly to that slide.

6. Tap outside of the list of slides to dismiss the list.

7. Pinch in at the center of the screen to end the presentation and return to editing mode.

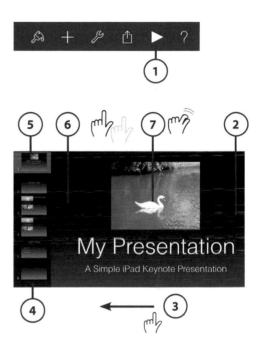

WHICH VIDEO ADAPTER?

One way to get Keynote's presentation out to an external screen is to use an adapter. There are two main choices: the VGA adapter or the HDMI adapter. Get the VGA adapter if you plan to present over a traditional meeting room projector. However, newer televisions and maybe some advanced projectors would use an HDMI connection. You can also convert VGA to fit other video connections. For instance, if you need to connect to a TV using a component or s-video, you should find some VGA adapters that work. See if you can find one that has been verified to work with an iPad before buying.

Presenting on an External Display

Presenting on your iPad with people looking over your shoulder probably isn't your goal. You want to present on a large monitor or a projector, which you can do with an Lightning to VGA Adapter (see Chapter 18, "iPad Accessories," for more information).

1. When you have your VGA adapter connected, the Play button has a box around it to indicate that your iPad is ready to present on an external video device. Tap the Play button.

2. Tap in the middle or right side of the screen to move forward to the next slide or build the next object on the current slide.

3. Tap the left edge of the screen to bring up a list of slides.

4. Tap on one of the slides on the left to jump to it.
5. Tap the Done button to stop the presentation.
6. Tap the Layouts button to bring up different layout options. You can choose to view both the current slide and next slide or the current slide with your slide notes at the bottom.

7. Tap and hold your finger on the slide to bring up a red dot that you can use as a pointer.

Presenting with Apple TV

You can also use the AirPlay ability of an Apple TV (2nd generation or newer) to send your presentation to a TV wirelessly. See "Using AirPlay to Play Music and Video on Other Devices" in Chapter 4 to set up AirPlay mirroring. But when you tap the Play button to play your presentation, mirroring will go into a special mode with the actual presentation on the TV and your presenter layout on your iPad's screen so you can control the slides.

Search for locations or
get directions with Maps.

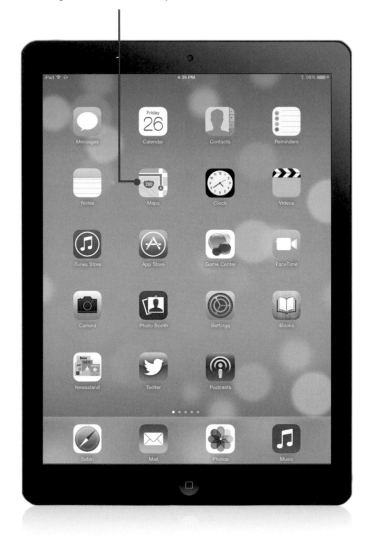

In this chapter, you learn to use the Maps app to find locations and get directions.

→ Finding a Location
→ Searching for Places and Things
→ Getting Directions
→ Setting Bookmarks
→ Using Views
→ Getting Traffic Reports

Navigating with Maps

The Maps app is a great way to plan a trip—whether you're going across the country or to the grocery store. You can search for locations on the map, view satellite images, see optimized driving routes, and even get information and reviews of local businesses.

Finding a Location

The simplest thing you can probably do with Maps is to find a location.

1. Tap the Maps app on your Home screen.

2. Type an address or the name of a place in the field.

3. As you type, you get a list of suggestions. You can tap one of these if you notice it matches your search closely.

4. Otherwise, finish typing the address or name and tap the Search button on the on-screen keyboard.

What Can You Search For?

You can search for a specific address. You can also use a general area or the name of a place or person, and Maps does the best it can to locate it. For example, you can try three-letter airport codes, landmark names, street intersections, and building names. The search keeps in mind your current Maps view, so if you search for a general area first, such as Denver, CO, and then for a building name, it attempts to find the building in Denver before looking elsewhere in the world.

5. The map shifts to that location and zooms in.

6. Tap the i button next to the location name to get more information.

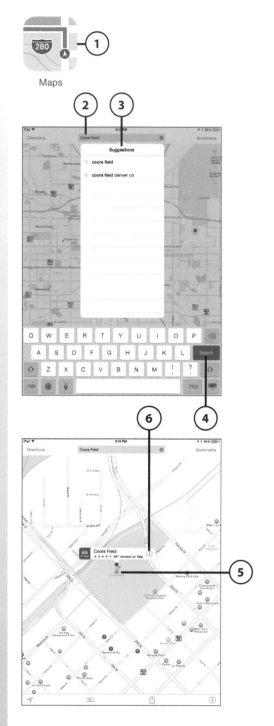

Maps

7. You see information about the location, such as the telephone number and website. You can click on these to call the location or visit the web page.

8. Tap Directions to Here to get directions to the address.

9. You can also switch to look at reviews for restaurants, stores, and other locations.

10. Tap Create New Contact or Add to Existing Contact to add the name, address, phone number, and other information to your Contacts app. Scroll down and you'll also find an option that lets you add the location as a book-mark in the Maps app.

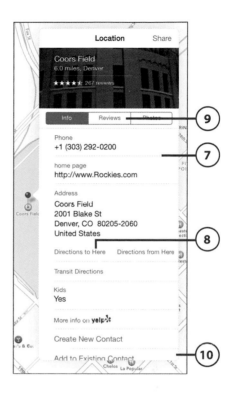

Where Am I?

Want to quickly center the map on your current location? Tap the GPS button (it looks like a small arrow) at the bottom-left corner of the screen. Even if your iPad doesn't have a GPS receiver, it takes a good guess as to your cur-rent location based on the local Wi-Fi networks it can see.

Searching for Places and Things

You can also use Maps to search for something that has more than one loca-tion. For instance, you could search for one location of your favorite com-puter store.

1. Start in Maps. You should see the last area you were viewing. If it is not your current location, search for that location or press the GPS button to go there.

2. Tap the search field and enter the name of a store.

3. Red pins appear on the map for all locations matching the search term in the general area. You might also see some dots representing other potential locations. Pinch to zoom in or unpinch to zoom out to see a wider area. You may need to try your search again after you have expanded the area.

4. Tap a red pin to get the name of the location and an i button to tap for more information.

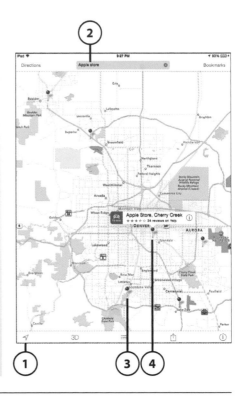

Sometimes Being General Is Good

Don't always restrict yourself to specific names such as "Apple store." You can type in general terms such as "coffee" or "restaurant" to get a broader selection of results.

Sometimes It Gets It Wrong

The maps database is huge, which means it also contains errors. Sometimes an address is wrong or the information is out of date, so you find yourself in front of a shoe shop instead of your favorite restaurant.

Siri: Finding Map Locations

You can ask Siri to find locations without even being in the Maps app. A small map will appear in the Siri interface, and you can tap on it to open up the Maps app, centered on that location. Try commands like:

"Where is Coors Field?"
"Show me Broadway and First Avenue on the map."
"Map 6th and Colorado Boulevard."

Getting Directions

The new iOS Maps app has something that the previous Maps app did not: turn-by-turn directions. If you are stationary, you'll need to settle for a map and a list of turns. But if you have a wireless mobile connection, you can use your iPad like a car's navigation system with spoken instructions.

1. In Maps, tap the Directions button. At this point, you may be asked to confirm whether the Maps app is allowed to use your current location.

2. Two fields appear at the top. The left field is already filled in with Current Location. Change the location by tapping in the field to clear it and typing a new address.

3. Tap in the second field and type the destination location. Suggestions appear underneath in a list. You can tap a suggestion to fill that into the destination box.

4. Select the mode of transportation. You can get directions for driving, walking, or public transportation.

5. Tap the Route button.

6. The directions show up as a blue line on the map. You might need to pinch to zoom out to see the whole route.

7. Alternate routes may also appear in a lighter shade of blue. Tap any route label to switch to that route.

8. Tap the Start button to go through the route turn-by-turn.

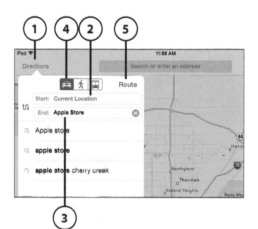

9. The current instruction appears at the top of the screen.

10. Tap on the next instruction to jump to it, or it will automatically shift over to the left as you accomplish the previous instruction. You can also swipe left to right to view future instructions.

11. Tap Overview to temporarily go to the map view that shows the entire route.

12. In Overview mode, you can tap the list button to view the directions as a simpler text list.

13. When you are done using the directions feature, tap End to exit back into normal map mode.

It's Not All Good

More Complex Routes

iOS originally included a maps app provided by Google and used Google maps. Today, the Maps app is provided by Apple and uses a different set of features and data. For instance, the Apple Maps app won't let you have more than two waypoints for a route. It also doesn't have biking directions. Google has since published a new Maps app that is available in the app store for free. So if you like maps and want to have two options available, search for Google Maps in the app store and add that to your iPad.

Spoken Turn-By-Turn Directions

For those who have a wireless mobile connection on their iPad, directions become much more useful. You can use your mobile connection as you drive and the Maps app will follow along, updating the steps in your route as you make progress. You even get spoken directions as you approach each turn, so you don't need to take your eyes off the road.

Siri: Getting Directions

The easiest way to get the Maps app to show you directions is to ask Siri. With or without the Maps app open, try phrases like:

"How do I get to Denver International Airport?"
"Take me to the nearest coffee shop."
"Plot a course to Colfax Avenue and Colorado Boulevard."
"Take me home."

Setting Bookmarks

If you find yourself requesting directions to or from the same location often, you might want to set a bookmark for that spot.

1. In Maps, search for a location.

2. Tap the i button for a location to bring up its info box.

3. Tap Add Bookmark.

4. Edit the name for the location if you want.

5. Tap Save.

6. Tap Bookmarks at the top of the screen to view your bookmarks.

7. At the bottom of the Bookmarks menu, tap Recents or Contacts to see a list of recently visited locations or pull up the address stored for a contact.

8. Tap the name of a bookmark to go to that location on the map.

9. You can also tap Edit to remove or rename bookmarks.

Add a Bookmark Manually

You can also create a bookmark by manually dropping a pin on the map. Tap and hold any location on the map, and a purple pin appears there. You can then drag the pin to another location if it isn't placed exactly where you want it. These pins have addresses and an i button just like any searched-for location. So, you can use the Add to Bookmarks button after tapping the i to add it as a bookmark. This comes in handy when the app doesn't quite get the address right.

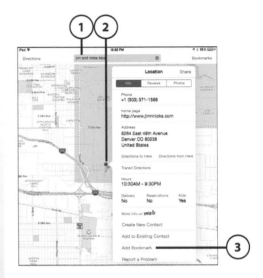

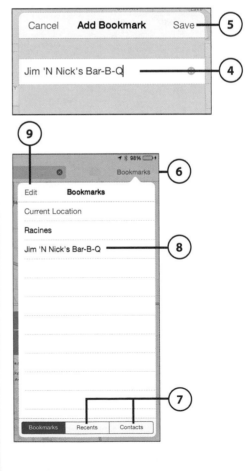

Using Views

One of the coolest things about online maps are the satellite and street views. Both are fun and helpful and a lot more interesting than a traditional map.

Using Satellite View

Satellite view is like the standard Map view in that you can search for places and get directions. But you can also get a better sense of what is at a location.

1. In Maps, tap the i button in the bottom-right corner.

2. Tap Satellite to see a satellite view of your location. Alternatively, select Hybrid to see a satellite view that also gives you map references to identify items on the map.

3. Unpinch in the center of the map to zoom in.

4. The closer view helps show you what the streets actually look like.

Using 3D View

The old Google Maps had street view, a way to view images taken at street level. However, the new Apple Maps app replaces that with 3D aerial views—images taken from airplanes that include all sides of buildings in major downtown areas.

1. Start by looking in Maps using the standard view. Tap the 3D button.

2. The flat top-down view is replaced by a perspective view. Pinch to zoom in closer.

3. Larger buildings in downtown areas are now 3D objects. Use two fingers to rotate the image, and you can see the buildings from all angles.

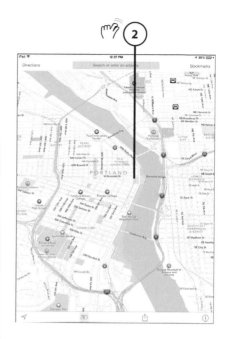

4. Tap the info button in the bottom-right corner.

5. Select Satellite view. You can still zoom and rotate in satellite view, even getting so close to the ground that you can virtually move between buildings.

6. Use two fingers and swipe up. This will tilt the 3D effect for a more horizontal view.

7. Tap to turn off 3D mode and return to standard top-down flat mode. Notice that when you are zoomed in on a city, you see a city buildings icon instead of the 3D button.

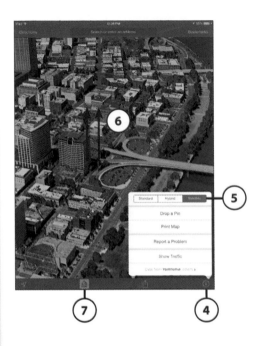

Not in My Town

Although 3D view is great for those of us who live in big cities, it isn't available for every location. For there to be 3D models and textures, an Apple-hired airplane has to take pictures of your city. They have gotten a lot of the world's major cities, but not everywhere yet.

Getting Traffic Reports

The Maps app includes a way for you to see up-to-date traffic flow and information.

1. Bring up a Map view that shows some highways and major boulevards.

2. Tap the i button.

3. Turn on Traffic overlays.

4. The map shows red or yellow dashed lines where traffic is slow.

5. You can also see the locations of accidents that are affecting traffic. Tap for details.

6. These symbols represent road closures. You can tap on them to see more information.

7. These icons show you where roadwork is taking place.

8. You can also see other events, like "police activity."

Siri: Traffic Reports

You can quickly bring up the map with traffic reports turned on by asking Siri:

What's the traffic like?
What's the traffic like in San Francisco?

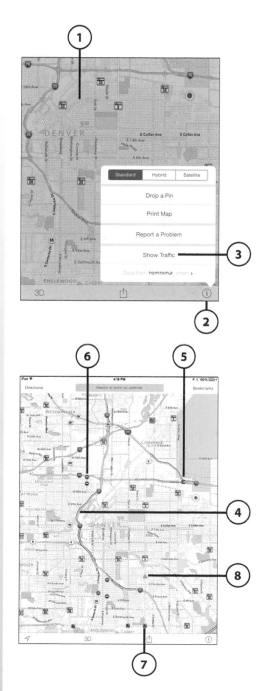

Search Apple's App Store for thousands of useful, educational, and entertaining apps.

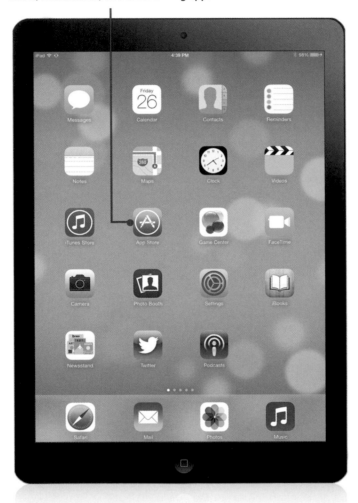

To go beyond the basic functionality of your iPad, you need to learn how to add more apps using the App Store.

The World of Apps

Apps that come with your iPad and Apple's office apps, Pages, Numbers, and Keynote are just the tip of the iceberg. The App Store contains hundreds of thousands of apps from third-party developers, with more added each day.

You use the App Store app to shop for and purchase new apps— although many are free. You can also rearrange the app icons on your Home screen pages to organize them.

Purchasing an App

Adding a new app to your iPad requires that you visit the App Store. You do that, not surprisingly, with the App Store app on your Home screen.

1. Tap the App Store icon on your Home screen.

App Store

2. If this is the first time you have used the App Store, you will see the featured apps at the top of the screen. Otherwise, tap the Featured button at the bottom.

3. Swipe left or right in the New & Noteworthy section to view more featured apps. You can do the same for the sections below, which often change to feature different types of apps.

4. Scroll down to see more featured apps.

5. Tap Top Charts to see the top paid apps and top free apps.

6. Tap More to see a list of app categories.

7. Tap any category to go to the page of featured apps in that category.

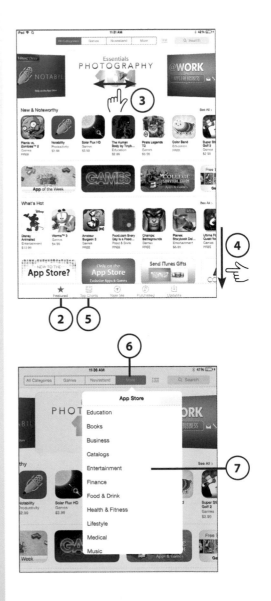

8. Use the search box to search for an app by keyword.

9. The button at the top lets you filter between iPad apps and iPhone apps. Apps that are optimized to work well with both screen sizes will appear in both.

10. Select whether you want to see apps that are free or both free and paid.

11. Select a category to narrow down the search results.

12. Choose how you want the results to be ordered: relevance, popularity, ratings, or release date.

13. Tap an app to read more about it.

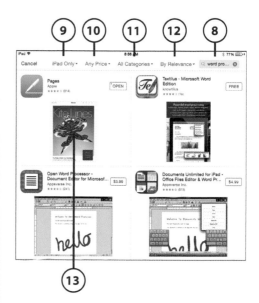

Redeem Codes

If you go to the bottom of the Featured page in the App Store, you will see a button marked Redeem. Use this to enter any redemption code you get for a free app. You may get a code because someone sends you an app as a gift. Developers also send out a handful of these codes when they release a new app or app version.

Automatically Download New Apps

If you go to the Settings app, look for the iTunes & App Store category. There you can turn on automatic downloads for apps, as well as music and books. Once you turn this on, purchasing an app on your Mac or PC in iTunes, or on another iOS device with the same Apple ID, will automatically send this app to your iPad as well.

14. The app's page displays screenshots, other apps by the same company, and user reviews.

15. Tap on the price on the left under the large icon to purchase an app. It changes to a Buy App button. Tap it again. If you have already purchased the app, the button will simply say OPEN and you can launch the app by tapping the button.

16. Scroll down to read the description of the app.

17. Tap Reviews to look at reviews for the app.

18. Scroll left and right to flip through the screenshots for the app.

19. When you purchase an app, it starts installing, and you can watch the progress from the app's information page in the App Store app or from the location of the app's icon on your Home screen.

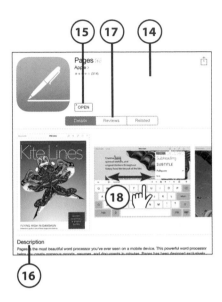

Redownloading an App You Already Purchased

Once you buy an app, you own it forever—at least as long as you keep using the same Apple ID. At the bottom of the App Store app, you see a button marked Purchased. Tap that to see a list of all apps you have bought, even if you have removed them from this iPad, or maybe never even downloaded them in the first place. Perhaps you previously bought an app on your iPhone or iPod Touch. You can quickly jump to any of these apps and download them to your iPad without paying for it a second time.

FREE, PAID, AND FREEMIUM

Some apps in the App Store are free, and others you need to pay for before downloading and installing. But some apps are free for the basic version, and then you need to make in-app purchases to use advanced functions or buy more content. These are called "freemium" apps.

It is up to the developer of the app to design the method of making purchases. Most apps show you a preview of the function or content and then include a purchase or buy button. Before any app can charge your iTunes account for an in-app purchase, you will see a standard Confirm Your In-App Purchase prompt.

Photo apps may use in-app purchases to charge you for additional filters or effects. Drawing apps may charge for new brushes or tools. Some free apps have advertising and allow you to make an in-app purchase to be able to use the app ad-free.

Often games will have a variety of items you can purchase to alter gameplay. But instead of a long list of in-app purchases, they simply charge you for in-game currency such as tokens, gems, or gold. Then you can use these to purchase items inside the game.

There's no risk in trying free apps that offer in-app purchases. If you find that the purchases in the app are not worth it for you, simply do not purchase anything. If the app isn't useful, you can delete it without spending a penny.

Arranging Apps on Your iPad

It doesn't take long to have several pages of apps. Fortunately, you can rearrange your app icons in two ways. The first is to do it on the iPad.

1. Tap and hold an icon until all the icons start to jiggle.

2. The icon you are holding is a little larger than the others. Drag it and drop it in a new location. To carry the icon to the next page of apps, drag it to the right side of the screen.

3. Delete an app from your iPad by tapping the X at the upper left of the icon. Note that the X does not appear over all apps, as the default set of apps that come with your iPad cannot be removed.

4. When finished, press the Home button.

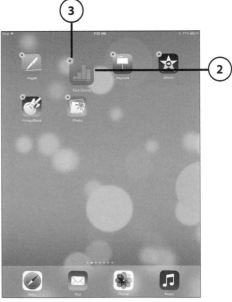

Deleting Is Not Forever

If you sync your iPad to iTunes on a computer, you do not delete apps forever. All apps remain in your iTunes library on your computer unless you remove them. So, you can get rid of the app from your iPad and find it is still on your computer if you want to select it to sync back to your iPad. Additionally, you can always redownload an app from the app store that you purchased previously, without paying again. If you don't think you'll need an app for a while, you can delete it and then add it back again later.

WHAT ELSE CAN I DO?

Here are a few more tips that might make your app housekeeping easier:

- You can release an app and then grab another to move it. If the apps still jiggle, you can keep moving app icons.

- You can drag apps into and out of the dock along the bottom where you can fit up to six apps. Apps in the dock appear on all pages of your Home screen.

- You can drag an app to the right on the last page of apps to create a new page of your Home screen.

Arranging Apps with iTunes

You can also arrange your apps when you sync with iTunes on your Mac or PC. Simply select the iPad in the left sidebar of your iTunes window, and then select Apps on the right. You can move apps between screens and also decide which apps get synced between your computer and your iPad.

Creating App Folders

In addition to spreading your apps across multiple pages, you can also group them together in folders so that several apps take up only one icon position on a screen.

1. Identify several apps that you want to group together. Tap and hold one of those apps until the icons start to jiggle.

2. Continue to hold your finger down, and drag the icon over another one you wish to group it with.

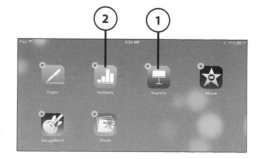

3. An app folder appears and enlarges to fill the center of the screen.

4. Change the name of the app folder.

5. Press the Home button once to dismiss the name editor, and again to return to your home screen.

6. You now see the app folder on your home screen. You can drag other apps to this folder using steps 1 and 2.

   After you have created an app folder, you can access the apps in it by first tapping on the folder and then tapping the app you want to launch. Tapping and holding any app in the folder gives you the opportunity to rename the folder, rearrange the icons in the folder, or drag an app out of the folder.

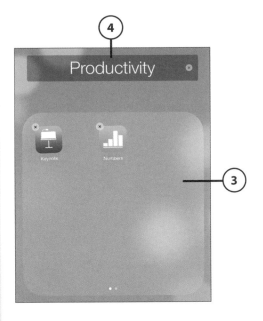

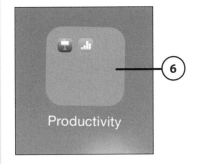

>>>Go Further

WORKING WITH APP FOLDERS

Here are a few more things you can do inside app folders:

- To remove an app from a folder and put it back into a position on the Home screen, tap and hold the icon until it jiggles. Then drag it out to the surrounding area outside of the folder.

- Inside app folders you can have more than one page if you have more then 9 apps stored in it. You can swipe left and right to move between pages while the folder is open.

- While apps in the app folder are jiggling, you can move them around inside the folder and off to the left or right to move them between pages inside the folder.

- You can move app folders around your Home screen and between Home screen pages just as you can with an app icon.

Viewing Currently Running Apps

You can have many apps running at once on your iPad. In fact, after you launch an app, it will remain running by default even if you switch back to the home screen and run another app. Apps running in the background use little or no resources. You can think of them as paused apps. You can switch back to them at any time, and most apps will resume right where you left off.

1. Double-press the Home button.

2. This gives you a new view that shows all your currently running apps in a large horizontal list. The app you currently are using appears to the left, and the previous app that you used is in the middle. This lets you easily switch between the current app and the previous app.

3. Swipe left and right to see more items in the list. The further to the right in the list the app is located, the longer it has been since you last used it.

4. Icons for each app also appear at the bottom. You can tap on these icons just as you can tap on the screens. You can also swipe left and right among the icons to scroll through the list faster than by swiping left and right between the screens.

Moving from App to App with a Gesture

If you have several apps running, you can quickly move between them by using four-finger gestures. Just swipe left or right with four fingers at the same time. This will move you from app to app without needing to go back to the Home screen, or use the list of recent apps.

Quitting Apps

Although it is rarely necessary to completely quit an app, you can do it in one of two ways. This will force the app to shut down if it has frozen, or if you simply want to start the app fresh to see an introduction sequence or work around problems the app may be having.

1. Press the home button twice to see the list of your currently running apps.

2. Swipe to the left or right so the app you want to force to quit is in the center of the screen.

3. Tap the preview of the app and swipe upward quickly until your finger is almost at the top of the screen, and then let go. The app will quit and will be removed from the list.

A second method works when the app is the one currently on the screen.

1. Press and hold the wake/sleep button on the top of your iPad for about 3 seconds. You will see the "Slide to power off" control appear.

2. Don't use the "Slide to power off" control or press the Cancel button. Instead, hold the Home button down for several seconds. This will quit the app and return you to your Home Screen, or for some apps it will restart the app.

   The app will also remain in the list you see when you double-press the Home button since it is one you recently used, even though it is not currently running.

Finding Good Apps

Finding good apps might be the biggest problem that iPad users have. With more than 900,000 apps in the App Store, it can be hard to find what you want, so here are some tips.

1. Check out the featured apps in the App Store, but be wary because they tend to be heavy on apps by large companies with well-established brands.

2. In the App Store app, find an app close to what you want and then check out the Related section.

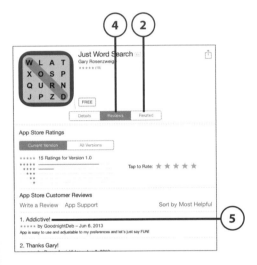

3. Look for trial versions, which often have names with "Lite" or "Free" at the end. Search for the name of the app and see if other versions turn up. Use free versions of apps to determine if it is worth paying for the full or enhanced version.

4. Tap on Reviews.

5. Read reviews, but don't trust them completely. Casual users are not always the best at providing balanced reviews.

USING RESOURCES OUTSIDE THE APP STORE

Many good resources for finding apps aren't part of the App Store. Following are a few suggestions:

- Search using Google. For example, if you want another spreadsheet app, search "iPad App Spreadsheet."

- After you find an app that you want, try another Google search using the name of the app followed by the word "review."

- Find sites that feature and review apps. Many are out there, but be aware that some sites are paid by developers to review an app, so the review might not be the most objective.

- The author provides a list of recommended apps at http://macmost.com/featurediphoneapps.

Using iPhone/iPod touch Apps

One of the great things about using apps on the iPad is that you can use almost every app in Apple's App Store—including those originally made for the iPhone and iPod touch.

Four types of apps are in the store from an iPad-owner's perspective. A few are iPhone/iPod touch only. Avoid those, naturally. The majority are iPhone/iPod touch apps that also work on the iPad. These apps appear in the middle of the screen or scale to double the size. Some might work better than others on the iPad. You can also find apps that work only on the iPad. If you select iPad Apps from the switch at the top of a search results screen, you will see apps that are either for the iPad only, or are for both the iPhone and iPad but have been designed to use the iPad's full screen size. Otherwise, if you pick iPhone apps, you will see apps that work for both, as well as apps that work only at the iPhone screen size.

For the apps that only work at the iPhone's screen size, you can scale them up so they are easier to work with on the iPad. In some cases, made-for-iPhone apps actually work better on the iPad because it is easier to see the graphics and touch the buttons.

1. To enlarge the app, tap the 2x button at the lower-right corner.

2. If the app looks blurry when it's enlarged, tap the 1x button to return to normal size.

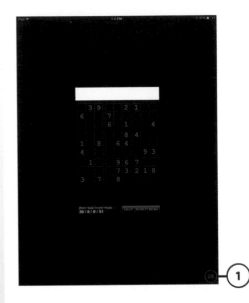

Getting Help with Apps

Apps are developed rapidly by both large and small companies. And apps are difficult to test because of Apple's restrictions on app distribution. So it is common to find bugs, have problems, or simply need to ask a question.

1. Check in the app to see if you can contact the developer. For example, in the Word Spell game app, there is a FAQ/Feedback button that takes you to a page of frequently asked questions and contact information.

2. If you don't find a way to contact support in the app, launch the App Store app and search for the app there.

3. Select the app to view its information.

4. Go to the Reviews section.

5. Tap the App Support button.

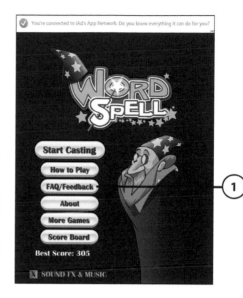

Family Sharing

When you buy an app, it can be put on any iPad (or iPhone/iPod touch if it works there, too) registered to your iTunes account. So if you share an iTunes account with your entire family, you can share your apps as well. No need to buy them again for a second iPad.

Authorizing Multiple Accounts

In iTunes on your Mac or PC, click the Store, Authorize This Computer menu item to authorize that copy of iTunes with more than one account. Then you can download apps to iTunes purchased from any of those accounts. In addition, the Home Sharing feature of iTunes lets you grab apps from one computer to another on the same network so that they can be loaded into iTunes and then synced to different iOS devices. But to update these shared apps, you sometimes are asked for the password that goes along with the Apple ID used to purchase the app originally.

Keep up with news and interesting posts.

View and control your desktop computer.

Store and view documents.

Make phone calls using your iPad.

Keep up with your friends on Facebook.

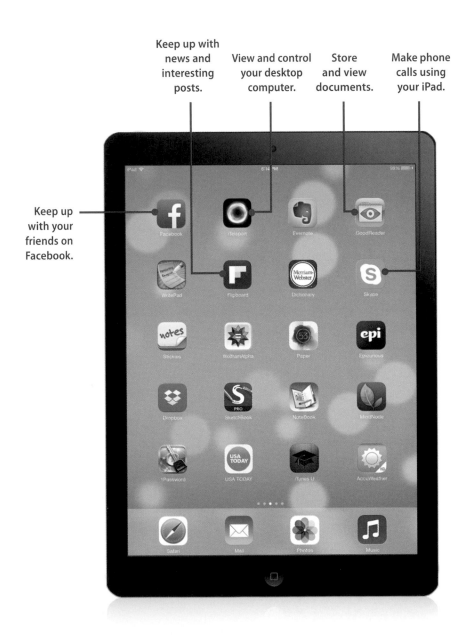

In this chapter, we take a look at various apps that you should add to your iPad to make it even more useful.

16

→ Connecting with Friends on Facebook

→ Controlling Your Computer with iTeleport

→ Reading Documents with GoodReader

→ Reading the News with Flipboard

→ Adding a Dictionary

→ Making Phone Calls with Skype

→ Putting Notes on Your Home/Lock Screen

→ Creating Multimedia Cloud Notes with Evernote

→ Handwriting Notes with WritePad

→ Sketching Ideas with Paper

→ Solving Math Problems with MyScript Calculator

→ Finding Recipes with Epicurious

→ Checking the Weather with AccuWeather

→ Learning New Things with iTunes U

→ Other Useful Apps

Using Popular and Critical Apps

Ask almost anyone what the best feature of the iPad is and you'll get the same answer: all the apps! The App Store is not only a source of hundreds of thousands of useful, interesting, and fun apps, but it grows each day as third-party developers and Apple add more. Here's a look at how to use some of the most popular apps for the iPad to perform various useful tasks.

Connecting with Friends on Facebook

Many people now spend more time on Facebook than the rest of the Internet combined. If you are one of those people, the official Facebook app is probably the first third-party app you should put on your iPad.

With it you can browse your wall, post status updates, send messages, post photos, and do most things that you can do on the Facebook website, but inside an environment designed for iPad users.

1. Search the App Store for the Facebook app. Tap FREE to download and install it.

2. Enter the email address and password you use to log into Facebook.

3. Tap Log In.

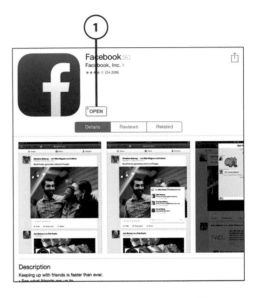

4. Scroll up and down to view your news feed.

5. You can Like posts just as you would on the Facebook website.

6. You can also tap Comment to add a comment to a post.

7. View and handle friend requests.

8. View direct messages and send messages to friends.

9. See your list of Facebook notifications.

10. Tap the menu button or swipe left to right to bring up the sidebar.

11. Tap your name to examine your own wall and edit your profile.

12. Tap the gear button next to News Feed to switch between only showing top posts or all recent items.

13. See a list of your friends and view their information and their wall.

14. You can also post to walls of Facebook pages that you manage.

15. Tap Status to update your Facebook status, adding a post to your wall.

16. Type the text of your update.

17. Add friends who are with you to the update.

18. Add a photo from your Photos library, or take a new photo using your iPad's cameras.

19. Choose groups you want to allow to see your update.

20. Post the update to Facebook.

It All Looks Different

If there is one consistent thing about Facebook, it is change. Facebook loves to change how its website and apps look. So if the Facebook app looks different than what you see here, it could simply be that Facebook has, once again, decided to redesign the interface.

Post from Outside

You don't need to use the Facebook app to post pictures. You can do it right from the Photos app and other image-handling apps. But you first need to go to the Settings app, then the Facebook section, and enter your email and password again. This gives iOS permission to use your Facebook account for posting. Then you can do things like post pictures from the Photos app, post links from Safari, and ask Siri to "update my Facebook status."

Controlling Your Computer with iTeleport

Your iPad can be a window to your Mac or PC. By using Virtual Network Computing (VNC) technology, you can control your computer just like it was sitting in front of you (except you can't hear the sound output).

1. Search the App Store for "VNC" to find a VNC client app for your iPad. There are many to choose from. As an example, we'll use iTeleport. Tap FREE to download and install it.

2. iTeleport has a system where you can install software on your Mac or PC and log into an account. See the app's help or the developer's website for more information. This will let your iPad find your computer easily. But you can also manually enter the IP address and login information to connect. Tap the Manual button to do that.

3. Then tap the + button to add a new connection.

4. Enter the IP address and port that your computer is using for VNC. On a Mac, you would find this in System Preferences, Network.

5. Enter the authentication information, such as the user ID and password. Make sure you set the authentication type to "Mac" if you are using Mac screen sharing.

6. Set the computer type.

7. Tap Save Server.

8. Tap the new entry on the Manual screen to connect to the computer.

9. After you are connected, you will see a portion of your computer's screen.

10. Tap and drag to move around to see your whole screen. This takes some getting used to, as you are both moving the cursor and the portion of the screen you are viewing. Practice a little and you'll be moving around like a pro. A quick tap without dragging is the equivalent of a mouse click.

11. Pinch to zoom in and out.

12. To type into an application from a keyboard, first select the application to type in by tapping, as you would click it on your computer.

13. Tap the keyboard button to bring up a keyboard. The keys you type will be relayed to the computer you are controlling. The other buttons across the top bring up modifier keys and special function keys like arrows.

Setting Up VNC on Your Computer

It takes two to VNC. You need to set up your Mac or Windows computer to accept the connection and allow your iPad to take over the screen. On a Mac, you can do this by turning on Screen Sharing in the Sharing pane of System Preferences. On Windows, it is called Remote Desktop, or you can install a third-party VNC server.

Other VNC Apps

There are many other VNC apps like iTeleport. Also check out VNC Viewer, Mocha VNC Lite, and Screens VNC. A slightly different app to look at is Air Display. It lets you use your iPad as an extra screen with your Mac or Windows PC.

Why Won't It Work?

Getting VNC connections to work can be frustrating. It has nothing to do with the iPad. Getting them to work between a laptop and a desktop has the same difficulties. If your network router or Internet modem isn't set up just right, it won't connect and you have little indication as to why. Most of the time, VNC connections work right away, but if you are one of the unlucky few, you might need to tinker around with your network equipment settings or even call in an expert to get it to work. If you are trying to set up the connection manually using an IP address, you may want to instead use iTeleport's desktop software to make the connection process easier.

Reading Documents with GoodReader

Although iBooks is great for basic document viewing, those more serious about collecting documents to read on their iPad have looked to apps that have even more features. Apps such as GoodReader enable you to create a library of viewable files such as PDFs, Word, images, text, and so on. You can then access these documents any time.

1. Search the App Store for GoodReader. Tap FREE to download and install it.

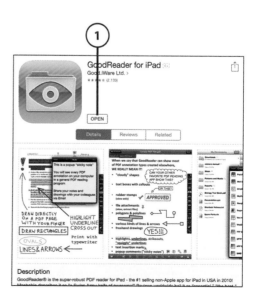

2. On the left side of GoodReader's main screen, you see the documents you have on your iPad.

3. On the right side are various controls. For instance, you can browse the web or enter a URL to download a document from the web.

4. You can also see Internet locations you have set up access to, such as your Dropbox account.

5. Tap Add to add more Internet services.

6. You can access documents stored on your Google Drive or created with Google apps.

7. You can use Dropbox or one of the other major cloud file storage services.

8. You can use a standard Internet sharing service, such as FTP.

9. You can also access Macs and PCs using standard file sharing.

10. Tap a document to open it.

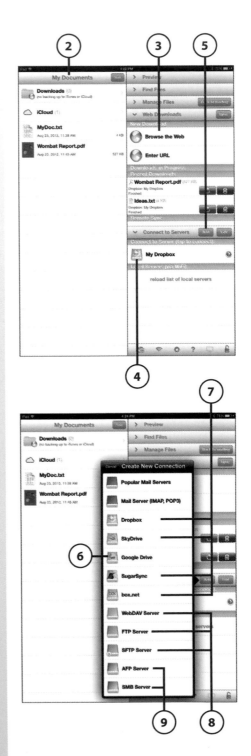

11. Documents of all different types, such as PDF, Pages, Word, text, images, and audio files can be viewed.

12. Documents open in tabs, allowing you to switch easily between several documents.

13. Use annotation tools to mark up the document.

14. You can search the document and use various reading tools. If the document is editable, such as a text document, then you can also use editing tools here.

15. Tap to return to your list of documents and services.

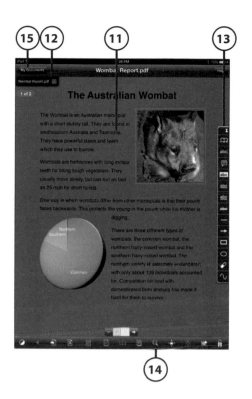

Transfer via iTunes

You can also transfer files between your Mac or PC and your iPad into GoodReader when you sync, without using any special Internet services or setting up file sharing. See "Syncing Documents" in Chapter 3.

Or, Use the Dropbox App

If you plan on using only the Dropbox service to transfer documents to your iPad, you can just use the Dropbox app to view them. The app shows you everything you have in your Dropbox folder and can display standard formats like PDF and Microsoft Word documents. You can even view a document when you have an Internet connection, and then it will be cached for the next time you view it, even if you do not have a connection at that moment. Go to www.dropbox.com to learn more about Dropbox.

Reading the News with Flipboard

Your iPad is a great device for catching up on the latest news. It is easier to hold than a newspaper, and you can get up-to-the-minute articles from sources all over the world.

Flipboard is a news app that uses information from your Facebook, Twitter, and other social media accounts to show news stories, pictures, and posts from your friends. It also uses your RSS feeds to show you news you are interested in. To see page after page of things that should interest you, just keep flipping.

1. Search for Flipboard in the App Store. Tap FREE to download and install it.

2. The front page contains featured Flipboard stories that change every few seconds. Tap on the image to read more.

3. Swipe the Flip button to the left to continue to your main Flipboard page.

4. Sign up for a Flipboard account for additional functionality like the ability to compile articles into magazines and share them.

5. Sections match either a subject or a social network that you have added to your Flipboard. Tap a section to view stories in it.

6. Swipe to move to the next page of sections.

7. Tap here to open your preferences.

8. To add more news sources, tap a category.

9. Then select a source and tap here to add it.

10. Tap the Accounts button to add social networks to your sources.

11. Tap Twitter to add your Twitter account. Flipboard will then check for articles shared by the people you follow on Twitter.

12. Likewise, add your Facebook account to get more articles from there.

13. Add more social networks that you use as sources.

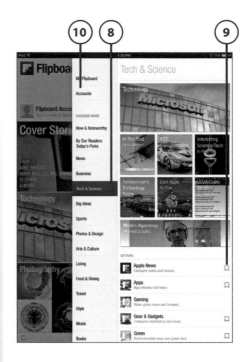

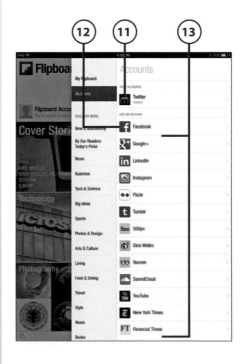

MAKE THE IPAD YOUR NEW NEWSPAPER

No need to get a physical paper dropped on your doorstep anymore. Many major newspapers and magazines deliver via their iPad apps. Look for apps from *USA Today*, the *New York Times*, the *Wall Street Journal*, *Newsweek*, *Time*, and *Wired*. You can even create your own newspaper using multiple sources with the app The Early Edition.

In some cases, the app and the daily content are free. Sometimes you need to pay for the app, but the content is free. Other times, such as with magazines, you pay for each issue you download.

Newspapers that don't have a custom app can still be viewed in the iPad's web browser, often with more up-to-date content than you can get with a paper edition.

Adding a Dictionary

It would be a crime to have to carry a dictionary with you in addition to your iPad. Of course, the solution is to get a dictionary app for your iPad. The Merriam-Webster Dictionary HD app is a free download from the App Store. There is also a premium version that removes the ads and adds illustrations and other features for a few dollars.

1. Find the Merriam-Webster Dictionary HD app in the App Store. Tap FREE to download and install it.

Use Any Online Dictionary

Of course, if you prefer another dictionary that doesn't have an iPad app, you can always just bookmark that site in Safari. You can also create a Home screen bookmark as we did in Chapter 7.

2. Tap in the search box and enter a word to look up.

3. You can also tap the microphone button and speak the word to look it up. Handy if you don't know how to spell the word.

4. The word and definition appears.

5. You can tap the speaker icon to have the word spoken so you can hear its pronunciation.

6. The app can also be used as a thesaurus. A list of synonyms appears at the bottom. Tap any one to jump to that word. In fact, any blue word in the definition can also be tapped to jump to that word for further clarification.

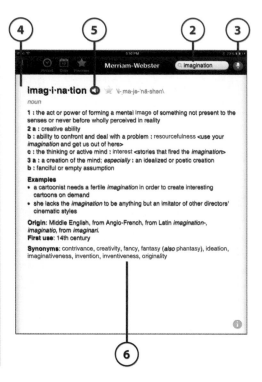

Making Phone Calls with Skype

Your iPad works quite well as a phone when you use a VoIP (voice over IP) app. Skype is probably the most well-known.

1. Search for Skype in the App Store. Make sure you look for the iPad app, not the iPhone/iPod touch app of the same name. Tap FREE to download and install it.

2. When you run the Skype app, you need to enter your ID and password and then sign in. After you do this the first time, you can skip this screen.

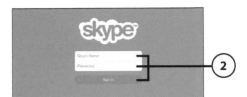

Get a Skype Account
You need a Skype account to use the Skype app. You can get a free one at http://www.skype.com/. If you find the service useful, you might want to upgrade to a paid account, which lets you call land lines and other phones. The free account lets you call only other Skype users.

3. Use the on-screen keypad to enter a phone number. You need a country code, too, which means using a 1 for U.S. calls. It should be there by default.

4. Tap Call.

5. While placing a call, you see the status, and eventually the elapsed time.

6. Additional buttons are available across the bottom for things like mute, volume, voice call, recent chats, and accessing your profile.

7. Tap the end call button to hang up.

How Do You Hold Your iPad to Talk?
The microphone is at the top of your iPad. The speaker is at the bottom on the back. The best way may be to just put the iPad in front of you and ignore the locations of both. Or, you can get a set of iPhone EarPods, which include the speakers and the microphone.

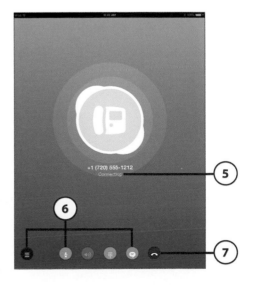

How About Skype Video?

You can also make video calls with Skype using your iPad's cameras. But you must be connecting to another Skype user who also has a video camera connected to their computer, or perhaps they are using an iPad as well.

Putting Notes on Your Home/Lock Screen

Your Lock screen and Home screen backgrounds look pretty. But can they be functional? One app attempts to make them more useful by enabling you to put sticky notes on them. Search in the App Store for Sticky Notes HD and add it to your collection of apps.

1. Search for Sticky Notes HD in the App Store. Tap FREE to download and install it.

2. Tap + to create a new note. You may be asked to choose Small or Large. Choose Large.

3. Select a color from the list. You can also select different note types, such as talk bubbles, pieces of paper, or even just plain text boxes.

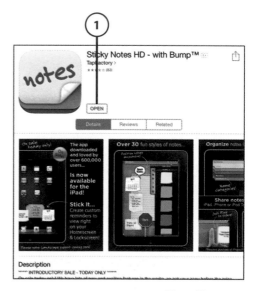

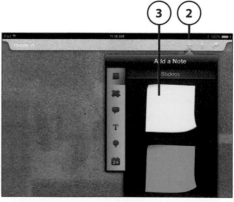

4. Type a note using the on-screen keyboard.

5. Tap Done.

6. Drag the note into a better position.

7. Tap the bottom-left corner to pick a background image.

8. Choose a background from the Library, Colors, or Photos buttons. Tap a new background.

9. Tap Done.

10. Tap the Export button.

11. Tap Save to Camera Roll.

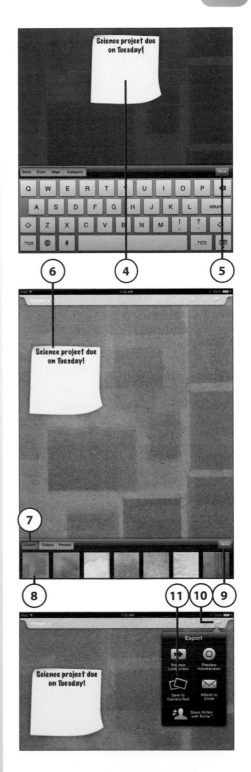

12. Tap Dismiss.

The App Can't Do It for You

Although the Sticky Notes app is great for making backgrounds with notes on them, it can't make these backgrounds your Lock or Home screen. You have to do that yourself using the Photos app or the Brightness & Wallpaper settings in the Settings app.

13. Press your Home button to return to the Home screen and then tap the Photos icon.

14. Find the photo you just took and tap it.

15. Tap the Share button in the lower-left corner.

16. Tap Use as Wallpaper.

17. Tap Set Lock Screen.

18. Press the Wake/Sleep Button at the top of your iPad.

19. Press the Home button.

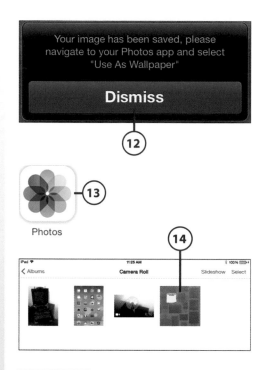

Your image has been saved, please navigate to your Photos app and select "Use As Wallpaper"

Dismiss

Photos

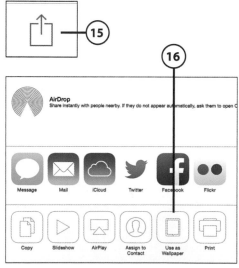

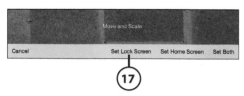

20. The background, complete with the sticky note, now appears on your Lock screen.

Emergency Contact Info

Another use for this app is to quickly and easily put your emergency contact information on the Lock screen. You can just put a "In case of emergency" phone number and instructions on the screen, or "If found, please call:" phone number.

Creating Multimedia Cloud Notes with Evernote

One of the most popular productivity apps on the iPad and iPhone, as well as Macs and PCs, is Evernote. At its heart, it is like the built-in Notes app on your iPad. You can create text notes, and they will sync across your devices.

But Evernote has several advanced features that endear it to users. First, you can easily record audio and take photos and add them to your notes. Second, it is independent of an email service like iCloud or Gmail. Third, there are Evernote clients for almost every computer and device. You can even view your notes in a web-based interface if you need to.

1. Search for Evernote in the App Store. Tap FREE to download and install it.

2. If you have never used Evernote, you can create a new account on your iPad. Basic accounts are free.

3. If you already have an Evernote account, just enter your ID and password to log on.

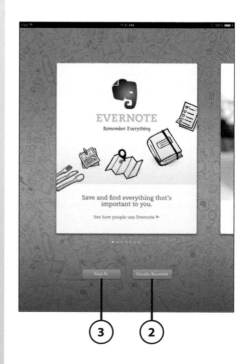

4. The main screen will show your notes. Tap a note to view it.

5. To create a new note, tap the top button on the left.

6. Tap in the title area to type a name for the note.

7. Tap in the body area to type text into the note.

8. At any time you can tap the photo button to take a picture with your iPad and add it to the note at the current cursor location. The button next to it allows you to select a photo from your photo library.

9. Tap Evernote's microphone button to record a voice memo or simply record the sound around you.

10. You can format text with a variety of controls, even creating checkboxes and lists.

11. Tap the info button to get info on a note.

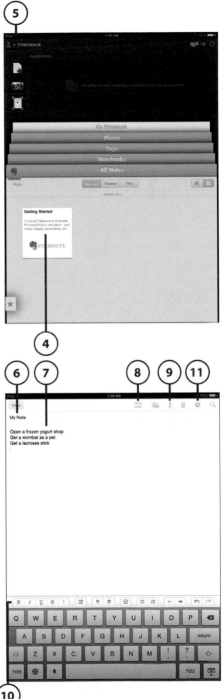

12. You can add tags to notes as one way to organize them.

13. If you allow it, notes will include location information about where you were when you created the note.

14. You can share the note on Facebook, Twitter, via Email, or print it.

15. Tap the search button to search the content of notes.

The real power of Evernote involves how it syncs quickly and wirelessly over the Internet. For instance, you can use it to write notes, record audio, and take pictures with your iPad while out of the office, and then find them all on your Mac or PC when you get back to your desk. Often, the picture-taking ability is used to grab snapshots of sketches on napkins or product information on the back of a box.

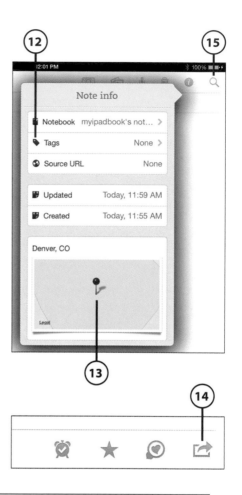

You Want Audio While Taking Notes?

If you want to record audio and take notes at the same time, try the app SoundNote. You can tap out text with the keyboard and draw with your finger all while audio is being recorded. Then it remembers where the audio stream was for each word. So tap a word to hear the audio at that moment.

Another app that does this is Circus Ponies NoteBook. You can type text, draw, take photos, and so on. You can turn on audio recording, and then each line in your note will match up with a portion of a recording. So you can sit in a lecture or meeting and take notes, and then refer back to the audio that matches each portion of your note. Wish I had these back in college!

Handwriting Notes with WritePad

You'd think with a touch screen that the iPad could recognize your handwriting instead of making you type on an on-screen keyboard. The WritePad app enables you to take notes by typing or by using the touch screen to write with your finger.

1. Search for WritePad in the App Store. Tap FREE to download and Install it.

2. Tap the My Documents button to view your current documents.

3. Tap + to start a new document.

4. Tap + on the list screen create folders to organize your documents if you want.

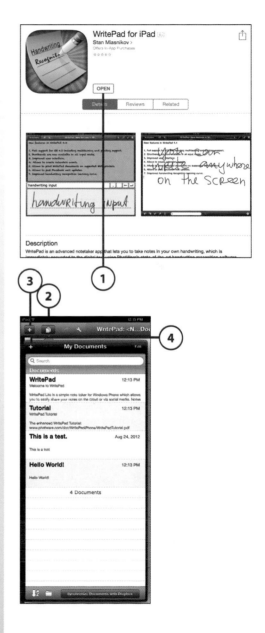

5. Tap and drag around the screen using the tip of your finger like a pen or pencil. Start in the upper-left corner. You can use printed letters, cursive, or a mixture.

6. Stop writing and wait for the text to process. When it does, the text appears at the cursor location.

7. Tap the buttons at the top-right corner to switch between Reading mode, Writing mode, and Keyboard mode.

8. Tap the Undo button to undo the last text processed.

Sketching Ideas with Paper

Perhaps you don't want your handwriting converted to text, but instead want to sketch out ideas or doodle on your iPad. Probably the most popular app for that is the simple Paper by FiftyThree.

1. Search the App Store for Paper by FiftyThree. Tap FREE to download and install it.

2. You can create a new notebook to sketch in, but there are already several empty notebooks waiting for you when you first install the app.

3. Tap a notebook to open it.

4. Anything you may have sketched previously appears on the first page.

5. You can swipe left to flip through the pages in the book.

6. Tap in the middle or pinch out to zoom in on a page so you can sketch.

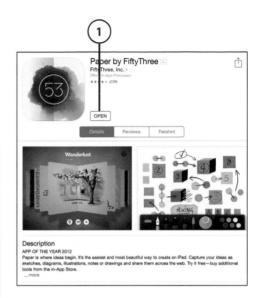

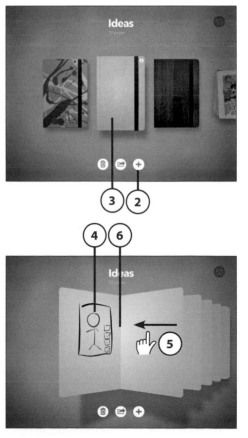

7. Select the pen tool to draw.

8. Tap and drag your finger to draw lines.

9. Tap a color to change colors.

10. Tap the eraser tool and drag your finger on the page to erase.

11. Pinch in to zoom back out to view the whole notebook. Pinch in again to zoom out to see all your notebooks.

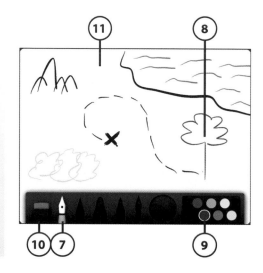

WHAT ELSE CAN I DO?

>>>Go Further

Here are some more things you can do with Paper by FiftyThree:

- The blank spots next to the eraser and pen are more drawing tools such as pencil, marker, more pens, and a color mixer. The basic Paper is free, but you need to pay with in-app purchases to get these tools.

- You can undo by tapping with two fingers and making a counter-clockwise circle. The more you circle, the further back in time you will go. You can reverse the direction of the circle to redo.

- When flipping through the pages of a notebook, you can use the Share button below the notebook to send the currently visible page to your Camera Roll for use in other apps, or even as your lock screen or home screen.

- You can also send a page to Tumblr, Facebook, Twitter, or to a friend via email.

Looking for a Different Handwriting App?

A similar app to Paper is Penultimate. You create notebooks and write in them by drawing with your finger. You can also mark up PDF documents and enter text using the on-screen keyboard. Another advantage of Penultimate is that it syncs with an Evernote account, if you are already using Evernote.

Solving Math Problems with MyScript Calculator

While it is impressive that some apps can translate your handwriting to characters, it is even more impressive when it can then take those characters and do something with them. MyScript Calculator is an app that lets you handwrite math equations and will then solve them for you.

1. Search for MyScript Calculator in the App Store. Tap FREE to download and install.

2. When you run it, you get a blank canvas. Start handwriting a number.

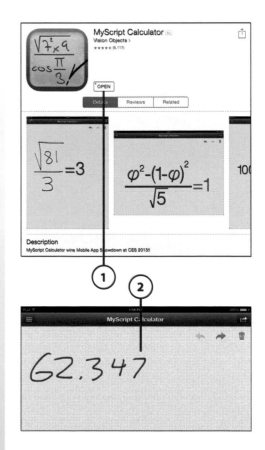

3. When you pause while writing out numbers and parts of an equation, the app translates them to characters, confirming that it understands them.

4. The app also automatically completes equations. In this case, the 62.347, the dividing line, and the 15.21 were drawn; then the =4.099... was filled in automatically by the app.

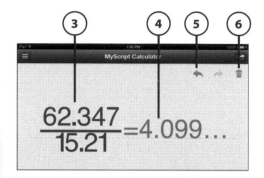

5. Use the Undo button if you have made a mistake, or if the app has made a mistake in translating your handwriting.

6. Use the Trash button to clear the canvas.

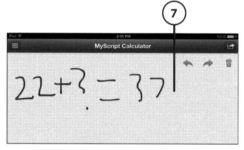

7. You can leave a blank space in an equation, or use a question mark.

8. The app will fill in the blank with the appropriate number to make the equation work.

9. Tap here to access the tutorial, which shows you what else you can use in your equations. You can use parenthesis, superscript to represent powers, and symbols like square root and pi. You can also use functions like cos, sin, tan, and log.

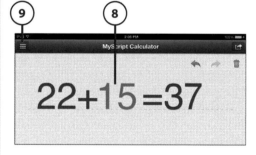

Finding Recipes with Epicurious

One application for early personal computers was to store and recall recipes. With the Internet, we can also share those recipes. And now with the iPad, there is finally a way to easily have these recipes with you in the kitchen while cooking. The Epicurious app is a favorite for such tasks.

1. Search for Epicurious in the App Store. Tap FREE to download and install it.

2. Tap the Control Panel to see a list of featured sections.

3. Or, use the search box to search for a recipe.

4. Tap Featured, and then select a category from the list.

5. Tap a recipe.

6. You'll get a list of ingredients needed.

7. You can then follow the recipe. If only cooking were that easy! Bon Appetit!

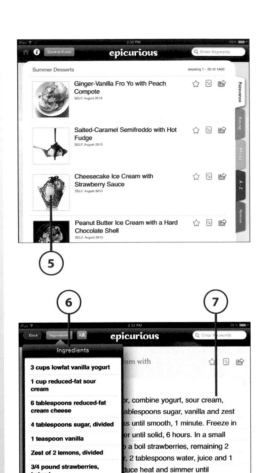

Checking the Weather with AccuWeather

The iPhone comes with a Weather app preinstalled, but the iPad does not. However, you can find many good weather apps in the App Store. Download any one of those to add this important information to your iPad. As an example, let's look at using the AccuWeather app.

1. Search the App Store for AccuWeather. Tap FREE to download and install it.

2. The first screen you see shows you the current conditions for your location.

3. You can slide this control to the right to advance the time to any hour later in the day to see a prediction of the conditions then.

4. Tap the menu button for more options.

5. Tap the Forecast button to see the 5-day forecast.

6. Tap the Maps button to see weather maps.

7. Drag up the menu at the bottom of the screen for map options.

8. There are options to change the type of map you are viewing.

9. You can also tap and drag the map around to see other areas. Pinch and unpinch to zoom works as well.

10. Tap the menu button to return to the current conditions or forecast.

Lots of Weather Apps

There are dozens of good weather apps in the App Store. Other popular ones include Weather+, The Weather Channel, Weather Live, WeatherBug, and Living Earth.

You can also find weather sections in many local television news apps and newspaper apps. Or, you can just bookmark the web page for your favorite weather site.

Learning New Things with iTunes U

You have an entire school in your iPad—many universities, in fact. Apple's iTunes U app is your gateway to free educational content provided by many of the world's top colleges.

1. Search the App Store for the iTunes U app. Tap FREE to download and install it.

2. If you start with a blank library of courses, tap the button at the upper left to enter the course catalog, which would be labeled "Catalog."

3. Tap the More button for a complete list of categories.

4. Tap in the search field to search the catalog for a course.

5. Tap a course to view more information.

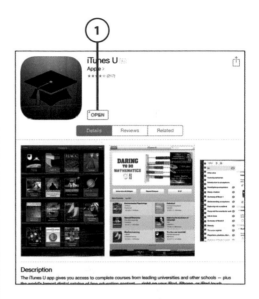

6. Read the description of the course.

7. Swipe up the page to move down and see all the course materials. Icons to the right of the names indicate what type of material: audio, document, video, and so on.

8. You can tap to download an individual item.

9. You can subscribe to the whole course, which will put it in your library and take you to your library screen.

10. To return to the library, tap the Library button at the top of the screen. Then, tap the course in your library.

11. When viewing the course, tap Posts to see a chronological list of the course materials.

12. The list can be arranged in many different ways, according to the author of the course. In this case, the course is broken into weeks.

13. Tap an item to expand it.

14. You can download and listen/read/view the item.

15. When you have completed an item, you can check it off the list.

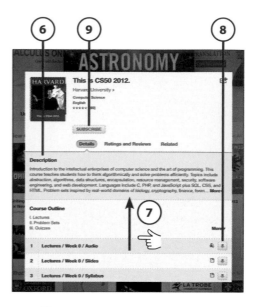

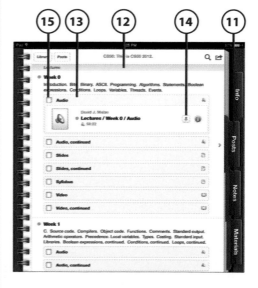

Is It Really Free?

Yes, for the most part. Many major universities provide these courses for free. However, just like with a real course, you sometimes need to purchase extra materials to follow along. For instance, there may be a book, app, or other item listed. Sometimes you can purchase the item right on your iPad, such as a book in the iBookstore.

Keep on Learning

Another learning app is Craftsy. You can purchase video courses for things like crochet, kitting, quilting, baking, weaving, and other crafts. You browse their catalog and buy the course with an in-app purchase. Then you follow along with video tutorials. You can also take notes and ask questions of your instructor.

If you search the app store, you can find apps that teach you just about anything. Want to learn to play guitar? How to Bowl? How to repair your car? There are all sorts of apps for these. And when you can't find an app, you can use the YouTube app to search for tutorial videos.

Other Useful Apps

So many useful apps are in the store that it is impossible to cover them all in a book. Here are some quick mentions of others you can check out. Some are free, others you have to pay for.

- **SketchBook Pro**: This drawing app lets you paint with your fingers. Unlike Paper by FiftyThree, SketchBook Pro is specifically for illustration. Professional artists have used it to create some amazing pieces. There is even a Flickr gallery of SketchBook pro art. You should also check out **Brushes 3**, **ArtStudio**, and the free **Adobe Ideas** app.

- **1Password**: Mac users already know about the popular 1Password for Mac. The iPad version doesn't integrate with Safari, but it does give you a place to securely store passwords and other important information.

- **Things**: If you are into productivity apps and to-do lists, check out Things. It is the king of to-do list apps on the iPad. Also check out **Wunderlist**.

- **MindNode**: If you use mind mapping software to organize your ideas and plan projects, then you'll be happy to know there is a pretty advanced tool that lets you do this on the iPad.

- **OmniGraffle**: If you need to create organizational charts, or like to use graphics to plan out projects, check out the iPad version of this popular graphics tool.

- **WordPress**: The official WordPress app lets you write, edit, and maintain your blog posts. It works for the WordPress.com blogging service and for WordPress blogs set up on independent sites.

- **StarWalk**: This is a must-have app for anyone even vaguely interested in astronomy. Even if you aren't, the beautiful, up-to-the-minute renderings of the night sky on your iPad will impress your friends. You can see what the sky looks like right now, right where you are, and use it as a guide to identifying what you see. Also check out **The Elements: A Visual Exploration** for more cool science learning.

- **Wolfram Alpha**: Want to compare two stocks, see the molecular structure of sulfuric acid, or calculate the amount of sodium in your breakfast? Would you believe that one app does all three and has hundreds of other interesting answers to all sorts of questions? It is also the answer engine behind a lot of what the iPhone's Siri feature does, so you get a little bit of Siri on your iPad.

- **USA Today**: While other national newspapers are playing around with pay-to-read models, *USA Today* is sticking with free. It provides a great summary of what is going on around the country. If you are looking for a more European perspective, the **BBC News** app also provides news, plus a lot of video.

Compose music.

Stream video.

Listen to music.

Read magazines.

Play games.

Track your best scores and challenge friends.

In this chapter, we look at apps that exist for entertainment purposes such as viewing movies, reading comics, listening to music, or playing games.

→ Composing Music with GarageBand

→ Watching Videos with YouTube

→ Watching Movies and TV Shows with Netflix

→ Subscribing to Magazines with Newsstand

→ Using Game Center

→ iPad Games and Entertainment

Games and Entertainment

You can view a lot of information and get a lot of work done on the iPad, but it is still a great device for entertainment. The majority of entertainment apps out there are games, but there are also some general entertainment apps that we can take a look at.

Composing Music with GarageBand

It is hard to sum up GarageBand in just a few pages. This brother to the Mac GarageBand application is a very big app. It could almost deserve a book all to itself. Let's look at how to create a simple song.

1. Download and install GarageBand from the App Store. Launch it from the home screen. See "Purchasing an App," in Chapter 15 for instructions on how to find and download apps.

2. If this is the first time you are using GarageBand, you can skip to step 3. Otherwise, you will see a list of songs you have created. Tap the + button and then New Song.

3. Now you can choose an instrument to start. Select the keyboard.

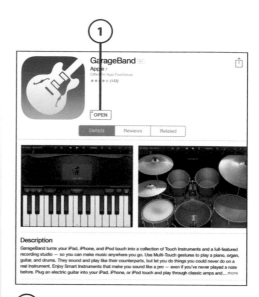

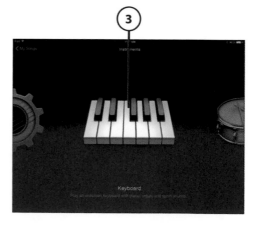

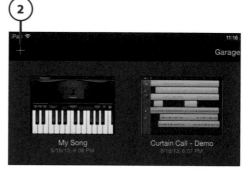

4. Tap the keys to play notes. The force at which you hit the keys and the spot on the key determines the exact sound it produces.

5. Tap the instrument button and swipe left or right to change from Grand Piano to one of dozens of other instruments.

6. Tap the record button to record what you are playing. A metronome will count down, so wait one measure before starting. Try just a few notes, only one or two measures.

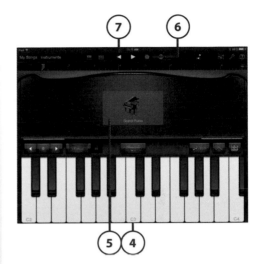

7. Tap the Stop button when you are done recording.

8. Tap the Undo button if you didn't quite get the notes right. Then try again.

9. After you have recorded a bit of music, the View button will appear. You can use that to switch to the Tracks view.

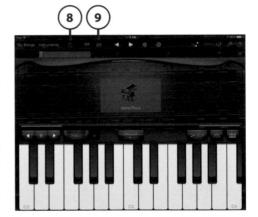

10. In Tracks view, you will see the bit of music you recorded. Tap on it once to select it. Tap again to bring up a menu that includes Cut, Copy, Delete, Loop, Split, and Edit. Tap Loop.

11. The music you recorded is now set to loop for the entire section of the song. Tap the Play button to test it.

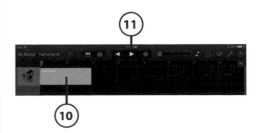

12. Tap the Loop button to view pre-made loops that you can add to your song.

13. Tap Instrument to select the type of loop you want to add.

14. Tap an Instrument.

15. Select a loop to test it. You can even have your loop playing at the same time by tapping the Play button at the top and then tapping a loop from the Apple Loops menu to see how they sound together.

16. Drag a loop from the list to the area right under the loop you created.

17. Now you have your original loop and a bass loop. Tap play to hear them together.

You can continue to add loops. Add a bass line and maybe some guitar. You can also double-tap on the left side of each track where you see the image of the instrument, to return to the instrument view and switch instruments or record more notes.

Besides the piano, you can also play guitar, bass, or drums. And each instrument has several variations. Plus, there are smart instruments, such as the smart guitar, that only allow you to play notes and chords that fit well together.

See http://macmost.com/ipad-guide/ for more tutorials on using GarageBand for iPad.

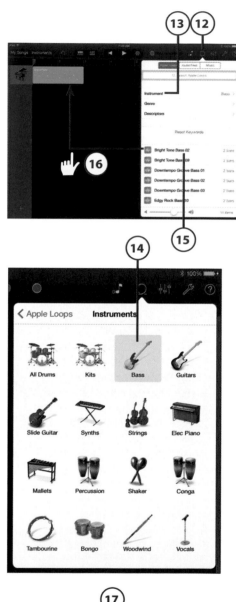

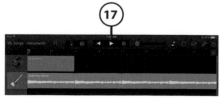

Watching Videos with YouTube

Originally, the iPad came with a YouTube app preinstalled. It is no longer built into the iOS, so you need to go to the App Store to get the official YouTube app from Google. Although you can watch YouTube videos by browsing YouTube.com with Safari, the YouTube app gives you a dedicated video player for the millions of user-created videos on the service.

1. Search the App Store for the YouTube app for iPad. Tap FREE to download and install it.

2. When you run the app, you see a list of popular videos.

3. Tap the menu button to bring up a list of options on the left.

4. Tap Sign In to sign in using your YouTube account. This allows you to rate and comment videos, create playlists, and user other options that you might be used to using on the YouTube website. But to simply search and view videos, you do not need an account.

5. Select a category to see a list of popular videos in a specific topic.

6. Use the search tool to search for any video on YouTube.

7. Tap a video to view it.

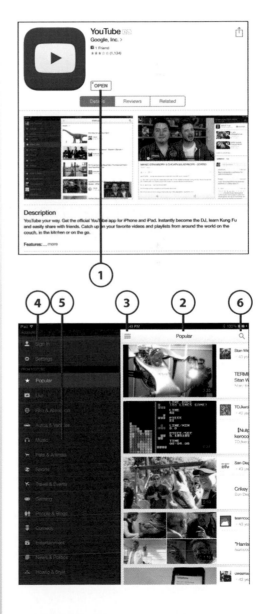

8. Use the pause/play button to pause and resume the video.

9. You can tap and drag the circle left and right to move back and forth in the video.

10. Tap the expand button to expand the video to full screen. Then turn your iPad so it is in horizontal orientation to see the video fill the screen.

11. You can add a video to Playlist, Favorites, or the Watch Later list. You need to be signed in to your YouTube account to see this button. You can also share it with friends using email, messages, or social networks.

12. Tap the back button to return to the list, or search results you were looking at before choosing this particular video.

WHAT ELSE CAN I DO?

>>>Go Further

The YouTube app is essentially an exploration tool, allowing you to find interesting videos to watch. Here are some more ways to discover new videos:

- Turn your iPad so it is in horizontal orientation—you see a list of suggested videos to the right of any video you are viewing. Tap on a suggestion to jump to that video.

- If you sign into your YouTube/Google account in the app, you can subscribe to any YouTube channel with the Subscribe button under the video. Then, you see a My Subscriptions option in the left-side menu where you can view all new videos from the channels you subscribe to.

- When you are signed in, you also see a "What to watch" option in the left menu that gives you suggestions of videos you might like.

- You can also search by channel instead of for a specific video. To do this, search for a keyword or phrase to get video results; then tap the Channels button at the top of the screen to switch to channels results. This may help you find a set of videos or a YouTube personality that you like, rather than a single video. You can also choose Playlists to search for user-created video playlists that match your search terms.

- Want to contribute? Another app from Google called YouTube Capture lets you record video with your iPad's camera and upload it to YouTube. You can also share your videos from the Photos app or iMovie to YouTube with the Share buttons in those apps. Get ready for your 15 minutes of fame!

Watching Movies and TV Shows with Netflix

Netflix started as a DVD rental service using home delivery by mail rather than retail stores, but it is quickly changing into an online video rental service. One of the first acclaimed apps for the iPad was the Netflix app. Netflix subscribers can use it to rent and watch movies right on their iPads.

1. After installing Netflix from the App Store, run it and enter your email address and password, and then tap Sign In. If you don't have an account, you can actually sign up for a trial account right on your iPad.

2. Tap an image to find out more about the movie or TV series.

3. Read information to find out more about the item.

4. In this case, the item is actually a TV series, so there is a list of episodes. Tap the play button next to an episode to watch it.

5. The movie should start after a few seconds. It plays in horizontal orientation, so you need to turn your iPad on its side. There are Play and Pause controls at the bottom of the screen.

6. After the video starts playing, the controls disappear. To bring up the controls again, tap in the center of the screen. You can double-tap in the center of the screen to enlarge the video, or just turn your iPad sideways for a better view.

7. Use the large slider at the bottom to jump around in the video.

8. Tap the back button to return to the previous screen.

Connection Required

Although watching movies in the Netflix app is unlimited, you can't download and store the movie for later viewing. You need to be online to watch. iTunes rentals, on the other hand, can be stored and watched while offline, like on an airplane flight.

More Streaming Video

Netflix is not the only main choice for streaming video. Another app called Amazon Instant Video gives you access to similar content with lots of movies and TV shows. Instead of subscribing to Netflix, you can subscribe to Amazon's service through your Amazon Prime account.

Hulu, another service that streams TV shows and movies, also has an iPad app called Hulu Plus. It works with the same Hulu account that you may already be using to view shows on the Hulu website.

In addition, many TV networks provide their own app that lets you watch videos provided you get that channel through your local cable network or satellite provider. For instance, the app HBO Go lets you watch HBO shows on your iPad after you have proven that you get HBO at home.

Subscribing to Magazines with Newsstand

A special app that comes with your iPad is really an app folder with a special purpose. This folder is the Newsstand. Inside you will find apps that have been created to contain periodic content, like magazines.

When you install a magazine app, it usually goes into your Newsstand folder automatically. The developer of the app has to submit the app to Apple as a special Newsstand app in order for this to happen, so you may find that some apps behave just like normal apps, and won't go into Newsstand.

1. Tap the Newsstand icon on the Home screen.

Newsstand

2. Tap Store to go to the App Store. This is basically a shortcut to the Newsstand section of the App Store. You can also get to it by launching the App Store app and going to this section.

3. Tap a magazine to run the app. What you find when you run the app depends on the app developer. You usually find a list of issues you have downloaded, more issues that you can download for free or purchase, and often the ability to "subscribe" so that you pay once and get a year or more of issues.

4. As an example, here is what the Wired magazine app looks like. After you sign in with your Wired account information, you can see a list of magazine issues. If you do not subscribe to Wired, you can buy an issue with an in-app purchase.

5. Tap to download an issue and add it to the content on your iPad. Once downloaded, it can be viewed here in the Wired app, even if you do not currently have a connection to the Internet. However, some online content embedded into magazine pages may require a connection.

6. After it has been downloaded, you can tap the issue to view it.

Already a Subscriber?

Some magazines offer the iPad version for free to those who get the print edition of a magazine. When you launch the app, you might see a button or feature that allows you to enter a code from the mailing label on your magazine, and uses that to verify you are a subscriber. Then, the downloads are free.

Often the iPad version of the magazine has interactive features like videos, music, and clickable areas on the page. So it is worth it to get it on your iPad, even if the print copy is lying on your coffee table.

Zinio

Although some magazines have their own apps, many others can be found inside the app called Zinio. It is kind of a clearinghouse for hundreds of magazines that publish with a standard format. Browse sample articles for free, and then look for magazines you can purchase either as a single issue or as a subscription. You can even get European and Asian magazines that are hard to find in the U.S.

Using Game Center

Apple has created a single unified system for high scores, achievements, and multiplayer gameplay. A large portion of the best games in the App Store have adopted this system, called Game Center.

Your game center account is the same one you use to purchase apps in the App Store. After you use the Game Center app to log in, you won't have to log in directly in any of the games. It all works seamlessly.

1. Tap the Game Center app to launch it. The app comes with your iPad.

Game Center

2. Enter your Apple ID and password and Sign In.

3. You see the number of games you have that connect to Game Center. You can also see how many friends you have connected to, how many pending friend requests, and how many challenges your friends have made to you.

4. Tap Friends to see a list of people you have connected with in Game Center. You can challenge them to play a game.

5. Tap Games to see your scores and achievements for each game.

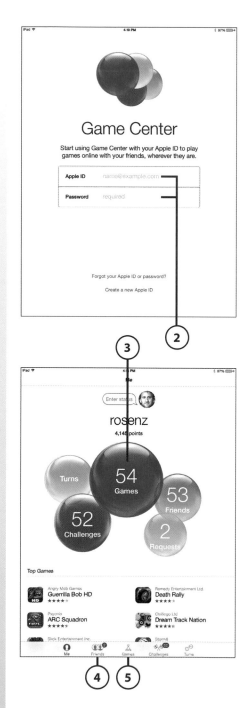

6. In the list of games, you can see your high scores. Tap a game to get more details. At the top of the screen, you see some recommended games based on ones you have played.

7. You can view a list of the world's best scores and see how you compare. Note that when you appear in the high scores list, you will be listed as "me." Others looking on their iPads see your name.

You can often also see high scores and achievements inside the games themselves, even though they are stored in the Game Center system. You can challenge friends to games or to beat your scores from inside some games.

What's in a Name?

You don't need to use your real name in Game Center. If you go into the Settings app and select Game Center on the left, you can examine your Game Center Profile settings. You can pick any nickname you want, and that will be used in the Game Center high score lists. You can choose to have your real name visible or private in your Game Center profile.

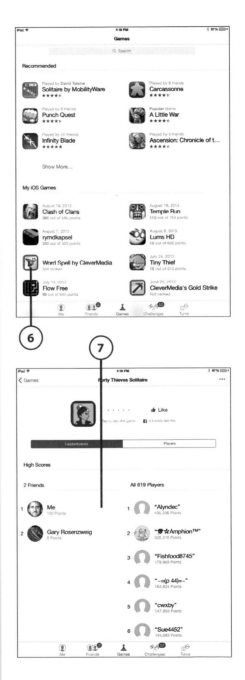

iPad Games and Entertainment

Even if you purchased your iPad to stay connected, get work done, or watch videos, you might want to check out the rich and wonderful world of games.

With the touch screen and accelerometer control, the iPhone and iPod touch turned out to be fertile ground for game developers. Add to that the large screen and fast processor of the iPad and you have a powerful and unique gaming device.

Let's take a look at some of the best games for the iPad.

Where's My Water

Some of the best iPad games have premises that are a little bizarre. For instance, Disney's Where's My Water game has you digging in the dirt to let water flow down to some pipes so an alligator can take a bath. Yes, that's the game.

But what makes this crazy game so good is the realism—at least how real-istically the water flows as you swipe through the environment. Each level presents a more difficult challenge. You can buy new packs of levels that tell sto-ries as in-app purchases.

Cut the Rope

Another strange premise is needing to cut ropes to swing candy into a monster's mouth. This time the physics puzzle is about the way the ropes react as you cut them. Not only do you need to break the ropes in the right places, but you need to be quick so you do it at the right time.

Cut the Rope has a free version with ads and a paid version without. Each level presents new challenges, such as puffs of air and spiders that crawl on the ropes.

Harbor Master HD

One of the new game genres that appeared on the iPhone was the draw-to-direct type of game. It first appeared with a game called Flight Control, which is also available on the iPad.

Harbor Master HD takes the genre a little further. The idea is you direct ships into docks by drawing with your finger. Simply draw a line from the ship to the dock and the ship follows the path.

The game gets harder as you go along, with more and more ships unloading cargo and then sailing away. You have to make sure the ships find a dock and that they never collide.

Angry Birds HD

Many people purchase games to play on an iPad. But some people buy an iPad to play a game. When that is the case, the game responsible is usually Angry Birds HD.

In this game, you shoot birds at a structure using a slingshot. Your goal is to destroy the pigs living in the building. Sounds a bit strange, but behind the premise is a good physics simulation that presents challenges with every level. And it has also spawned some sequels, like Angry Birds Seasons HD, Angry Birds Rio, Angry Birds Space HD, and Angry Birds Star Wars HDGalcon Fusion

Galcon

Galcon was a huge hit on the iPhone, and all the time you couldn't help but wonder how much better it would be on a larger touch screen. Now we know, because we have Galcon Fusion for the iPad.

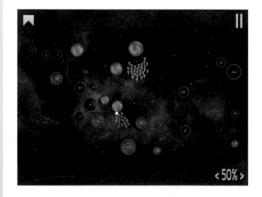

In this game, you conquer a small cluster of planets using ships. The game looks like a strategy game, and you must use strategy to win. But it plays like an arcade game because all you do is tap and drag to send ships from one planet to another.

Plants vs. Zombies HD

Zombies are attacking your house, and you need to defend it. So, what do you use? Strange mutant fighting plants, of course.

It sounds weird, and it is. But as a fun strategy game, it works. It plays like a tower-defense style game but with fun elements that you find in those $20 PC game downloads. Plus, if you like it there is a sequel: Plants vs. Zombies 2.

Monkey Island 2 Special Edition

If you played this game back when it was first a hit on the PC, then you'll be excited to know that it has been re-imagined for the iPad. It is the same adventure, but with beautiful graphics and sound.

If you have never heard of Monkey Island, then you really shouldn't wait any longer. This game probably represents the pinnacle of computer adventure games and can give you hours of head-scratching and gut-busting fun.

Scrabble for iPad

There are thousands of word games for the iPad, and one of the best is one of the original word board games, Scrabble. Not only can you play against a tough computer opponent, a friend on Facebook, or your local network, but you can also play against a friend in the same room, using your iPhones.

You just both download the Tile Rack app for the iPhone and then use the iPad as the main game board; your tiles appear only on your iPhones.

Fieldrunners for iPad

A major genre of touch device gaming is tower defense. In these games, you build walls and armaments to defend against a never-ending onslaught of enemy troops. Probably the best in this group is Fieldrunners.

The enemies come out of specific spots at the sides of the board and try to move across it. You have to gun them down before they reach the other side. But you are on a budget. So, choose your weapons and place them carefully.

Temple Run 2

The original Temple Run spawned an entire genre of iOS apps called "endless runners." The character you control in the game runs forward at full speed. All you do is control whether the character jumps, slides, turns left, or turns right.

It sounds pretty simple, and when you start you only last for a few seconds. This leads to wanting to try it again and again to improve your score. Before you know it, you'll be making impossibly long runs and challenging your friends on Game Center.

The Room

Here's a mystery puzzle game with beautiful graphics. You manipulate objects in a room using natural gestures to solve puzzles. As you progress, a story unfolds.

You need to explore the small 3D game environment in order to notice tiny clues and interpret messages. It is a slow-paced game for those who like to think instead of furiously tap and swipe. Anyone who is a fan of old-style games like Myst will like this game.

Gold Strike

I'll go ahead and mention two of my own games here. Gold Strike was first a web-based game, then a PC game, and then an iPhone game. Once you try it, you'll see that it was really an iPad game all along, just waiting for the iPad to come along.

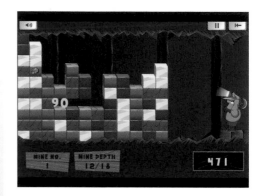

You tap groups of blocks to remove them before the mine fills up. Gold blocks give you points, and the larger the group, the more points you get. The iPad version also includes some game variations for extended play.

Just Jigsaw Puzzles

With your iPad, there is no need to take up the entire dining room table for the next week to do a puzzle. You can work on one using your iPad's touch screen.

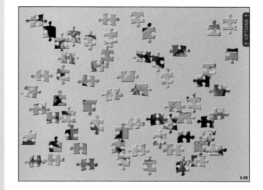

You move the pieces around and connect them until you have completed the picture. You can adjust the size of the pieces and use helpful tools to solve the puzzle. The game comes with a free set of puzzles, and you can buy more sets in various themes like paintings, landscapes, and animals.

iTunes Radio Alternatives

The Music app isn't the only way to listen to music on your iPad, and iTunes Radio isn't the only streaming music option. In addition to the many streaming Internet radio station apps, there is Pandora, which also enables you to make your own radio station based on a song or artist.

The stations you create on the iPad also show up in your Pandora account wherever you log on. You can use Pandora on your computer by just going to www.pandora.com/ and logging in. You can also use Pandora on many mobile phones. There are even television sets and car radios that play your Pandora radio stations.

Another streaming service is Spotify. Unlike Pandora and iTunes Radio, you can search for and play specific artists, albums, and songs. So you don't need to hope for a song you like to come up next—you can actually pick the song.

After you have the Spotify app, you can sign up for a free account and get a time-limited amount of streaming. For an annual fee, you get unlimited streaming, and even the ability to save some songs to your iPad temporarily so that you can listen to them when you do not have a connection.

**Extend your iPad with printers,
cases, connectors, and keyboards.**

In this chapter, we use some optional accessories like cases, docks, keyboards, and adapters.

→ Printing from Your iPad
→ AirPlay Mirroring with Apple TV
→ Video Output Adapters
→ Using Wireless Keyboards
→ Importing Photos with SD Card and USB Adapters
→ Charging Your iPad with Power Accessories
→ Listening with EarPods
→ Protecting Your iPad

iPad Accessories

Many accessories available for your iPad perform a variety of tasks, protect it, or just make it look pretty.

You might already have some things that work with your iPad—printers and wireless keyboards, for instance. Let's look at a variety of accessories to see how to use them.

Printing from Your iPad

Sometime after the release of the first iPad, Apple added wireless printing to the iOS operating system. They call it AirPrint. You can print a web page or document directly from your iPad over your wireless network.

The one catch? It works only with printers that support AirPrint. Fortunately, the list is growing fast and now includes printers by many companies. You can find an updated list of AirPrint printers at http://support.apple.com/kb/HT4356.

Assuming you have one of these printers and have set it up on your local network, here's how you print, using the Notes app as an example.

1. In Notes, with the note you want to print open, tap the Share button.

2. Tap Print.

3. Listed next to Printer you will see the name of the last printer you used, as long as the iPad is still connected through the network to this printer. But if you have never printed before, or the printers available have changed, you need to tap Select Printer.

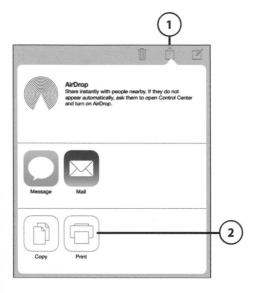

4. If the printer is on and has been configured to your network, it should appear in a list. Tap it to select it.

5. The printer name will now appear. You can tap its name again to select a different printer.

6. Tap Range to specify a range of pages to print, or leave it at All Pages. The Range option appears only if you have more than one page in your document.

7. Tap the -/+ buttons to set the number of copies to print, or leave it at 1 Copy.

8. Tap the Print button to send to the printer.

   At this point, your iPad will launch a special Printer Center app. You may not notice it unless you quickly double-press the Home button to bring up the list of apps. You will then see this Print Center app running as the left-most app in the list.

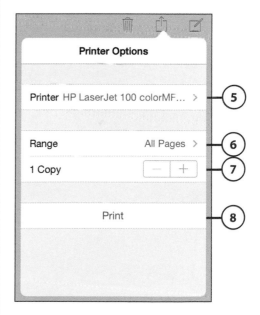

9. Double-press the Home button to bring up the list of apps currently running on your iPad. Swipe left to right to go all the way to the left side of the list.

10. Tap the Print Center icon.

11. You can see the status of the printing process and other information.

12. Tap Cancel Printing to stop printing.

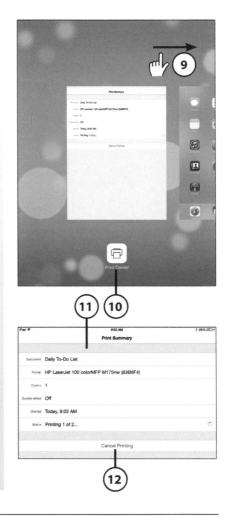

Different for Other Apps

How you initiate printing differs from app to app. Using Pages, for example, you go to the Tools button at the top of the screen and select Share and Print. You see Print as one of the options. But for most apps, you initiate printing by looking for a Print option in the Share button that looks like a box with an arrow pointing up.

Printing When You Can't Print

Not all apps include the ability to print. But that doesn't mean you can't print what you see on the screen. Just capture the screen by pressing the sleep/wake button and home button simultaneously (see "Capturing the Screen" in Chapter 9). Then, go to the Photos app and look in your Camera Roll for the new image. You can print that image using the Share button in the Photos app. This is handy for printing out maps, since most maps apps don't include a print function.

Bypassing Apple's AirPrint

Although not all Wi-Fi printers support AirPrint, there is a way to cheat. Some enterprising third-party developers have come up with software for desktop computers that sets up a printer connected to the computer as an AirPrint printer. You aren't really printing directly to a printer—you are going through the computer. Still, it may be a good option for some. Search on the web for the Printopia (Mac), handyPrint (Mac), or Presto (PC).

AirPlay Mirroring with Apple TV

The Apple TV may be the best iPad accessory of them all. It enables you to display the screen of the iPad on a high definition television. And it does this wirelessly, using the local Wi-Fi network and something called AirPlay mirroring.

You need to make sure several things are in place before you can use AirPlay Mirroring.

1. Make sure that both your iPad and Apple TV are connected to the same local network.

2. Make sure both your iPad and Apple TV are up-to-date. Using older or mismatched versions of software on the devices could prevent AirPlay from working.

3. Turn on AirPlay on your Apple TV. To do this, go into Settings, AirPlay, and turn it on.

4. On your iPad, swipe from the bottom of the screen up to bring up the Control Center. See "Using Control Center" in Chapter 1.

5. Tap the AirPlay button. Note that it will only appear if you have at least one AirPlay device, such as an Apple TV, connected to your network and enabled.

6. Select which Apple TV you want to mirror the iPad's screen.

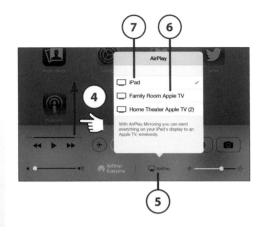

7. When you want to stop mirroring, repeat steps 4 and 5, but select iPad to turn off AirPlay mirroring.

The $99 for an Apple TV may be worth it just as an AirPlay accessory for the iPad. But you also get all the other Apple TV features, such as iTunes movie rentals, YouTube, Netflix and Hulu apps, and streaming for iTunes on Macs and PCs.

The Mirror Crack'd

Some apps won't mirror to Apple TV at all. Certain video streaming apps have purposely restricted mirroring due to licensing issues and other reasons. So you might not be able to mirror when using apps from certain cable networks.

MORE ABOUT AIRPLAY

Go Further

Mirroring your iPad's screen through an Apple TV is just one of many functions of AirPlay. You can also find AirPlay buttons in other apps, such as the Music app and other third-party audio apps. You can send just the audio stream from these apps to Apple TV to play music through your TV or home theater system.

You can also get audio-only AirPlay devices, such as Apple's own Airport Express base station and many small speaker systems and home theater attachments. These devices will appear when you try to use AirPlay from an audio app.

You can also use the Bluetooth ability of your iPad to send audio from some apps to wireless speakers. Check out http://store.apple.com/us/ipad/ipad-accessories/speakers for Apple's list of audio devices that use either AirPlay or Bluetooth to connect to your iPad.

Video Output Adapters

In addition to using an Apple TV to wirelessly mirror your iPad's screen to a TV or projector, you can also use one of two cables to directly connect your iPad to a screen.

There are two models. One is for VGA connections, such as you may find on many boardroom and classroom projectors. The other is an HDMI connector, which works for most HD televisions produced in the last few years. However, you will find televisions with VGA connectors and projectors with HDMI connectors. Check your device first before purchasing one of the two adapters. If you have both types of connections, get the adapter for the more modern and versatile HDMI connection.

Apple's Lightning Digital AV Adapter   **Apple's Lightning to VGA Adapter**

Both adapters have a Lightning connector on the one end that plugs into the bottom of your iPad. The other end has either the HDMI or VGA connector, plus a port to connect a Lightning cable. This is for connecting your iPad's power adapter so your iPad is receiving power at the same time it is sending the video signal to the TV or projector.

You don't need to use this Lightning port—you can run your iPad on its battery while connected to the screen. However, connecting your iPad to AC power prevents your battery from draining and your iPad from running out of power while you are presenting. Wouldn't want to have to stop your presentation just before the slide where you ask the board members for money, would you?

1. Connect the adapter to the dock port on your iPad.

2. Connect the other end of the adapter to a standard HDMI or VGA cable. You cannot hook the adapters directly to a TV or projector because they have female connectors. A male-to-male connector bridges the gap between the adapter and the TV or projector, just like it would if you were connecting to a laptop computer.

3. Connect the other end of the cable to a monitor or projector that accepts either HDMI or VGA.

4. If you are using the VGA adapter and also want audio, then use an audio mini jack to connect the headphone port of the iPad to the line in the projector. The exact type of cable you need depends on what audio input the projector takes.

5. At this point, the video on the projector or monitor should mirror that of the iPad. Some apps may show different things on the iPad's screen and the external display. For example, Keynote will show the presentation on the external display, while you have the presentation plus controls on the iPad's screen.

TV Compatibility

The video coming from the iPad is compatible with both 720p and 1080p HD televisions and video devices. It also includes audio over the HDMI cable. Many televisions support only 1080i, not 1080p. In that case, the video may be shown in 720p instead.

No Lightning?

If you are using a first, second, or third-generation iPad, you have a 30-pin dock connector at the bottom instead of a Lightning connector. These two adapters won't work with your older iPad, but you can still find the old 30-pin versions of these adapters if you search online retailers.

Using Wireless Keyboards

If you have a lot of typing to do and are sitting at a desk anyway, you can use Apple's wireless keyboard with your iPad. This is the same wireless keyboard that you would use with a Mac. You can also use just about any other Bluetooth-compatible wireless keyboard.

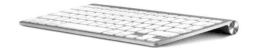

Apple Wireless Keyboard

Choosing the Right Wireless Keyboard

If you have an older Apple wireless keyboard, it might not work with your iPad. The Apple Store warns that only "newer" keyboards can successfully connect to the iPad. Reports from people with older wireless keyboards indicate that this is true. However, you don't need to stick with Apple's wireless keyboard. Most Bluetooth keyboards work fine with the iPad. Search your favorite online store for all kinds of compact wireless Bluetooth keyboards. Check reviews to see if anyone has mentioned trying the model with an iPad.

1. To connect to the Apple Wireless Keyboard, first make sure you have good batteries in it.

2. Go to the Settings app on your iPad and tap Bluetooth.

3. In the Bluetooth settings screen, make sure Bluetooth is turned on. Switch it on if not.

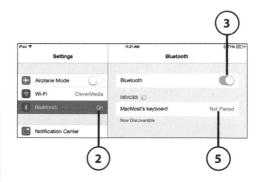

4. Turn on your Apple Wireless Keyboard by pressing the button on its right side. You should see a small green light turn on at the upper-right corner of the main face of the keyboard.

5. After a second or two, the keyboard should appear on your iPad screen. Tap where you see Not Paired on the iPad screen.

6. Look for a 4-digit number in the message displayed. Type that on your keyboard. Then press the Return key.

7. After the connection is established, you should see Connected next to the name of your keyboard.

8. After you connect, the iPad automatically uses the physical keyboard by default, rather than bringing up the on-screen keyboard. To use the on-screen keyboard again, you can either disconnect or power off your Apple Wireless Keyboard, or you can press the Eject button at the upper-right corner of the keyboard to switch to the on-screen keyboard at any time.

9. If you want to disconnect the keyboard so it is no longer paired with your iPad, tap the i button, and then tap Forget this Device.

SPECIAL KEYS

The Apple wireless keyboard was not made for the iPad—it existed first. But the iPad recognizes many special keys on it and uses those keys in various ways.

- Brightness (F1 and F2): Changes the brightness of the iPad screen

- Volume (F10, F11, and F12): Mutes, lowers, and raises the volume

- Eject (To the right of F12): Brings up or dismisses the on-screen keyboard

- Arrows: Navigates around in editable text

- Arrows+Shift: Selects editable text

- ⌘: Can be used with X, C, and V for cut, copy, and paste inside editable text

- ⌘+Z: In many writing apps you can use this to undo, just like when typing on a desktop computer.

- Audio Playback Keys (F7, F8, and F9): Goes to previous track, play/pause, and next track

- ⌘+Space: Switches between keyboard layouts if you have multiple keyboards selected in the Settings app.

Importing Photos with SD Card and USB Adapters

Apple sells two adapters that can be used to connect your camera to your iPad. The first is a Lightning to SD Card Camera Reader that lets you take an SD card and connect it to your iPad. The second is the Lightning to USB Camera Adapter that lets you plug your camera and other devices directly into your iPad. If you have a 3rd generation or older iPad, you need to get the old Apple iPad Camera Connection Kit which includes both of these adapters, but designed for the 30-pin dock connector, not the Lightning connector.

Here is how to import photos directly from your camera or SD card.

1. Connect either the camera connector or the SD card reader to your iPad's dock port. Connect your camera using the USB cable that came with it, or slide the SD card into the card reader. If you are connecting a camera, you will most likely need to switch the camera on and into the same mode you use to transfer pictures to a computer.

**Apple Lightning to SD
Card Camera Reader**

2. After a slight delay, the Photos app should launch and images on the camera or card should appear on your iPad's screen. You may need to tap the Import button at the bottom of the screen to see the photos.

3. Tap Import All to import all the photos on the card.

4. Tap the Delete All button if you want to delete the images without ever importing them into your iPad.

5. If you don't want to import or delete all of the images, tap one or more images to select them.

6. Tap Import.

7. Tap Import Selected to bring in only the selected photos.

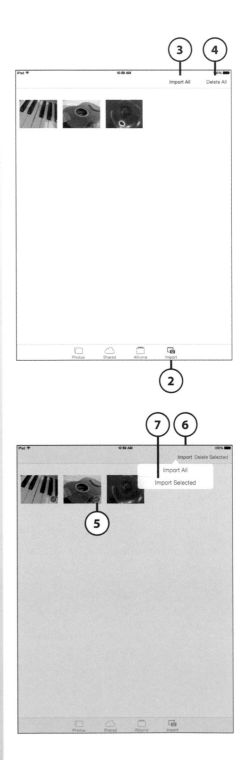

8. After importing the photos, you are given the chance to delete them from the camera or card. Tap Delete to remove them.

9. Tap Keep to leave the images on the camera or card.

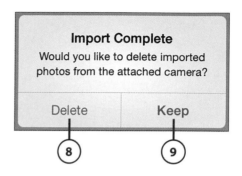

Wirelessly Transfer from Camera to iPad

With the Eye-Fi card (www.eye.fi), you can take pictures with your digital camera and wirelessly transfer them from your camera to your iPad. You can even do this while you are taking more pictures. The card is something you install in your camera that acts like a regular SD card, but it also contains a tiny wireless transmitter. Then you use a free iPad app to connect the card to your iPad. Snap a picture and it appears on your iPad.

Charging Your iPad with Power Accessories

A power user of any gadget usually acquires additional power chargers and cables. For instance, you might want to charge your iPad at home and at work, or even while travelling. Here are some suggestions for accessories that will keep your iPad charged. All of these are available in Apple Stores, the Apple online store, other online retailers, and many computer and electronics stores.

If you travel between two locations, such as home and work, or home and school, then carrying your one and only power adapter with you may be a problem. It is too easy to forget to bring it along.

You can buy a second charger and dock cable from Apple that is the equivalent of the one that came with your iPad. Alternatively, the iPad Dock from Apple enables you to stand the iPad up vertically while it's either plugged in to a power outlet or docked with your computer. You can also use the iPad in this position and even pipe the audio into external speakers through the dock.

Here is a list of items you might want to consider:

- **Apple Lightning to USB cable**: An extra dock cable to plug your iPad into a Mac or PC for syncing and slow charging. Many cars and some public places like airports now have USB outlets that you can use with this cable or the one that came with your iPad. It is always good to have a spare cable, as losing your only one means you can't charge your iPad. If you have a 3rd generation or older iPad, you need the old 30-pin dock connector instead of this Lightning cable.

- **Apple iPad 12W USB power adapter**: A 12-watt adapter that charges the iPad at full speed, faster than a standard USB port. This doesn't come with a cable, so if the plan is to have a complete set of power adapters and cables in two locations, make sure you pick up the aforementioned USB cable too.

**Apple iPad 12W
USB power adapter**

Just Wireless Car Charger

- **Car Charger**: You can find car USB phone chargers very cheap at superstores and online, and then use your own Lightning cable to connect your iPad. Make sure that the device outputs at least 10 watts of power, or it will charge your iPad slowly or not at all. Apple doesn't have an official car charger, but it sells several third-party brands in the Apple Store

- **External Battery**: If your needs are extreme, and the 10+ hour normal battery life of your iPad isn't enough, you can shop for an external battery pack. They all work by charging them up before you leave home, and then you plug your iPad into them with your Lightning cable. The iPad thinks it is getting power from a wall charger—it doesn't care that it is a battery pack instead. Apple sells some in its store that can add a few more hours, or even as much as a full charge, to your iPad.

Not All Power Is the Same

Your iPad requires extra power to charge properly. With the power supply that came with your iPad, a 10- or 12-watt model, it should charge fully after about 4 hours. But with a smaller 5-watt iPhone power supply, or while hooked up to a standard 6-watt USB port on a computer, it takes twice that amount of time. Some low-power USB ports on computers won't charge the iPad at all.

Listening with EarPods

Although you can use any standard earphones with your iPad, the official Apple EarPods headphones come with a controller on the cord that gives you additional functionality.

You don't get a set of EarPods when you buy an iPad, but you do get a set when you buy a new iPhone or iPod, so you may already have these. You can also purchase them separately from Apple in Apple Stores and online.

In addition to the controls, the EarPods have a microphone that usually gives you better quality recording than using the one on the body of the iPad, which is typically farther from your mouth. It is a good idea to use the EarPods mic when making FaceTime or Skype calls, or recording using audio apps.

Here's what you can do with the controller on the EarPods while you have music playing with the Music app. These also work in many third-party music apps and even audiobook players. You don't need to have the audio app on the screen, or even your iPad unlocked to use these. The audio just needs to be playing.

1. Press the + button to raise the volume.

2. Press the – button to lower the volume.

3. Press the center button once quickly to pause the music. Press again to resume.

4. Press the center button twice quickly to skip to the next song. If you hold the second press, the current song will fast-forward until you release.

5. Press the center button three times quickly to go to the previous song. If you hold the third press, the current song will rewind until you release.

EarPod Alternatives

The EarPods are not only inexpensive, but regarded as pretty high quality. However, if you do prefer other headphones, note that they usually do not come with controls on the cord. Sometimes you will find only the volume controls, and other times you will find all three buttons—but the center button only serves to pause music and won't perform other actions. You can also find adapters for other headphones that extend the cord and add these buttons, but only some are fully compatible with all the button actions mentioned here.

>>>Go Further

MORE FUN WITH EARPODS

FaceTime: If you get an incoming FaceTime call while the EarPods are connected, you can press the center button to answer the call. To decline the call, hold the button down for a few seconds.

Siri: You can also use the center button to activate Siri. Just press and hold the center button for a few seconds until Siri appears. Then the microphone on the EarPods comes in handy so you can talk to Siri through it as well.

Camera: What? There's a camera in your EarPods headphones? No. But you can use the + button on the cord to trigger taking a photo with the Photos app. It works just like the onscreen camera button. You can also use the volume up button on the side of the iPad. This allows you to take a photo while not physically holding your iPad.

Protecting Your iPad

Most iPad users buy something to protect their iPad. Protection ranges from large impact- and weather-resistant cases to thin screen coverings. Some users even buy multiple cases to use in different situations.

iPad Smart Cover and Smart Case

A cover is just a cover, right? But Apple didn't make "just a cover" for the iPad. They made a "smart cover." By using magnets, this cover sticks to the front of the iPad without hiding the rest of the iPad's design. And it is highly functional, acting as a stand as well. It does not, however, work with the original iPad.

The Smart Cover also performs two other functions. First, your iPad can detect when it is closed or opened. You can turn this option on or off by going to the Settings app, under General settings, and looking for the Lock / Unlock option.

Another function your Smart Cover performs is to clean the screen. The material on the inside of the cover gently wipes the screen each time you open and close the cover. Your screen might still need a good wipe-down with a soft cloth every once in a while, but the Smart Cover does keep it a little neater.

The Smart Case is basically the same as the Smart Cover, but it includes a cover for the back of the iPad as well and only fits the full-size iPad. You can get the Smart Cover in several colors made from either polyurethane or leather material.

The iPad Air Smart Case

Protective Covers

Instead of the Smart Cover, or in addition to it, you may want to get a protective cover for your iPad. The problem here is not finding one, but choosing from the hundreds of models already available.

Some covers cover only the back and sides of the iPad, leaving the screen open. Often these covers work in conjunction with an Apple Smart Cover, allowing you to use both at the same time.

The advantage of a cover over a case is that the cover stays on the iPad while you use it. So if you drop your iPad while trying to use it, the cover provides some protection.

Protective Cases

A case or sleeve, on the other hand, is something you would put your iPad inside of in order to protect it while not using the iPad. Then you would take the iPad out to use it.

Some cases fit loosely enough to allow you to also put a cover on the iPad, giving double the protection. There are also many products that are between a cover and a case, offering the protection of a case, but allowing you to still use the iPad without taking it out—at least to a certain extent. Some manufacturers use the terms "cover" and "case" interchangeably.

When looking for a case, there are many things to consider. Don't just look in a local Apple Store—it stocks only a few cases. Look online to discover a wide variety. Pick one that fits your needs and style.

Size Matters

Remember that each version of the iPad is physically different. The original iPad and the iPad 2 are different shapes. The 3rd and 4rth generation are slightly larger than the iPad 2, and the iPad Air is much thinner than its predecessors. The iPad mini is much smaller than the full-size iPads. The 4th and 5th generation iPads, iPad Air, and iPad mini have a small lightning port on the bottom, whereas the older iPads had a larger 30-pin dock port, which means some cases may not have a properly sized or aligned opening. Check the product carefully to make sure you are getting one that fits your device.

A Keyboard and a Cover

Some covers and cases combine protection with a keyboard. They allow you to unfold the cover so the iPad, and a keyboard built into the case, resemble a small laptop computer. If you like using an external keyboard, and want to carry the keyboard around with your iPad, this may be the best setup.

Index

J

K

Q-R

T

Y-Z

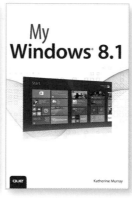

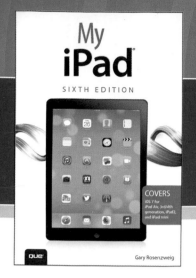

My iPad
SIXTH EDITION

COVERS
iOS 7 for
iPad Air, 3rd/4th
generation, iPad2,
and iPad mini

que

Gary Rosenzweig

Safari
Books Online

FREE
Online Edition

Your purchase of **My iPad®, Sixth Edition** includes access to a free online edition for 45 days through the **Safari Books Online** subscription service. Nearly every Que book is available online through **Safari Books Online**, along with thousands of books and videos from publishers such as Addison-Wesley Professional, Cisco Press, Exam Cram, IBM Press, O'Reilly Media, Prentice Hall, Sams, and VMware Press.

Safari Books On   'o thousands
of technology, digit   leading
publishers. With o   s to learning
tools and informat   ps and tricks
on using your favo   nd much more.

STEP

STEP   orm.

Addison
Wesley   Adobe   O'REILLY

Peachpit
Press   ILEY

PRES

Atlanta-Fulton Public Library